FATHER BOB

and his

BOYS

FATHER BOB

FATHER BOB
and his
BOYS

EMILY GARDINER NEAL

THE **BOBBS-MERRILL** COMPANY, INC.
A SUBSIDIARY OF HOWARD W. SAMS & CO., INC.
Publishers • INDIANAPOLIS • NEW YORK

Also by Emily Gardiner Neal

IN THE MIDST OF LIFE
THE LORD IS OUR HEALER
GOD CAN HEAL YOU NOW
A REPORTER FINDS GOD

PRAYER OF ST. FRANCIS

O Lord, Our Christ, may we have thy mind and thy spirit.
Make us instruments of thy peace;
Where there is hatred, let us sow love;
Where there is injury, pardon;
Where there is discord, union;
Where there is doubt, faith;
Where there is despair, hope;
Where there is darkness, light;
And where there is sadness, joy.

O divine Master, grant that we may not so much
*   seek to be consoled as to console;*
To be understood as to understand;
To be loved, as to love;
For it is in giving that we receive;
It is in pardoning that we are pardoned;
And it is in dying that we are born to eternal life.

                                    Amen.

CONTENTS

CONTENTS

FATHER BOB

and his

BOYS

CHAPTER 1

ON THE THRESHOLD

NOT MANY YEARS AGO, a dream was born in the heart of a young priest, Robert Herbert Mize, Jr. It was to create a home for adolescent boys where the requirement for admission would be not indigency or lack of a family, but trouble with the law. In other words, the candidates for his home would be juvenile delinquents: boys whom no one wanted, and for whom there was no place to go except jails or state correctional institutions.

Although the youngsters would be embryonic or even full-fledged criminals, the home would have no fences or walls, nor in any way be segregated from the community. Wherever it might be located, the boys who lived there would attend the public schools, mingle with the local young people, play on the school teams, date the local girls, and share in every respect in the normal life of the town.

It would be a small home—two dozen or so boys at most, so that a real family atmosphere, with no hint of the institutional, could prevail. The priest would live with the youngsters as head of the "family," and be, by title and in image, "Father" to each one in his care.

The method of rehabilitation would be simple; "therapy in

Christ," the priest would call it: a therapy to be founded on the love and forgiveness of God, through which erring boys would learn to be young men responsible to themselves and to others. The home's contribution to every child who came there would be to give him Christ as his closest companion.

This book is the story of Robert Mize's dream and of how "Father Bob," heartbreakingly alone, pioneered a great Christian experiment which most doubted, many feared, and not a few scoffed at. It is the story of the St. Francis Boys' Homes in western Kansas, which are unique in their "public life" program, unique in their Christ-centered therapy, and unique in their high rehabilitation rate.

People sometimes refer to the St. Francis Homes as "a great humanitarian work," which they are; but, far more than that, they are a demonstration of the power of the Christian Faith practiced in something of its fullness, unweakened for expediency's sake, and undiluted by false "practicality."

The stocky, sandy-haired, gray-eyed founder seems not quite to belong in the twentieth century. He is unashamedly a "fool for Christ's sake," who turns the other cheek, returns good for evil, and, when someone steals his coat, insists that he take his overcoat also. Fashionable or not, such Christlike methods still work. The priest who was called "hopelessly impractical" made his dream a reality without subsidy from Church or state, with no psychological training, and with no professional knowledge of juvenile delinquency.

He was called "incredibly naive" because he took in suspicious, unrepentant kids whose crimes ranged all the way from truancy to homicide and, following the example of Christ, loved and forgave them before they had even tried to do better; but his way succeeded where punishment and preaching had failed. Never sentimental, he knew very well how bad his boys were, but he also had an unshakable vision of the men they were meant to be. His boys astounded everyone by becoming the men Father Bob saw and trusted in them from the first.

14

In 1961, Father Bob became the Bishop of Damaraland in the Anglican Province of South Africa; his diocese includes all the vast and desolate United Nations protectorate of South-West Africa. When I approached him about the writing of this book, he gave the project his blessing, but said emphatically that it must be the story of the boys and the Homes—not his. "Here," he said, as we looked over some pictures which showed him flanked by St. Francis boys, "this is dandy of Jack and Eddie. Use it in the book, but make sure *I'm* taken out of it!" Of course the thing could not be done; he was standing so that his outline touched the boys, the buildings, everything that made the photograph valuable. Neither can he be left out of the story, for the boys, the Homes and Father Bob are inseparable. The struggle to found the St. Francis Homes, to keep them going, and, once, to keep them from being abolished, was *his* struggle; the altar-centered campuses are *his* creation, achieved by the grace of God. Although he is now in Africa, his spirit and his philosophy continue to rescue many hundreds of boys with desolate hearts and lonely spirits, but he remains an unassuming and diffident man ("I learned real humility by the mistakes I made at St. Francis," he says with a grin) who, as Bishop, signs his notes, "an erring son of St. Francis."

Father Bob contends that any story of the Homes must begin with Johnny, whom the priest calls his co-founder.

He first saw Johnny in early June of 1945. Father Bob and the fifteen-year-old boy lingered behind after a Young People's Conference held at St. John's Military School in Salina. Sitting by the side of the priest before the dying embers of the campfire, the youngster turned.

"May I tell you something, Father?" he asked in a low tone.

"Sure, go ahead. I'm all ears."

"You won't tell anybody?"

"No, of course not."

The boy hesitated briefly, and then said very softly, "I'm from the Industrial School at Topeka. Father Moore arranged for me

15

to come to the Conference, but I've got to go back there first thing tomorrow morning."

Johnny was well aware that Father Bob was a sitting duck for such a carefully drawn shot; by then all Kansas knew of the mission priest's concern and compassion for boys in trouble. Within seconds came the hoped-for and fully expected reply.

"Tell you what, Johnny. If you'd like, I'll ask Mr. Gardner at the Industrial School to let you come stay with me this summer, and when the Boys' Home starts in September at Ellsworth, you can be there."

Two days later, Johnny had been remanded to the custody of Father Bob, and was sharing the priest's tiny three-room cottage at WaKeeney. The two were not there much that summer, for not only was there the vast western Kansas mission field to cover as usual, but if the Home was actually to open in September as planned, a lot more money would have to be found, and that meant many additional trips throughout Kansas to raise it.

Johnny was the priest's constant companion on all his travels, and his presence proved an unexpected asset. Those who listened to the priest at the same time saw at his side a living example of those for whom he pleaded so intensely.

Their response was sympathetic and generous; people who might have resisted an appeal for money to house anonymous dead-end kids dug deep into their pockets to help nice-looking, intelligent "boys like Johnny."

"I had never considered that angle of it," Father Bob smiled—"but Johnny certainly earned the title of co-founder that summer."

Johnny had been thrown simultaneously into religion and the mission life on his first morning at WaKeeney with Father Bob, and his first day with the priest set the pattern for the many full days to come, a pattern which was to mark his life ever after.

It began at 5:45 A.M. when Father Bob shook him with a cheery, "Time to get up, Johnny! We have a whale of a lot of miles to cover today."

Johnny groaned once, but then was up like a shot, throwing his

16

clothes on as fast as he could. Travel! Adventure! They would be a lot more exciting than life at the Industrial School! When he walked into the kitchen, dressed and ready for breakfast, he stopped in surprise: he was hungry as a bear, but there were no signs whatsoever of food. The kitchen table held only a clean white cloth and a crucifix. He looked wonderingly at the priest, who was waiting for him. "First, we celebrate Holy Communion," Father Bob said; and then, knowing what was foremost on the boy's mind, he added, "We'll have some breakfast afterward on the road." As the priest made ready to offer the Eucharist, he told Johnny briefly of our Lord's sacramental presence under the elements of bread and wine, rapidly explained the ritual to him, and handed him a Prayer Book; then, while the boy tried bewilderedly to find his place in the book and to follow the actions, the priest proceeded with his daily offering of the Holy Communion.

Afterward, the vested priest turned from the makeshift altar beside which Johnny was kneeling for the first time in his young life, and saw in the hungry boy, so lately branded a thief and confined in the State Industrial School, the good thief forgiven by Christ from the cross. The youth was not yet very good, or even penitent, but he had almost unknowingly taken his first steps toward knowing and loving his Saviour.

The plains of Kansas are vast, and the mission area was widespread. The hours which separated one point from another allowed plenty of time for talk. Interspersed with chatter about life in general and baseball and cars in particular (which one was Johnny's greater passion would have been hard to say), Father Bob contrived to tell his young charge about Christ: of His endless love and limitless forgiveness, of His promise to be always with us so that Johnny need never again feel abandoned and alone, of His assured and Real Presence in the blessed Sacrament. He told Johnny what prayer is and that he could always talk to God, who is ready to listen and to understand; he taught him that the Church is Christ's Mystical Body, bound together by the Holy Spirit and filled with His Life. He found Johnny receptive and eager to

17

learn, as most boys then and later found it easy to learn from Father Bob, because his words and his actions taught the same lesson. Slowly, Johnny began to know God as something more than an expletive.

Each day began faithfully with the Holy Communion, wherever the priest and the boy happened to be—in the kitchen at home or in the kitchen or dining room of whatever ranch family had offered them hospitality; never a day passed that the two did not read together the Offices of Morning and Evening Prayer. Frequently they would be speeding along the road between farms when Father Bob would take his Prayer Book out of his pocket, hand it over to the youngster, and say, "Here, Johnny—you read the responses and I'll do the rest." Gradually the devotions became to Johnny a normal part of his life.

Months of close association with Father Bob did a lot for the boy, but the priest wondered many times who was helping whom, as Johnny made himself useful in a hundred ways. The old Plymouth in particular benefited from his care and instinctive understanding of how things worked, for Father Bob drove his decrepit cars as hard and fast as he did himself. Evening always found the vehicle encrusted with dust and the wreckage of thousands of grasshoppers, but by morning Johnny had it spotless and gleaming again. He also tended to the needs of the engine; because of its advanced age and the primitive roads, the car would falter two or three times a week, but the occasions were few when Johnny could not put his finger quickly on the trouble spot and as quickly repair it. The boy's presence also allowed Father Bob to enjoy what was for him a rare privilege: when he felt that all too familiar plop which signaled a flat tire, someone was there to jump out of the car with a "Stay where you are, Father—I'll have it changed in a jiffy," and, in the blaze of a Kansas summer day, prove himself as good as his word.

Johnny's prowess and delight in wielding a hammer and screw driver were even more useful than his passion for cars. In those church-poor and immense mission areas where funds were not available to put up buildings, Father Bob sought to convert any available unused structures into places of worship. Such reconstruction projects found Johnny an excellent and eager helper. Still sharp is the priest's memory of the last job they undertook together before the Home was to open in September.

On a white-hot day in August, Father Bob and Johnny had got up at daybreak to begin to transform a deserted hotel at remote Russell Springs into a chapel for the mission congregation which had purchased the building. All day long they had pounded down existing walls with sledge hammers and mallets, until at last the four small rooms had become a spacious one. On the whole, the work had been easier than they had anticipated, for the original structure had been flimsily built.

Toward the end of the day, the boy knocked down the last intervening wall, which stood at the proposed altar end of the new chapel. The wall fell as readily as the others, but a low barrier remained. Johnny pounded at it first with the hammer and then with his hatchet; but, impervious to the one and impenetrable by the other, the base of the wall continued to stand. The boy stopped to mop the sweat pouring down his face. Suddenly he pointed to the three-foot-high solid foundation and said quizzically, "You know, Father Bob, that's a natural altar rail, just as it is." Johnny was right; and whatever the reason that one wall in a pioneer frame hotel had been given such a secure base, it served that mission ten years as an altar rail. Fifteen years later, Father Bob was to say, "Whenever I visit that chapel, I think of the young boy, burned dark like the Syrian Jesus and standing ankle-deep in the dirt with his dust-laden jeans, who saw in the wall he couldn't knock down the place where followers of our Lord would kneel to receive His Holy Life."

The road to Johnny's rehabilitation was to be as long and rough as the ones he traveled that summer. The sometimes sullen, recalcitrant youth was not miraculously transformed overnight from a thief to a saint, but during the heat of that summer the leaven of love had begun to work. Johnny at last was happily married, has become the father of three children, and today is the head of his own construction company. He was born in 1930, but his true life began in 1945 when his toughness met the gentleness of a priest, his rebellion was countered with understanding, and he began to realize that gentleness is not weakness, nor rebellion strength. As a guardian to the boy, Father Bob had made him feel wanted for the first time in his life; as a friend, he had shared his interests and confidence; and as a priest, he had shown him the Redeemer and communicated to him the benefits of His redemption. Through His priestly instrument, Johnny caught his first glimmer of the reality of the love of God and of the power of forgiveness conveyed in His name.

Father Bob is at peace only when he is fighting for a cause which he feels sure is the will of God, and the harder the fight the better he likes it. That summer, he did not anticipate that the fight for boys like Johnny would bring near despair as well as joy, nor did he know that the opening of St. Francis would mark not the end but the beginning of the battle.

CHAPTER 2

HEREDITY IS ONLY
HALF THE STORY

CONSIDERING HIS FAMILY, it is hardly remarkable that Father Bob should have entered the priesthood. However, little in the sheltered environment in which he was raised suggests the sort of man and priest he was to become, or explains his extraordinary ability to reach and help boys in trouble with the law and themselves.

He was born with the proverbial silver spoon in his mouth, yet he turned from a comfortable home to a life of austerity; he had known ease, but he chose hardship; his family offered him financial security, but he adopted personal poverty with the zeal of St. Francis, whom he considers to have been the most Christlike of all the saints.

The extent of his reversal perhaps can be most truly measured by his renunciation of a personal family life. The Mize family was and is a particularly close and happy one; yet Father Bob has been a lonely man who has ministered to the lonely and who has offered himself, mind and soul and body, in marriage only to the Church for the fulfilment of God's will and purpose.

Robert Herbert Mize, Jr., was born in Emporia, Kansas, on

February 4, 1907, the second son of the Reverend Robert Mize and his wife, Margaret. As the attending nurse handed him to his mother, she remarked, "He's a lucky baby to be born into such a fine family!" She probably voiced the opinion of many.

The Mize family was one of the first in Kansas (some jokingly say that the Mizes were there before the Indians), and is one of the state's wealthiest and most respected.

It is prolific as well, and on the campus at Lawrence, generations have said, "There's always a Mize at Kansas University."

When young Bob's father entered Holy Orders, he was the first clergyman to come from the elite and rather worldly family which had made its name and money in business. Members of the Mize clan are scattered throughout Kansas, but Atchison is the headquarters of the prosperous wholesale houses founded by the family years ago. A casual visitor who happened to glance at the local telephone directory might think the town is populated exclusively by Mizes and their relatives.

If Robert Mize's black coat and clerical collar looked out of place at a family gathering, they were right at home among his wife's kin. Margaret Moore Mize could claim that every male relative on her side was a member of the clergy and had been since the time of Bishop Moore, second Bishop of New York. Her family record was not broken by her marriage; her two sons, Edward and Robert, followed in their father's footsteps.

Two years after Bob Jr. was born, Margaret gave birth to a daughter. The young mother, always frail, was discovered to have tuberculosis when baby Marge was only three months old. Until she died in 1923, she spent long months in sanitariums, and during her visits home was not strong enough to take part in a normal family life. The all-but-motherless household and the three children were largely in the care of Julia, the old Negro cook who had been with the Mizes for years.

She was the one who removed splinters and bandaged cut knees, kissing away the hurts. She heard the children's prayers, and her lap often held little Bob, his arms wound around her neck as she told him Bible stories by the hour. His sister remembers, "He was the most sentimental and loving of the three of us, and seemed to miss Mother the most."

On those occasions that his mother was able to be at home, he spent hours visiting with her and reading aloud to her even when he was small. The boy who was so much denied his mother and the mother who was so often separated from her children grew very close. She died when he was sixteen.

The affectionate and sensitive boy had no unhappy childhood. The three children, with only two years' age difference between each, were drawn together by an unusually strong bond, one both created and extenuated by loneliness. They also had the close companionship and loving oversight of a father who managed to spend considerable time with his small brood while he was a parish priest in Kansas City.

When Bob was at the crucial age of thirteen, the situation changed. His father was consecrated Bishop of Salina and his considerable diocese, which comprised western and central Kansas, kept him away more than he was at home. With Marge away at school, and Ed immersed in high school activities, Bob's family circle shrank to just two others—the faithful Julia and his dog.

The seeds for the Homes may have been sown in the heart of a lonely thirteen-year-old boy who longed for a real home; certainly his own experiences make understandable his instant sympathy and compassion for the lonely.

His need for love in those years intensified his relationship with his sister. She says: "I'll never forget what Bob meant to me those years when I was in boarding school. It's always lonely when there's no one to greet you when you arrive somewhere and no one to say good-bye when you leave. Bob seemed to know, and I could always count on him to be on hand, no matter what, to welcome me when I came home for vacations, and to see me off when I went back, with a cheery, 'Be sure to write, Marge; I'll be waiting for your letter.' It may seem like a small thing, but to a girl without a mother, and a father mostly away, it made all the difference in the world to me. It gave me the feeling of having a real home."

Bob attended St. John's Military Academy in Salina for a few months, but he seemed to have a growing distaste for the family money which could send him to a private Episcopal school, but couldn't secure him a normal home life.

"*Please*, Dad, let me go to the public high school," he pleaded with his father; "I feel like a snob going to St. John's."

His father did not understand his viewpoint; he was never to understand his son's attitude toward money and personal possessions, but he acceded to his request. Bob graduated with honors from Salina High School.

In one respect only was Bob a typical Mize: he could sell, a talent which he was to find unusually useful in the priesthood. While still in high school, he had acquired a *Saturday Evening Post* route, and quickly had outstripped all his competitors. His magazine route soon grew so big that he couldn't handle it alone, and he was forced to give half of his territory to his closest friend, Ted Coffin.

That night at dinner he told his father what he had done. The Bishop said, "I suppose you mean you *sold* your half to Ted?"

"Of course not," Bob replied indignantly. "You don't *sell* things to friends!"

The Bishop shook his head. "You'll never make a businessman," he said, but he smiled as he said it; it seemed that his impractical son was at least half a Mize.

Bishop Mize managed every summer to herd his three children and some of their friends to the family cabin in Allenspark, Colorado. The youngsters looked forward to the holiday; but the Bishop told them after they were grown, "For years, whenever I thought of Colorado all I could conjure up was the sight of potatoes, bushels of them, that I peeled for you kids!"

His Colorado efforts, even the endless potato peeling, were not wasted, however—least of all on Bob. From his earliest memories the cabin represented a cherished, great and happy part of his life, and it does still. As a priest, he returned to it often to make retreats, and he shared it with many of his boys after the Homes were established. It is one possession he *can't* give away, because

24

it is owned equally with his brother and sister; and he considers it his only home outside of the Boys' Homes.

Bob's spirit of adventure was acquired as a youngster. When he was fifteen, he wrote long letters to his mother in a Denver sanitarium, which described in detail and illustrated with maps the hikes he and Ted Coffin had taken. He and his friend explored all the nearby lakes, and climbed all over the surrounding Rocky Mountains; they scorned the tourists' trails and blazed their own to reach the mountain peaks. Once, when he was only slightly older, he spent two days making his own trail alone across the Continental Divide. When he was eighteen, Bob asked his father's permission to thumb his way to the West Coast. The Bishop promptly denied it, but the next day brought a postcard from his son, saying he was on his way. It was probably his most serious act of disobedience, although, like any other youngster, Bob frequently tested the reins of authority. The memory of one runaway, and of all the other times he had longed to kick over the traces, became a part of the understanding he had for the rebellious hearts of the juvenile delinquents who later became his life.

That summer, he caught rides all the way to the Pacific Northwest, down the West Coast, and back to Salina; and thereafter he could never resist picking up any and all hitchhikers. He stopped at the sight of a suitcase or waving thumb beside the road, and he rarely returned from a trip without two or three strangers in the car. His friends repeatedly cautioned him of the danger, but he never listened, and never came to harm.

"Bob's faith in people must have saved him," his sister says, "because he has taken some awful risks!"

She tells one story about their trip home together from college for the Christmas holidays the year following his West Coast trip. At the time Bob was enamored of a Wellesley girl he had met through Marge, and he wanted to stop by her house in Abilene on the way home to arrange a date for New Year's Eve. Before they arrived, they passed five hitchhikers standing in a group on the side of the road.

25

"They were unkempt, dirty, and unshaven—real bums if I ever saw any," Marge recalls with a smiling shudder, "but of course, being Bob, he insisted upon picking them up. He put four in the back, and one in the front between him and me."

In Abilene, Bob parked in front of his girl's house, got out of the car, and disappeared with an airy, "Be out in a minute."

"All of a sudden," relates Marge, "I realized I was in the car with five bums I'd never seen before. Bob didn't come and he didn't come, and I got more and more scared. Finally I couldn't stand it any longer, and said, 'I'm going to go get him,' and jumped out."

She ran in to try to drag her brother away from Betty, but the project took a few minutes, and she realized suddenly that she had left the keys in the car. She lacked both her brother's faith in humanity and his indifference to property, and she fully expected the car to be gone when they went out. It was intact, however, and the men, who no longer looked so fierce to her, were happily and quietly talking while they waited to proceed on the trip. "One of them," says Marge, "actually got out and opened the door for me."

No Mize, however unconventional, could attend another school than the University of Kansas, and Bob spent four years there, living in the Phi Delta Theta house. He distinguished himself as a student; he was elected to Phi Beta Kappa, and was chosen a Rhodes scholar alternate. With his gregarious nature and readiness for a good time, he also was popular, and engaged in multitudinous activities. "The only disappointment I can remember during those years," he says fondly, "was my failure to make the varsity basketball team."

His quick temper and sense of justice made him a crusader from the beginning; he never lacked a cause, and for a while he orated eloquently, and frequently far into the night, on the virtues of the socialism of Norman Thomas. Because he was an outstanding English student and was particularly interested in journalism, he was made editor-in-chief of the college newspaper. He also was a contributing staff member of the radical periodical entitled, rather ironically, *Dove*. One of his contributions soon created an uproar within his own fraternity, to which he was almost fanatically loyal; he wrote an article on Hell Week which violently condemned some practices of which his own fraternity brothers were not blameless. A few long held his "treachery" against him, but most came to acknowledge, however reluctantly, that he was right.

He dated as many girls as he could afford, but his attitude toward money greatly handicapped his social life. He could have had more money at his disposal than most students, but he refused to take from his father any more than he needed just to exist.

"He lived on far less money than any of the fifty boys in the fraternity," a friend recalls, "and he cared nothing whatever about clothes. He often wore shoes that didn't match, and his socks almost never did!"

During Bob's second summer at the University, Bishop Mize offered all three of his children a trip to Europe. The gay and luxury-loving Marge quite naturally elected to go first class on the "grand tour." Ed went tourist with friends. Bob worked his way over on a cattle boat and rode a bicycle around the Continent. He lived so frugally that he saved enough money to pay his college tuition the next fall.

His years at the University were happy ones. They provided an outlet for his quick and volatile mind, and kept him surrounded by the people he likes and needs to have around him. For the first time he was thrown in with different tastes and backgrounds, and he loved it. He sought out the Negro and foreign students and found many friends among them. He was elected president of the Cosmopolitan Club on campus, and throughout his University years worked hard and successfully to promote it. A Denver grandmother remembers him well: he cast her in a club play when she was a young Hindu student. "The only religious influence I ever had when I was young," she says, "was just knowing Bob. He never realized it, but his example was responsible for bringing us all into the Church."

Bob was a journalism student, but he was acting more like an evangelist. A list of his college activities sounds suspiciously like

"Religious Emphasis Week"; no one but he had any doubt about where his major interest lay. His friends at the University accused him of continually trying to make Episcopalians of them; and although he had not at the time seriously thought of the priesthood for himself, he tried to talk his Episcopal classmates into it. In deciding on journalism, Father Bob does not recall if it was an effort to test himself, to avoid following the footsteps of his father and brother, or just what it was; but in looking back later he could tell where his heart had been all the time. In any case, he went to work for the United Press in Kansas City immediately after he was graduated from the University in 1928—the same year the newspaper play, *The Front Page,* was a hit on the Broadway stage.

Bob Mize might have been happy in such a fictional city room with its excitement and cries of "Stop the press!"—but the reality was very different. He found himself sitting at a machine by the hour and retyping the news as it came in; after the newness had worn away, the job seemed to him unbearably routine and uninteresting. He needed challenge and an opportunity to help people, and had neither. He grew increasingly discontented. He wrote his family frequently that he was "just plugging along, doing practically nothing worth while."

A transfer to Oklahoma City brought brief contentment—his job bored him more than ever, but there he had under his wing a little newsboy.

"He likes to hang around the office," Bob wrote his family, "and I kind of like to have him pester me. He thinks the office is mighty luxurious and I guess it is, compared with the one room over a cigar store where he lives with his mother and father."

His letters from Oklahoma were filled with tales of little Jimmy: how the lad was interested in learning how everything worked at the office, how he was quick to pick up the tricks of the trade, how he enjoyed the trip to the zoo on Bob's day off, how his family had given permission for him to go with Bob to church, and how afterward they had lunch together while Bob answered the child's eager questions about the experience.

Bob was also leading a pleasant social life. He never lacked an invitation to spend an enjoyable evening somewhere; and an increase in salary after sixteen months with United Press let him date a girl without worrying about the money for dinner and a movie. Nevertheless, he felt increasingly restless and frustrated, and the apparent futility of his work never stopped nagging him. His church associations gave him many friends in the clergy; and the more he contrasted his life to those of the priests he knew, the more useless seemed his own.

Bishop Mize and Marge were having breakfast when the telegram came. "I hope this does not spoil your morning coffee," it read, "but I'd like to go back to seminary with my brother Ed this fall." Too moved for words, the Bishop silently handed the night letter to Marge to read, and folded his hands tightly over his pectoral cross. Spoil his coffee? It seemed to become a cup of happiness. Both boys in the sacred ministry: he would never be happier than he was just then.

CHAPTER 3

FROM JOURNALIST TO PRIEST

AT GENERAL THEOLOGICAL SEMINARY in New York City, Bob Mize became an ex-journalist, and began the journey to the priesthood. During his three years at the school in Chelsea Square, an area already rundown before the great Depression, his studies in the Gospel united with his compassion for the misery all around to conceive the dream that was to direct his life.

Independent as always, it never occurred to Bob that his father would pay for his seminary training. When his sister stopped by Oklahoma City after he had given notice to United Press, Bob had told her elatedly, "I've gone over my accounts with a fine-tooth comb and things are much better than I'd thought. With the money I've saved, I oughtn't to be more than $1,000 in debt by the time I get out of seminary if I'm careful and don't eat too much!"

His father persuaded him to accept some help by pointing out that a young priest who starts out in debt is likely to find his ministry handicapped. "Your main concern," said the Bishop to his son, "would then have to be repayment of the loan, not working where you may be most needed." Bob saw the truth of the argument, and agreed to accept from his father just enough aid to get by without borrowing. He then made ends meet by living with monastic austerity, working during vacations, and picking up an occasional $2.50 for taking noon and evening services at local parishes. Sometimes what he considered to be a great windfall came his way. "Great news!" he wrote his father excitedly on one such occasion. "I've been asked to take *eight* evening services in a row at the Church of the Ascension!" At the end of that unusually prosperous month, he found himself with five dollars left over, and promptly gave the sum to a poverty-stricken family he knew in the nearby St. Peter's Parish.

Early in seminary Bob manifested the will and compulsion to meet and overcome any and all obstacles that impede God's purpose, which fighting spirit has characterized his ministry. Not for him was the comfortable and prosperous parish where the Gospel was too often muted lest a wealthy parishioner be offended by a reminder that "the wages of sin is death." With a passionate and single heart, he believed that the need of the world was to hear and live by the pure and complete Gospel of Jesus Christ; and he was determined to take the real thing to people who might not otherwise know it. He therefore cast about for the most challenging and difficult situations the Church had to offer.

"He was always talking about going to some distant, isolated spot to do missionary work," a friend recalls of the period that he was president of the seminary missionary society. "He was on fire to do anything, to kill himself doing it if necessary, to win souls for Christ." Distance and isolation, however, were as plentiful in Kansas as anywhere else and he began to develop the idea of what he called an associate mission, to bring Christ and the Church to the isolated inhabitants of the Kansas prairies. The plan was a good one, and later would play a vital role in his ministry.

Late-night bull sessions to prove and tie down ideas loosed in daytime classes are a necessary part of any higher education; Bob's room at seminary provided the arena for many of them, and none of his classmates could hold on to a bucking discussion longer than he. He brightened as the hour latened, and as long as his company could stay awake, passersby in the corridor were likely

31

to catch the sound of his quick, excited voice, punctuated by his ready laughter, pleading his current cause. Pacifism was then one of his enthusiasms.

"If you believe in war," he'd say with passionate intensity, "you'll have to preach a compromised Christ—a Christ who is all right to follow when the going is smooth, but who must step aside in an emergency like war, when the world is at its worst."

When someone would object to his single-minded reasoning, he'd listen intently, then answer with a vehement "No! You can't change the Gospel just because it seems expedient or just to suit the purpose of any one group. You must face it: in choosing war, you choose the world over Christ. It's as simple as that."

Bob could never understand why everyone did not share his own strong convictions, whatever they happened to be. He preached the first sermon after his ordination on pacifism, and was dismayed at the uproar it caused in the congregation. As years went by and the United States became involved in World War II and the Korean conflict and his brother became a permanent chaplain in the United States Army, Bob discovered that the choice between Christ and the world was, if simple, not easy; but he has never lost his belief that war should not be an instrument of national policy.

Always active, Bob found his energy only partially exhausted by meetings, studies, discussion, and work. In the seminary gymnasium he discovered how much he had missed athletics during his brief journalistic career, and he worked out there every day. At Kansas University he had failed to make the varsity basketball team; he made good that disappointment by becoming the captain of the seminary team. He also was an avid tennis player who seized his all-too-infrequent opportunities to get in a few sets.

At about the same time, Bob's social life was looking up, and he was happy with the world. When his father asked him how he liked General Seminary, he exclaimed, "It's a whale of a place!" Then he added, "It just couldn't be any better, especially since Betty has moved closer to New York. She's a peach, Dad, and I've invited her up for next weekend."

In his excitement over the prospect of her visit, Bob was the butt of much teasing from his classmates the night before she was due to arrive. "Better get up early," his roommate advised, "and give yourself plenty of time to find two shoes that match. She'll take a dim view of one brown and one black shoe, no matter how much she likes you."

Bob was up early all right, and dressed with what was for him unusual care, but even matching shoes did not get the visit off on the right foot. He had a lifelong propensity for being late; if he knew a trip took twenty minutes, he'd allow ten—and so it was that morning. He hurried into the station twenty minutes after Betty's train arrived, and took an additional fifteen minutes to find her. She was tapping her foot with irritation in front of the information booth; but with Bob at hand, she quickly forgot his lapse in anticipation of her thrilling first visit to New York.

It didn't turn out exactly that way. Bob had made meticulous plans, but they were not ones to please a romantic young girl. He took her from one end of the city to the other—but underground, because the subway was all he could afford. At the end of each subway trip was a church which Bob wanted to show her. "I must have seen every Episcopal Church in New York," she told Marge years later. Bob had overlooked two things: Betty might have some ideas of her own about what constituted a "good time," and she was not even an Episcopalian. She had one moment of cheer when Bob told her of the gala plans he had made for Saturday night: dinner, the theater, and dancing. It sounded too good to be true—and it was. Bob had no interest in the theater and he didn't know how to dance, so he had given the theater tickets and supper club reservations to a fellow seminarian, and forthwith turned Betty over to his friend for the evening.

Sunday's "entertainment" consisted of going to church: however proper to the day, it was one church too many for the disillusioned girl. Betty took a train home immediately after luncheon. She never came to see Bob again. Her first visit was the end of their romance.

St. Peter's Church, Chelsea, is just down Twentieth Street from the seminary. One of its founders was Bob's great-grandfather on his mother's side, Clement Clarke Moore, who wrote "A Visit from Saint Nicholas." There Bob was assigned to teach Sunday School, and there he first made friends with great numbers of under-privileged boys.

Enthusiastic, fun-loving and athletic as he was, the young seminarian immediately won the admiration of the youngsters in his charge; in turn, he soon was deeply interested in them and their problems. He quickly set up an athletic program for them, organized around a basketball team which he coached; and he beamed with pride as his team scored victory after victory only a few weeks after they began to take on competition. He spent at least three nights a week with "his boys," and hours more of his time listening to their problems and counseling them. Again and again he wrote his father, "Work with the boys is what I like best. If my school work didn't keep me humming so fast, I'd spend every evening of the week with them."

While he was teaching Sunday School at St. Peter's, all former attendance records were broken. "We set a new record again today," he wrote his father exuberantly during his second year at General; "one hundred and twenty in class. Last Sunday the Rector was away and my boys put on the eleven o'clock Service—and they did a mighty fine job. Pretty good, eh, Pop?"

Bob was popular with almost everyone he met. A priest who knew him in seminary says, "He was then, as he is now, one of the most charming and consecrated men it has ever been my privilege to know." He smiled in recollection of the time Bob visited him at his camp in Maine. A job needed doing which required the use of hammer and saw. Bob, who was never handy with tools and disliked working with them, looked scornfully the other way. Someone remarked casually, "Our Lord didn't mind carpentering." Bob reflected for a moment, and then was off like a shot.

"An hour later," the priest said, "he called me and with a wide grin pointed to the job he had finished. He'd managed it very well, I might add."

Bob worked hard at seminary, and since it was work he loved, he probably had more fun than he ever has had in his life, before or since. He was not always diligent—one letter to his father told of three bridge games in one week, and ended by saying, "Such a social whirl! This sounds like one of Marge's letters! I wish like sixty I didn't have to, but I guess I'd better get back to work unless I want to graduate at the foot of the class!" Discipline came hard, however, and he was likely to solve his problems simply by adding more hours to his day.

In the summer of 1929, Bishop Mize first called upon his sons for assistance, and unwittingly nurtured the growing interest of his younger son in young people. The year was a tough one for every-body, but missionary bishops had particular problems. Wall Street crashed in October, and soon even the farmer on the most remote plains of western Kansas felt the financial pinch. When the farmer was pinched, the small-town merchant was pinched, and the Church soon felt the effects.

The situation in western Kansas was worsened by the beginnings of a seven-year drought and ensuing dust storms of the "dirty thirties." The Bishop, with fewer priests than ever, found himself holding three backbreaking jobs: Bishop of Salina, responsible for all the churches in his jurisdiction; Dean of his Cathedral Church; and, perhaps the most difficult of all, Superintendent of St. John's Military School.

Private schools were hit hard during the Depression; St. John's enrollment fell off by more than half. Bishop Mize turned the problem over to his two sons. To Ed, a senior in seminary, he gave the chaplaincy. To Bob, who had completed his freshman year, he assigned the task of representing St. John's on the road during the summer months. No salary was possible—only expenses.

For three summers Bob traveled for the school, and the sales-manship he had exhibited as a youngster on his *Saturday Evening Post* route was again evidenced. His efforts first restored St. John's enrollment to the former number, and then increased it to more than it ever had been before.

While recruiting students, Bob learned there was a reason other than financial why boys could not attend St. John's: many were ineligible because of delinquency, including some who had the money for tuition. The young seminarian became increasingly concerned about the boys with court records; once he spoke earnestly to his father about changing St. John's policy to permit boys with court records to enroll. The Bishop could only veto the suggestion. "St. John's is a private boys' school, not an institution for delinquents," he reminded his son. "Parents who send their sons here have every right to be assured that their youngsters will be living with honorable and well-behaved companions."

Bob did not pursue his objections to his father's position, but he could not quiet the question ringing in his mind: "What's to become of such troubled youngsters?" There was no real help for the boy offender. Either he had to be remanded to a state correctional institution which too often "corrected" only whatever good impulses he had left, or he had to remain unshepherded in the home community where he had fallen into trouble in the first place. The lives of such boys offered little opportunity for Christ to enter, and without Him, Bob was even then convinced, there was no hope of lasting rehabilitation.

From that time, the dream of the Homes kicked and stirred within the young seminarian; it was not yet born, but, thereafter, the boy in trouble with the law and in need of the redeeming love of Christ was never far from Bob's mind or heart.

The last few months before his graduation, Bob buried himself in his books. His social life was a thing of the past, and the shortening time forced him reluctantly to curtail even most of his work with the boys at St. Peter's. He wrote his sister, "Dear Squirt (I must learn to stop calling you that, but I haven't time to learn anything new just now), I'm so busy studying I can hardly find time for the parish calls I'm supposed to make. If I don't do better, I'll have to forfeit my small salary."

His concentration was worth while: in May, 1932, he graduated among the leaders of his class; and that same spring he was ordained deacon. Six months later, the time shortened to the minimum because of the diocese's need, he was ordained to the priest-hood by the Bishop of Salina, his father.

The Episcopal Church in the United States is a part of the Anglican Communion, the worldwide extension of the ancient and Catholic Church of England, whose faith and practice were reformed but whose order was not broken at the Reformation. It is "Protestant" only in the sense that its bishops protest medieval and modern additions to the Faith set forth in the Apostles' and Nicene Creeds. The "high" and "low" practices within the Church that so confuse outsiders do not affect the Catholic Faith it holds, but refer only to differences of ceremonial and a varying emphasis on traditions of the Church. The Book of Common Prayer is the Church's sole standard of worship, to which both the high churchman and the low churchman are equally bound. However muddled its witness at times and in places, it is still an historic part of the One Holy, Catholic and Apostolic Church planted on earth by Jesus Christ. Nevertheless, there is within the Church considerable latitude of opinion about how the Church's Catholic and reformed character may best be expressed. Bob described one extreme to his sister in a letter written shortly before he entered the seminary.

"I've never seen such nonsense in my life," he wrote. "The priest seemed to be continually blessing and crossing himself, and every time he moved, he did an abrupt 180-degree turn, taking a military step and turning back with the precision of a soldier at drill. Evidently he thought it poor 'dramatics' to take an ordinary side step. It seems a shame he learned all that at General Seminary!"

Father Bob has never been concerned about his "dramatic" impact upon a congregation, but has in his priesthood placed full emphasis on the continuity of the Church and dependable efficacy of the sacraments. Soon after his ordination, he became an associate of an Anglican religious community, the Society of St. John the Evangelist, commonly known as "The Cowley Fathers." As an associate, he lives by a definite Rule of Life, but is not required to take the vows of poverty, chastity and obedience, nor to live at the monastery.

A November grayness hung close over St. Michael's Church,

Hays, Kansas, the day that the Bishop of Salina, resplendent in his dazzling cope and mitre, prepared to convey the grace of the priesthood through the laying on of his Apostolic hands to his second son, Robert Herbert Mize, Jr., about to kneel before him. The younger man's heart beat fast on that most momentous occasion, for he was overwhelmingly mindful that he was about to receive a weighty responsibility, the indelible commission of a priest in the Church of God. The commission that the Twelve received directly from our Lord, its continuity unsevered, has been passed down and perpetuated through an unbroken succession of bishops, and shared in part by them and under their authority, with men chosen to be priests. To Bob, the sentences of the Gospel seemed to be spoken directly to him: "I am the good shepherd . . . and I lay down my life for the sheep. And other sheep I have, which are not of this fold: them also I must bring . . ."

The young deacon could not know how fraught with portent the words were, or how prophetic the Bishop's charge: ". . . ye are called . . . to seek for Christ's sheep that are dispersed abroad, and for his children who are in the midst of this naughty world, that they may be saved through Christ for ever." The Bishop's eyes met those of his son as he spoke the words, ". . . ye ought, and have need, to pray earnestly for his Holy Spirit . . . seeing that ye cannot by any other means compass the doing of so weighty a work . . ."

Bob knew well already his continual need for the Holy Spirit; but he could not foresee the "weight" of his work, which was to prove extraordinarily heavy; yet never a burden, because from the day of his ordination he was aware that the ministry in which he served was not his but Christ's, conducted not by him, but by the power of the Holy Spirit.

As the Apostles nearly two thousand years ago laid hands on chosen men, so did the Bishop reach out to touch his son.

"Receive the Holy Ghost for the Office and Work of a Priest in the Church of God, now committed unto thee by the Imposition of our hands."

Still on his knees, the new priest took the Holy Bible which was delivered into his hands, and received his stole, the symbol of Christ's yoke, over both his shoulders. Face radiant, the young man who had entered the church an hour earlier as the Reverend Robert Mize, deacon, rose to his feet as Father Robert Mize, priest, his soul forever marked by the Sacrament of Holy Orders conferred upon him by the Church. He is now empowered as were the men commissioned by Apostles, authorized as were they, to represent Christ in His Church by the grace of the Holy Spirit.

During his last year at seminary, Bob had abandoned all thought of foreign missionary work, and decided definitely to serve in Kansas. A few months before graduation, he had written his father to express a characteristic sentiment, "I sure hope you give me some place in the District that no one else wants—the weaker the better."

He got what he had asked for: ten thousand square miles of impoverished Kansas prairies. Heart aflame with the love of God, his old enthusiasm, and his new spiritual responsibility, the new Father Bob was ready to begin the first phase of that work for which he seemed to have been born.

CHAPTER **4**

WHEATBELT PASTOR

SOME OF Father Bob's seminary friends had questioned his decision to serve under his father, for such an arrangement may lead to as many difficulties in the Church as in business. The young priest never considered the warnings; he knew only that his father needed priests who could live on nothing, and that he could help. His sister remarked a short while ago, "Bob was the same then as he is now: if a task looked difficult, he was eager to do it; if it looked impossible, wild horses couldn't keep him away from it." In that spirit he plunged into his mission ministry.

However, no amount of enthusiasm and hard work could spread one lone priest over such an immense territory. Dust storms in summer and blizzards in winter often hampered his travels, and at the end of a half-day's drive he would be likely to find only one or two faithful families and no opportunity to seek out people who did not know the Church at all. He therefore was relieved and delighted that before his first year was ended, two other unmarried priests joined him, and his seminary-planned Associate Mission was organized, with headquarters at Hays, Kansas.

"Neither living conditions nor salary permitted a married priesthood," Father Bob comments. The three men traveled continuously to cover thousands of miles in the mission area and to try to establish the Church in those towns and villages where it was not known, while along the way, they visited long-neglected members of the Church on widely scattered farms and ranches, taking them the Sacraments and ministering to their spiritual needs.

Father Bob was in his element. He was doing new and difficult work; he was evangelizing; and he was among people who loved and needed him as much as he loved and needed them. Wherever he went, people responded to his unrestrained openheartedness.

"We lived for those times he came to see us," one woman comments. "Out there on the ranch, miles from our nearest neighbor, his visits brought us not only the Church which we had sadly missed but also a love and warmth and joy which lingered with us for days after he left. The minute he walked out the door, we began to count the days until he was to come by again. Everyone on his circuit felt the same way."

Father Bob's visits were mostly unannounced, but he did keep close to a regular schedule of celebrations of the Holy Eucharist at centrally located homes of parishioners whose neighbors happened to be Church families. He would be due at 6:30 the morning he was to come, but his early-rising host would not expect him to walk in the door before seven o'clock. A friend once said with an affectionate smile, "So far as I know, Father Bob has never been on time in his life."

Whatever the hour the Plymouth finally pulled up to the farmhouse, the little congregation would be gathered together in the dining room, patiently waiting for him. The table which would serve as the altar would be already covered with a spotless white cloth. There would be only a quick silent greeting before the celebration began; visiting would come later, as everybody sat down afterward to a typically generous farm breakfast.

Buckets of coffee later, the long day ahead already outdistancing him, the priest would be on his way, slowly. He would take a moment to hear about grandma's arthritis, move to the door for a

few words with fourteen-year-old Bill about the math he had
flunked the month before, and then walk to the car with his arm
around the shoulders of John Smith, who had been drinking more
than he ought but who as yet was sorrier for himself than for his
misdoings.

Father Bob was exceptionally able to deal with people of all
sorts and ages, but he had a special genius both with adolescents,
who accepted him, even as a young priest, as a respected "father,"
and with the elderly, who seemed to consider him a particularly
beloved son or nephew. "He's just like my own son to me," could
seldom before have been said by so many about one young man.

On the road at last, his next stop might be at the isolated prairie
farm of a Negro family whose home was divided into two sec-
tions: half for them, and half for their animals. The lambs, sheep,
and chickens in the room right next to the kitchen would make
conversation difficult at times, but Father Bob knew and loved the
people well, so as he sat in their tiny kitchen for over an hour, talking and drinking coffee with them, he never noticed the rich aroma
of the animals which mingled with that of the coffee. He was relaxed and unhurried with them, despite the miles he had to cover;
alone and between stops, he did everything rapidly, in a perpetual
and breathtaking race against time, but among his people Father
Bob never appeared impatient or anxious to get away. He had the
inestimable gift of making everyone he met feel supremely important, because, to him, they were.

Late morning might find the priest calling on a family like the
Joneses. Breakfast would seem a long time ago by the time Mrs.
Jones thought to say, "Aren't you hungry, Father?" He would
quickly reply, "By golly, I am at that!" When asked what he would
like for dinner, he would answer unabashedly and unhesitatingly,
"Fried chicken," because it was considered a treat, and was also
easy to fix and plentiful. Mrs. Jones would excuse herself, go to
the chicken yard, and come back within minutes with a bird
freshly killed for the occasion. With remarkable speed, dinner
would be on the table, and Father Bob would sit down to his

chicken dinner with all the trimmings—mounds of mashed potatoes and gravy, corn and homemade rolls.

Another call or two might make it close to four o'clock before he
got to the Frosts'. Mrs. Frost would be ironing, when suddenly the
squeal of tires coming to a sliding, noisy halt would tell her who
was there. Only Father Bob stopped a car that way. He did nothing slowly, especially in a car. Anything under seventy miles an
hour he called "crawling," and to slow down before he jammed on
the brakes was not in his book.

She would hurry to the door as the priest bounded from his car,
but before she could reach it, he would have flung open the door
and come striding in, his hands outstretched in greeting as he said,
"By golly, Elsie, it's mighty good to see you!"

Sitting at the table, he would say, "Tell me all the news since
last time"; but before she could answer, he would burst out, "How
did Paul make out over those broken school windows? He should
be home any minute, shouldn't he? I didn't want to miss him."

Within a half-hour, fifteen-year-old Paul would dash into the
room. "Hi, Father!" he would exclaim. "I saw your car outside.
Boy, am I ever glad to see you!"

Even though Paul's relationship with his parents was close,
somehow he could talk to the priest about some things better than
with his mother and father. Mrs. Frost knew and did not resent his
feelings. She would gladly remember some emergency far from
the kitchen, and leave discreetly so that her son could pour out
his heart to Father Bob, and get his advice on the problems which
burden the young. The broken window episode satisfactorily settled, Paul's problems would mostly concern basketball and girls.
Trivial? Not to Father Bob, who knew well that difficulties are as
important as the people who have them.

Mr. Frost would come in from the fields to interrupt the exchange of confidences and the priest would lead the gathered
family in evening prayer before he sped away. His day was not
quite over.

It would be late before his final visit was completed because the

43

last house boasted a piano. On his way out he had struck a few chords, and before anyone knew what was happening, a hymn sing was in progress. Father Bob had a good voice and played the piano well. The walls would still be reverberating from the rollicking spirituals he so loves when Father Bob glanced at his watch. He would start, and exclaim, "I've got to run—had no idea it was so late," and be halfway out the door, when his parishioners would call him back and invite him to stay the night. Many miles from home and more tired than he had realized, he would gratefully agree—glad also that to spend the night would provide an opportunity to offer Holy Communion with the family early next morning before he went on his way.

Bob's habit of dropping in on parishioners for meals used to disturb Bishop Mize, who felt that it was an unnecessary imposition on the household. The Bishop gradually learned that his son knew his people. They considered it no imposition but a great privilege to offer Father Bob their hospitality. There was no strain involved; he was part of every family. He knew all his parishioners by their first names, and never had to knock on any doors; he was at home wherever and with whomever he found himself, and his people loved his easy informality. He had no pretenses, no defenses, and one mark of all true religion—he laughed much. His people did more than love him: more importantly, they loved what he stood for in their lives. He brought the Church to them, and the goodness he was unconscious of in himself lit and illuminated their own better selves.

Father Bob's actions were always consistent with his faith, but in order to keep his spiritual life on schedule, he asked his body to take more than its share of the risks. More than one person had seen his familiar car lurching at an imprudent speed down a Kansas side-road with a Bible propped up on the steering wheel, while the priestly driver managed to read the lesson for the day and simultaneously keep the car on the road. Only the light traffic and the efforts of one of heaven's more skillful guardian angels let him get by with it as he did. His foibles as well as his dedication were making him known all over his area among both churchmen and the unchurched. People who did not understand what a priest was and who would never have thought of calling him "Father" nevertheless were beginning to think of him in just that way.

Few of the villages where he held regular Sunday worship had mission churches, so most often the services were held in schools or any other building or room which was available.

For some reason there was always a large congregation at the monthly services in the basement of an Oakley, Kansas, drugstore. Perhaps part of the attraction was the idea of going to church in what had been a barroom in earlier days. Father Bob would arrive several hours ahead of time each month to fix up the unused taproom as a reasonable facsimile of a chapel; and he always smiled at how impressive an altar the old bar made.

In most places, the size of a congregation could not be predicted; once the priest spent three blistering August days painting a church before the Feast of the Transfiguration. Considerable advance publicity had been sent out, and he wanted the Church to be beautiful for the day which commemorates the revelation of Christ's glory to His Apostles. One lone woman showed up for the service that morning.

One of the Associate Mission priests, Peter Francis, was by then engaged to be married, and his fiancee was teaching school temporarily in Russell Springs. Father Bob arranged to pick her up early the following Sunday so she could help him prepare an abandoned old school twelve miles south of town for a service—the first Prayer Book worship offered in the place.

As the young woman swept and dusted, the priest improvised an altar with two old desks. He spread the "fair linen"—the white cloth for the altar—and set on it the two candlesticks he had brought. They didn't match, but no matter—they did their work. Then Father Bob asked matter-of-factly what hymns she'd like to play. She replied with some surprise that she couldn't play *any;* but he said, "Oh, yes, you can—it's only a piano, not an organ."

"I'm sorry," she said, wondering why she felt guilty, "but I can't play even a piano."

Father Bob stared at her in disbelief, then said sadly, "Poor Pete. To think he's going to marry *you*."

Father Bob managed alone as he had many times before. He offered Holy Communion as he always did, but for the benefit of those who did not know the ways of the Episcopal Church, he first read Morning Prayer, with its Psalms and Bible readings, and also planned to use lots of hymns. He read the First Lesson, then dashed to the piano and substituted a hymn for the chant the congregation would not have known; then he read the Second Lesson, and ran back to the keyboard for another hymn. In the middle of the second verse, the piano broke down. The small congregation lost heart, and stopped singing entirely. Father Bob and the girl finished the hymn alone.

After they had struggled through and the last "good morning" had been said, Father Bob walked over to the young woman and said sorrowfully, "Poor Pete. You can't play the piano, and you can't sing, either!"

It was rumored at the time, although today there is no evidence and Father Bob isn't talking, that he himself had been seriously interested in a girl who had married someone else—a Lutheran. Whatever the truth of the story, Father Bob had his hands full with or without romancing during those days of the Associate Mission. He worked joyfully and indefatigably to bring Christ to people almost forgotten by the Church; but more and more he found the problems of the adolescent boys in his congregations claiming his time and interest. The demands of his work allowed him only chance encounters with the boys closest to his heart, the ones in trouble. Nevertheless, the conviction that such work was God's will for him continued to grow, and he was confident that in God's time the path would be pointed to by the Holy Spirit. Preparation for the future had already begun, although he didn't recognize it.

The young priest disliked traveling alone, and he picked up

every hitchhiking boy that he saw. He bought him a meal if there was a place to eat along the road; if not, he took him along on his next house-call and saw that the boy was fed there. Then he found him another ride to take him nearer to his destination. On more than one occasion, a boy asked to stay with the priest for a while, and Father Bob would get in touch with his parents for their permission. Some of the youngsters traveled with him for several weeks. The new way of life, the daily worship, the close relationship with a man of God, made real to the boys a part of life some of them had not even heard about. The mother of one such sixteen-year-old boy said, "That single month with Father Bob changed Frank's life."

At the outbreak of World War II, Bishop Mize retired. The new Bishop, with war making increased demands on his already thin ranks of priests, dissolved the Associate Mission, feeling he could not afford three priests in one underdeveloped locality. Both the people in the mission area and Father Bob were bitterly disappointed at the decision. However, the efforts of that little band of priests had prepared the way for a very different and greater work to come, a work to which the new Bishop of Salina, Shirley Hall Nichols, was to be godfather, helper, and friend.

CHAPTER 5

"FATHER, HELP ME!"

AFTER THE DEPARTURE of the two priests who had shared the work and the Associate Mission headquarters at Hays, Father Bob found himself in a very lonesome ministry. Once again he was covering singlehandedly a ten-county mission field with six church centers spotted around a 10,000-square-mile area. He stayed for a few days at a time with parishioners in the small towns or out on the ranches and farms. He began each day with the Eucharist wherever he was, and read Evening Prayer with the families and their guests at whatever house he happened to find himself at dusk.

A three-room cottage at WaKeeney became his center. It was so small that he used the bathroom, a bedroom before plumbing was installed, to store his books, boxes of beloved old vestments no longer wearable, and anything else the other rooms had no space for. The five dollars he paid for the place strained his monthly budget, and when the rent later was doubled, it was a severe shock.

He ate most of his meals with parishioners or at a nearby hamburger grill. When the lack of an invitation or the price of a meal forced him to use his small kitchen, he merely opened a can and rarely bothered to heat its contents. He was able to live in such hand-to-mouth fashion and make do on the offerings of his few and widely scattered parishioners only because he had no wife or family. "Aside from my car," he remembers, "my living expenses didn't run over $300 a year, if that." His way of life was the expression of something more than necessity.

During those early World War II days, he was moving closer and closer to a religious ideal of a personal life of strict poverty.

He has always had a curious otherworldly quality about his own affairs which is very different from his down-to-earth relationships with people and his realistic approach to their problems. He has needed to have people around him at all times, and yet he was, and is now as a bishop, austere in the detachment of his affections from the things of this world. His relatives and close friends sometimes questioned him about the reason for his rigorous self-denial. They could not understand why he frequently spent the night in his car instead of more comfortably in a hotel or motel, or why he bought most of his clothes at a secondhand store until the Homes were in operation, after which he outfitted himself, along with his boys, from the charitable donations of clothing received. His explanation was always the same: "The money can be better spent for extending the Kingdom of God."

His sister called for him one afternoon at the railroad station in Salina in her own car, bright with its shiny chrome. Her brother was always the last passenger to board a train (the man racing breathlessly down the platform and jumping on just as it began to pick up speed usually was he), but he also was always the first one off. As she caught sight of him that day, she noticed that he looked exactly as he had when she had put him on the train for New York the week before. His coat was out at the elbows, and his trousers were shiny and so threadbare they couldn't have supported the weight of the nickel he never had in his pocket.

She greeted him affectionately, and as they walked over to the car, he looked askance at her. "Is this yours?" he asked. When she nodded, he hesitated before climbing in, and then slumped low in the front seat as though he were ashamed to be seen riding in such grandeur.

"Isn't it a beauty?" she said with her usual exuberance as she let off the brake. He replied quietly, "I guess so, but for the same amount of money we could add another priest to the District of Salina." She was too sure of his love to take the reflection personally; she knew that her brother evaluated everything by one standard: what can it do for Christ's Church? He never intended to make anyone feel guilty or ill at ease for enjoying God's gifts; but he himself was content to find his joy in the one great gift of life—and he lived it then as well as now with high good humor. His sister says, "Bob's laugh makes a party, and that special quality of goodness he has only makes the gathering better. We all hoped that somehow a little of it would rub off on us." She and her husband recently sent their handsome young son to Africa to spend a few weeks of his twentieth summer with his uncle. "Everyone, no matter who, benefits by being close to Bob," she says with a smile.

However much the family accepted and approved Father Bob's dedication to poverty, even Bishop Mize, who was not a worldly man, found it hard to understand the extremes to which he went. The only serious quarrel father and son ever had was over the question of money.

On several occasions, the retired Bishop had attempted to speak with his son about the inheritance which would some day be his. At each mention Father Bob seemed to freeze, and finally he blurted out that he could not consider accepting his share of the family estate. Bishop Mize angrily retorted, "You've had a good home and a good life. You've gone to good schools, through four years of college and three years of seminary. What do you think paid for those things? The money earned by your grandfather and me made them possible—and now you piously refuse to accept your inheritance."

Father Bob could understand his father's irritation, and he could see the logic in his reasoning, but the mind's logic and the heart's conviction were irreconcilable. His reply to his father remained, "I'm sorry, but I just can't accept it." He gave no reason.

Wherever one goes in Kansas, Father Bob's extraordinary dedication to poverty was remarked. Since he has never married, many of his friends share his sister's belief that he has taken secret voluntary vows of chastity and poverty; but when he is questioned about the matter, he denies it and says only, "No, I've just been too busy to marry, and I never have had any desire for wealth." His answer seems singularly inadequate to explain the curious parallel between his life and that of his favorite saint, "God's little pauper," Francis of Assisi; both had well-to-do backgrounds, affluent relatives, a disinterest in physical comfort, a habit of rigid self-denial, a single-minded consciousness of the love of God, and a wide-open compassion for those in need. Consciously or unconsciously, Father Bob's footsteps fall close to those of Francis Bernardone as both follow their Lord.

During his days of working and living alone in WaKeeney, Father Bob first caught a glimpse of the work which awaited him in his future. The dream of the Homes began to be born when he met sixteen-year-old Eddie.

Early on a January morning, the priest was just closing the door of his cottage for the day, when the telephone rang. He dashed back inside to hear Father Clem, superintendent of St. John's School, ask for help with one of his students. Against the school's admission policy, Father Clem had accepted a boy with a delinquency record and had lost his gamble.

Eddie was the only son of two university professors. The youth's brilliant mind and his sturdy body were far more mature than those of other boys the same age; indeed, during his brief sixteen years he had experienced more of life, good and bad, than some adults ever did. After his father's death several years before, he had inexplicably been left for weeks at a time without any effective supervision whatsoever, and had become familiar with most

51

of the states from the Mississippi River to California; unfortunately he was equally familiar with several of their jails and detention centers. The preceding spring, he had progressed to armed robbery; he had held up a small-town store in Kansas, and after some shots were fired, he was captured.

Being arrested was nothing new to him, but the attitude of the county attorney was. Despite the serious charges against the lad, the man recognized his latent ability and wanted to see it put to better use. The boy was thus presented to Father Clem, who out of the kindness of his heart could not reject him. Eddie had entered St. John's in September as a regular student, and only the priest-superintendent knew his history.

By Christmas, Eddie's record was worthy of his potential and of his friends' trust. He was popular, good at school sports, and superior in his classwork. However, two weeks of vacation had been too great a temptation for him. He never reached home; he missed a bus connection in a large city on his way—perhaps on purpose. Instead of waiting in the terminal for the next bus, he decided to go out on the town and, once there, he stayed. Shortly after he had returned to St. John's, it was discovered that he had a venereal disease. For the safety of the other boys, he had to be dismissed immediately; and the distraught Father Clem had reached for the telephone.

The superintendent of St. John's put the alternatives squarely to Father Bob: Eddie would have to be returned to the county where he had staged the holdup to serve out his suspended sentence; or he could move into the little three-room house at Wa-Keeney.

"I'll pick him up within an hour," said the priest; and so the youngster, under a doctor's care, went to stay with Father Bob. Neither one knew it then, but the event was a momentous one for both the boy and the priest.

For several months Eddie made the mission-field rounds with Father Bob, as had many boys for shorter periods; together they read the daily Prayer Book offices wherever they found themselves. Sometimes it was in a chapel, sometimes in the basement taproom under the drugstore in Oakley, sometimes in an empty school, sometimes in a private home, and very frequently in the two-seated Plymouth as it sped down a prairie highway—the boy reading the prayers and Bible lessons of the Office, and the priest making the familiar responses to versicle and canticle. To the hospitable families of the mission stations, Eddie was just another of the numerous boys whom the priests of the former Associate Mission had often had accompanying them in their travels.

Eddie, however, was no usual boy. "Ed's mind grasped theological thinking with amazing quickness," the priest recalls, "and so much confidence did I have in him that on one or two occasions, I let him speak in church."

Only once was there a real mishap in the months they spent together. Father Bob was having great difficulty procuring tires because of rationing, and Father Peter Francis, then responsible for several outlying missions in his county, was having equal trouble in getting enough gas. The day came when Father Francis was housebound without gas and Father Bob was stranded on the highway with only three usable tires; Bishop Nichols heard of their plights at about the same time. He suggested that the two priests travel together again as long as the emergency lasted, using Father Francis' car with its four good tires, and Father Bob's ration card for additional gas. Thus the two men and the boy happened to be together the night they stopped at the Twell farmhouse.

Eddie's able mind and greater physical troubles had not reconciled him to a severe case of acne which he was trying hard to clear up. When the farm family offered the party beds for the night, he found there was no hot water for his evening ritual of washing his face and applying zinc oxide. No one paid much attention as he went into the kitchen to heat a pan of water on the kerosene stove; or thought to check after he finished. A city boy and unfamiliar with such equipment, he had not turned the stove off properly.

53

When Mrs. Twell started to light the fire the next morning for breakfast, she lit the whole floor of her kitchen. She screamed. Her husband saw the flames and jerked up a rug. Throwing his wife from the room, he smothered the burning floor with the carpet, while the two priests dashed upstairs and carried the two young daughters outside. Poor Eddie grabbed a bucket and ran to the pump, but his contribution did little to redeem his error. The old bucket had no bottom.

Fortunately no one was hurt, but the house was so badly damaged by smoke and heat that it had to be completely renovated. For once, Eddie had not done wrong intentionally, but his contrition was the deeper for that reason. The Twells responded magnificently. Their concern was not at all for their ruined house, but for the feelings of the boy. Over and over they assured him that the same thing might have happened to anyone who had used the stove on that particular night.

"It is kindness and understanding like theirs which reclaims errant boys," says Father Bob in grateful remembrance. Thereafter Eddie had little trouble. He finished high school and went on to a good university, spending every summer with his mother and writing frequently to Father Bob that "all goes well." He ultimately earned his doctorate in psychology, and is now teaching.

During the following months, Father Bob took under his wing several boys on parole, but he pondered long on the truth he first had seen confirmed in Eddie: that love and forgiveness have power to transform lives. The thought was no novelty; the priest knew by heart the many New Testament accounts in which our Lord approached sinners with forgiveness before they deserved to be forgiven and the sinners gladly turned from their sin to accept it. Practical men of the world, forgetting that God approached them in exactly the same way, had long since returned to the demand that the offender somehow earn society's favors, but Father Bob had always believed that Jesus Christ's way was the right one. In Eddie, he had proof that being trusted and wanted could mean life itself to a wayward boy. The priest's dream, conceived so long ago and growing so slowly, suddenly quickened and flared. Father Bob saw his future clearly: with God's help he had to build some sort of Home for boys like Eddie. To be born, the dream needed only a cradle to be laid in.

As he traveled, Father Bob found himself slowing down as he passed a likely site—an abandoned schoolhouse, a rundown farm —and wondering, "Might this be the place?" Time and again he paused in front of the old dilapidated hotel in Russell Springs. The little town, sleeping in the center of the county, once bustled with over a thousand inhabitants, but had declined over the years to less than a hundred. Nevertheless, its large stone courthouse still defied the constant wind of the surrounding prairie, and one of the few artesian wells in western Kansas kept alive a grove of trees in the courthouse square. To the priest it seemed an oasis in a desert.

He often gazed at the nearby Smoky Hill River, drought-thinned to only a thread of water joining tiny pools hidden in banks of mud and sand; he envisioned the water flowing again as a proper river should. He closed his eyes to think, "How my boys would love this!" and seemed to hear their shouts of laughter as they dove off the riverbank.

In the evenings as he read, his mind would wander as he planned how he would run the Home. He could see in his mind's eye multitudes of boys: hostile, belligerent, rebellious as they arrived—dangerous to themselves and to others. He could see them as they left, perhaps two years later—joyful, transformed by faith, by the unstinted love of a "family," and by a newly discovered function in life. His flights of imagination seemed sentimental, unrealistic, like wishful thinking then and afterward, but they proved to be remarkably accurate predictions of things to come.

Father Bob was highly impatient on the highway and at home, but he was never so in matters of the spirit. His preparation for the Homes was remarkably patient. He knew the poverty of the District, the severe difficulty of gathering such funds as the simplest kind of Home would require; but he knew also the power of

God. He was content to wait to be shown the way and the time. He was not disappointed.

A knock came on the cottage door after midnight on a cold and snow-filled night; he opened it and found a young boy standing there, shivering in the bitter Kansas wind. "Father, help me," he said. "I'm lost." The priest heard in those words the cry of all the thousands of "lost" boys everywhere—a plea which could not wait to be answered until time and money allowed, but which demanded a present and speedy reply.

Father Bob slept not at all the rest of that night; he prayed and thought and planned until the light came. During those hours, the Home-to-be was named for the beloved saint who had devoted his life to helping the poor, the lost, and the lonely: the saint who himself had nothing, yet possessed all. When the sun was fully up, Father Bob was ready.

CHAPTER 6

OUT OF THE DUST— THE ANSWER COMES

ALL DURING THE NIGHT, Father Bob had reviewed the various places his travels had suggested as possible sites for the Home; again and again his thoughts reverted to the town of Russell Springs. At dawn he sped off in his car for one more look before he presented his plan to Bishop Nichols.

Roosevelt's New Deal had been kind to the little town. In addition to contributing a modern schoolhouse, the government had built a dam over a draw emptying into the Smoky Hill River. The intended pond behind the dam was now dry, but it had been filled once and would be again—then what a fine swimming and boating spot it would make for the boys! The town itself sprawled out over about a mile and resembled the flimsy set for a Hollywood Western movie. Perhaps the spaces which gapped between the unpainted frame houses and the mostly unused store buildings on the two parallel dirt streets made it look more like an old man's smile. An ancient well pump on what had once been the main corner was still the town gathering place. The words "Post Office," almost obliterated by time and weather, could be distinguished faintly on three different buildings.

As Father Bob parked his car in front of the old hotel and walked around the quiet, deserted town, he could see the streets peopled with his boys as they helped to redevelop the village. He could see them painting and renovating the abandoned hotel which would be their home; he could see them unloading gravel in the dust-laden streets; he could see them worshiping in the repainted church; he could see them plugging up the hole in the dam and praying for rain; and he could see them crowding the large but almost empty school, where the four high school teachers nearly outnumbered their students. There was no doubt; it was the perfect spot! He jumped in his car and raced back up to Highway 40 and over through WaKeeney, Hays, Ellsworth, and Bavaria to Salina, where he dashed into the Bishop's study.

Bishop Nichols was sympathetic to the idea of the Home, but he was also practical. "What are you planning to use for money?" was his first question. He saw immediately that Father Bob had no answer at that moment, and also that his young mind was working at lightning speed. Bishop Nichols was taking no chances. "I'm all for your scheme," he said quickly, "but I have to tell you right now that you can't expect any money from the Missionary District. Furthermore, I want you to promise that you won't ask the National Council for appropriations."

The Bishop was being cautious, not difficult, and Father Bob respected his caution. "It was a necessary pledge," explains Father Bob, "and I knew it. The District of Salina was a rural community with only 700 Church families; our first goal was to make Salina a self-supporting diocese as soon as possible. To ask the National Council for an appropriation for the Home or to divert any other support from the area would perpetuate Salina as a missionary district."

Bishop Nichols was compelled to remind the priest of another circumstance he had overlooked in his excitement: the State Department of Social Welfare had to give its permission to start a Home, and had to approve the Russell Springs facilities.

Thanking his bishop, Father Bob immediately was off to

Topeka, another quarter of the state's length down Highway 40. He was both surprised and disappointed when his chosen site was instantly vetoed. "Look, Father," it was explained, "that is a backwoods area, the sort of place that would foster rather than curb delinquency. What would you do with the boys out there? There are no movies, no stores, no recreational facilities of any kind, nothing but barbed wire between you and the horizon!" They also pointed out something more important: the school system, despite its attractive building, was notoriously poor; moreover, the nearest doctor was over seventy-five miles away. The locality simply was not feasible for the priest's purpose.

Father Bob may have been disappointed, but he was undaunted. He plunged ahead with characteristic intensity into the search for a homesite which would be suitable to him and acceptable to the Welfare Department.

He covered hundreds of miles during the next few weeks, exploring likely possibilities and presenting them to the Topeka agency, only to have each suggestion rejected for some reason. Finally he seemed to have only one hope left; and he asked the Bishop to go with him to inspect the property. The Bishop by then was as interested in the project as was Father Bob, but his enthusiasm was more restrained. Before that trip was over, it was very restrained indeed.

The Bishop and his priest started out on a gray winter afternoon. About halfway to their destination Father Bob decided to take one of his frequent short cuts, which accounted in part for the fact that only unsuspecting hitchhikers and the reckless young were willing to ride with him. He seemed always to get lost and to add hours and miles to the trip he had thought to shorten. The Bishop fretting beside him, Father Bob realized he had no idea which way to turn—and the few flakes of snow were growing quickly in number and energy. Soon the ribbons of white had become a wall, and the wind was howling the snow into drifts across the road. Blinded and confused, Father Bob drove off the road into a deep bar ditch which held the Plymouth fast.

"I'll go phone for help," he said cheerfully to his dismayed passenger, who knew they had passed no dwelling for miles. Two hours later he was back at the car half-frozen, his mission unaccomplished: apparently there was neither house nor store for many miles in the other direction, either. They had to spend the night in the car, and if the priest had not frozen an ear during his fruitless search for a telephone, the comments of his irate Bishop might have scorched it.

Two days later Father Bob went alone to inspect the site, without short cuts. What he found was far from suitable, so he was hardly surprised when the Welfare Department turned it down. He was walking dejectedly out the door of the State office, feeling still lost in the snowstorm, when the Department's Miss Ferris called to him, "Father Bob, wait! Have you ever thought of the former Old People's Home at Ellsworth?"

He stopped short. He certainly had considered the brick poorhouse on the outskirts of the well-located cattle town of 2,000; he had driven past it often as he traveled from his mission field to the Bishop's headquarters at Salina.

"Yes," he replied to Miss Ferris, "but it's out of the question. The area I serve is in the westernmost part of the state, and Ellsworth is only two hundred and twenty-five miles from Kansas City. I must have a Home where I can serve as the nominal head while I continue my mission work. I plan to hire a good farmer and his wife actually to operate the Home, and an extra woman as a cook."

A smile crossed Miss Ferris's face; she knew the kind of staff essential to a Home for delinquent boys, and she knew how much time and effort such a Home would require. There was not time just then to disillusion the almost incredibly naive priest, so she only said kindly, "Well, do consider the property at Ellsworth." Father Bob did, simply because there seemed no other place to consider.

Bright and early in the morning, the priest set out for Ellsworth, thirty-eight miles from Salina. He was accompanied by Freddie, the young son of one of his parishioners. The place was as he had remembered it, but he looked from his car with new interest at the spacious brick structure, reminiscent of Southern Colonial style.

He rapped on the door, and an old lady greeted the two visitors and showed them around.

A dining room, kitchen, and two bedrooms were enclosed from the rest of the building, so they could be heated by a coal stove in the winter. A parlor, sunroom, and four small bedrooms made up the rest of the ground floor; eight small bedrooms and two larger dormitory rooms occupied the second floor. A roofed porch ran the length of the building in front; other roofless porches at each end, fenced with iron gratings, added to the security of the partially fireproof building. Under the building was a large basement with a concrete floor, and at one end, an old-fashioned furnace with overhead stoking. The place was all but abandoned; only one elderly couple remained.

The glow in Father Bob's heart was reflected in his eyes. It was the answer to prayer: a site ready-made for a Boys' Home. To be sure, the trim could stand a good paint job and the furnace would probably have to be replaced; but all that was immediately necessary was a chapel, which could be easily achieved by knocking down the wall between two small rooms downstairs. Already the Old Folks' Home was alive with boys in the imagination of Father Bob.

The priest strode outside to take in the surrounding eighty acres of land on which the house was situated; only the country club and golf course separated it from the town.

Directly in front of the poorhouse, overlooking the same Smoky Hill River that trickled by Russell Springs, were twenty acres of flat ground under cultivation. The high prairie then dropped off into draws and gullies which were good grazing land. In one relatively flat spot was a tiny cemetery overgrown with scrub cactus and yucca, the "Boot Hill" of the frontier days when Wild Bill Hickok and Calamity Jane claimed Ellsworth as their home.

Coyotes still barked there at night, and jackrabbits darted from clumps of weeds as Freddie drove the Plymouth across the pasture.

One corner of the property held a thick woods, a rarity in central Kansas; it had grown up by the inviting waters of a creek which meandered around a peninsula of land, and its trees were alive with birds and squirrels. Father Bob had seen enough. He would go the next day to see what sort of proposition he could work out with the Ellsworth County Commissioners. Meanwhile, he and Freddie looked at each other and at the creek and grinned. With unspoken common purpose they went to work at damming the creek enough to allow a shallow swim on a warm afternoon.

Father Bob found the county commissioners interested and generous. He was offered an option on the property for $10,000; but in addition he would have to raise enough money to take care of the Home's first year of operating expenses. When Father Bob consulted the Bishop, neither of the men had any idea what the expenses would be; the Bishop therefore urged the appointment of an advisory committee, to consist largely of civic-minded citizens from Ellsworth who would represent the town's various interests.

Unexpectedly, forming the committee was no easy task, for no one wished to serve on it. The plans for the Home had become common knowledge, and a very vocal part of the populace of Ellsworth was taking arms against the idea. Certainly, they knew about Father Flanagan's Boys' Town up in Nebraska, but his boys were merely needy and homeless; there were few delinquents among them, and they lived in their own village, segregated from other communities. Father Bob's idea was something else again. The citizens of Ellsworth didn't want a "bunch of hoodlums" taking over their town, disrupting their schools, being a bad influence on their sons and a worse one on their daughters. The man who was then sheriff was the most vocal of all the opponents: "I can't be responsible for maintaining law and order with a horde

of young criminals running around loose," he declared at every opportunity. Even the local parish church where Father Bob had
served often and was apparently loved and respected held a cold
and uncooperative silence.

Father Bob was amazed at the reaction. Through his daily
offices and offering of the Eucharist, he lived in the world of the
Gospels and believed that his plans were formed on their principles; he simply could not understand when people didn't agree
with him in an undertaking which was close to his heart. He was
not concerned with orderly civic affairs as such, or with the pros-
perity of the business community. He saw only one issue and that
crystal clear: boys who had broken the law could not be saved by
throwing them into jail to learn crime from professional criminals
or by crushing their human dignity and self-respect in strictly
institutionalized reformatories operated on secular principles; but
they could be brought to their true selves in a Christ-centered
Home where the boys would not be isolated from society. He
found it difficult to comprehend either the town's apprehension
or its reluctance to help in an endeavor which seemed to him to be
all-important and clearly the will of God. Whether it was holy
perseverance or human stubbornness, Father Bob's back was up,
and he was more determined than ever to provide a place where
his Eddies and Johnnies could find the rehabilitating power of
love.

A. H. Barofsky, who only recently retired from the Ellsworth
bank, remembers the night Father Bob came to see him. The priest
as usual had given no thought to the time or weather; he rang
the doorbell well after eleven. The banker opened the door to find
him standing in a pouring rain, drenched but with spirits un-
dampened. "Look, I'll be perfectly frank," he said without preliminaries; "we're having a hard time getting together an advisory committee for the Home. If you will serve, others will be
less reluctant to join us. Will you?"

The banker tried to beg off, but the dripping priest was prepared to hear only one answer. Mr. Barofsky approved the idea

of the Home, but knew nothing about running one. Father Bob laughed: neither did he.

"Father Bob was always persuasive," the banker recalls, "but that night he outdid himself. His rocklike conviction that errant boys could and must be saved impressed and moved me. He sold me so completely on the idea that I could help give them a chance that after an hour no one could have kept me off his committee!" Father Bob had found the right man. Mr. Barofsky was sword and shield to him in the days ahead.

With the banker enlisted, the Home no longer looked so much like an impractical priest's private delusion, and shortly twelve men had accepted places on the committee. They included a Presbyterian, a Baptist, a Lutheran and a Roman Catholic, and were the same men who a few months later were to act as the incorporators of St. Francis. Bishop Nichols was their chairman; he now makes light of his role and says, "The greatest contribution I made to St. Francis was to act as its brakes." Even if that were the whole truth, great credit would be his. The Homes owe their existence to Father Bob's enthusiasm and divine imprudence, but many times those same qualities very nearly brought disaster. The Bishop's good sense, steady hand and emotional detachment more than once averted a crack-up. It is difficult to imagine how the Home could have succeeded without his influence.

The committee agreed that the Home's first year of operating expenses would be at least $15,000. The figure seemed extravagantly high to Father Bob. He reminded the members that every boy would have a job for the dignity of knowing that he was helping to support himself, that no dishwashers or launderers or yardmen would be necessary, and that the farm itself would return a substantial income. He pointed out also that there would be no uniforms, since the boys would be wearing whatever they owned or was contributed to the Home. No teachers would be necessary, for the boys would go to the public schools, and such staff members as were necessary would work for subsistence salaries.

It all sounded plausible as the priest explained it, but the committee still thought it well to establish a budget of $25,000: $10,-000 to purchase the property and $15,000 to operate the Home for a year. That was the amount which would have to be collected before the Home could open. Even then, they were not so practical as they had thought—the year's operating expenses were over $22,000.

The Church approved the budget and the plan to buy the poorhouse; Bishop Nichols then offered Father Bob his blessing, but no salary.

Raising $25,000 was a formidable task in the far-from-affluent and sparsely settled district, few of whose missions could contribute much even to their own support. Father Bob, however, was confident as always that God never fails to provide the way for anything He wants done.

Father Bob is diffident as a man, but as the servant of a great work, he was uncharacteristically headstrong and aggressive. Once on the road to raise funds, his zeal transcended his diffidence, and his conviction that he pleaded in Christ's Name for His cause overwhelmed his long reluctance to ask for money. The naturally conservative people of Kansas—the farmers, the churchmen, and even the supposedly hardheaded businessmen—heard him gladly and responded with openhearted generosity. Perhaps they did so because many of them already knew and loved him; perhaps the highly respected Mize name helped; but most of all they seemed to respond to the priest's holy commitment to a noble ideal.

Organizations such as the Kansas D.A.R. made St. Francis one of their pet projects; and a leaflet appeal brought an exceptional number of answers. One bank official observed, "That priest is certainly Christlike, and he's also a genius at raising money."

All summer, a dream in his heart and holes in his shoes, he traveled the countryside with Johnny beside him. One happy day in mid-August, Father Bob informed the county commissioners that St. Francis was ready and able to purchase the property. His joy turned to foreboding as he saw that something was wrong. He was told he must see the County Attorney immediately.

"Father Bob," said the County Attorney as they sat alone in

the latter's office, "I hate to tell you, but we've been running down a blind alley. I've found an old statute on the books which requires the voters' approval on the sale of any property, such as the Old People's Home, which is valued at over five thousand dollars."

"What's so serious about that?" came the puzzled question.

"Only that the sheriff and a good many other people don't want delinquent boys in their town. They wouldn't vote to sell you the poorhouse in a million years."

"Let's just call a special election and find out!"

"No. I'm sorry, but that's impossible. It's too expensive. There can't be any decision for over a year."

With a sinking sensation of defeat, the priest fought to keep his hope alive. The money was in hand, all the arrangements were made, and the Home was to open in less than two weeks. To wait for the next election and near certainty of an adverse vote would be the death of the St. Francis dream. It was then or never. Out of desperation the priest pulled an idea. He said tensely, "St. Francis has to open. If we cannot buy it now, why can't we *rent* it?"

By late afternoon Father Bob had an agreement from the county commissioners: he could rent the property for a period of three years at the rate of $25.00 a month, but the arrangement was only a reprieve, not a pardon. Under those circumstances no renovations or improvements could be made on the Home, and there was no assurance that the property would ever belong to St. Francis. The Home would have to make do with the rickety furnace, which Father Bob had discovered heated only the first floor. The only two radiators which worked were in the boys' upstairs bedrooms. He worried also that further contributions might be stifled by so tentative an existence. Nevertheless, all the problems and worries receded before one glorious and all-important fact: the Home would open! It would open without security, with virtually no experience behind it, with no psychologist, no trained staff, no clinical program of any kind, and with only the love of God as therapy—but it would open. Father Bob was ready to begin his work that boys who were lost might be found.

CHAPTER **7**

THE FIRST WINTER—
DREAM OR NIGHTMARE?

ON SEPTEMBER 3, 1945, the St. Francis Home for Boys opened the doors of its rented poorhouse. Soon after dawn it received its first arrival. Johnny, the assistant fund-raiser, came lugging two battered old suitcases which contained the whole of his worldly possessions. He was an hour ahead of the Director and the rest of the staff: to greet him were only the old couple who were to stay on, and the nearly empty house.

Some miscellaneous furniture donated by a kindly churchwoman only made the rooms seem more vacant. Promptly at seven o'clock reinforcement appeared; a truck piled high with furniture rounded the bend in the driveway, and Father Bob jumped out of the driver's seat. Johnny ran to help unload the furniture—the priest's personal belongings and a goodly number of beds and bureaus and chairs begged or contributed by members of nearby parishes.

Within an hour the rest of the so-called staff had arrived: Helen Kueser, a jovial and buxom farm woman with two small sons; and Manetta Heidman, of whom Father Bob says, "Without her sustaining leadership, there would have been no Homes."

67

Miss Heidman had formerly been a teacher at Fort Hays College in Kansas, but was an assistant professor of Home Economics at Wayne University in Detroit when she had learned of the projected Home. Upon hearing that Father Bob was unable to find trained staff members, she had requested a year's leave of absence (subsequently extended to two) in order to help. The devoted churchwoman knew but didn't care that her University salary of $5,200 would be reduced to $1,800 at the Boys' Home. She was a born manager, and no job was too menial for her to do; she was always patient and understanding with the boys, and no less so with the constantly shifting staff over the next two years. She was as good a natural homemaker as she was a professional one; Manetta Heidman's contribution to the Homes cannot be overestimated.

The biggest problem at St. Francis from the first has been to enlist a staff trained to help boys and at the same time thoroughly committed to the Christian view of life and worship. The problem in 1945 was heightened by a war economy, and personnel had not yet been released from the military and industrial jobs created by the war. The only male staff member Father Bob had been able to recruit was Doyle, an Arkansas farm boy. All the priest knew about him was that he was an ex-Marine and had been active in 4-H clubs, but even he was considered a lucky find at the time.

Next to arrive were a couple from a neighboring town and their sad-eyed little son. Charlie was only seven and at that age could hardly be classified a juvenile delinquent, but when Father Bob saw the little curlyhead smile wistfully, he couldn't let the Home's age limits of twelve to eighteen keep the lad out. The priest was not told that the child's grandfather happened to be the sheriff who had waged so bitter a campaign against the establishment of the Home and would continue to fight its existence as long as he was in office. He had no idea that his grandson was there at the time.

Last on the scene, just in time for supper, was thirteen-year-old Jack, who had been in and out of the Boys' Industrial School in Topeka since he was eight. His latest offense had been car stealing. His life had begun on a treeless farm in Kansas, and to date had been unfortunate. His beloved father was an alcoholic. His mother had separated from her husband, and had taken Jack's little sister; his two older, better-behaved brothers had been placed with good foster families. Jack, the delinquent, was unwanted by anyone except his parents, whose constant tussling over the boy had only increased his unhappiness.

Johnny showed Jack where to sit at the long dining room table and nudged him, as he had everyone but Miss Heidman, to stand behind his chair until Father Bob said grace. Johnny was feeling definitely superior because he had been with the priest that summer and knew the ropes; at the end of the blessing, he made the sign of the Cross with rather unchristian smugness, and the other two boys furtively and fumblingly followed suit.

Father Bob smiled as he sat down at the table for the first meal with his beginning "family." None of the three scrubbed and cherubic faces before him or the polite voices murmuring "Please pass the potatoes" gave warning of the excitement their owners would generate over the next months.

Late that night after everyone was in bed and the house was quiet, the priest sat alone, offering a prayer of thanksgiving for the existence of the Home of which he had dreamed. He didn't expect an uneventful future, but in his happiness he did not suspect how serious would be the troubles that were about to begin. That first winter, as their number increased, his boys would almost tear the town apart.

Father Bob's family expanded rapidly. Raymond, a chronic runaway with a practice of spending nights in empty movie theaters, was remanded to St. Francis by the Industrial School. At thirteen he was an attractive, intelligent boy with a sweet and gentle disposition.

Mack was placed in the Home by the Probation Department in Kansas City for repeated car thefts.

Then came Melvin, whose good family background was counterbalanced by an overexacting father. The boy had twice stolen cars during runaways to Nebraska and New Mexico.

Wayne and Billy, at thirteen, were both victims of broken homes. They came together from the Industrial School where they had been committed because of thievery. The day they came to St. Francis, seven-year-old Charlie was taken away under protest by his irate grandfather, who had just learned of his presence in the Home.

One cold night a couple of weeks later, Jack was milking in the barn when he heard a rustle in the hay. Fearing snakes or wild animals, he hurled a pitchfork in the direction of the sound, and narrowly missed a human being.

"Hey, Jack, it's me," said a frightened voice—and not one but two Charlies crawled out of the hay. The original had run away from home to return to St. Francis, and had brought his twin brother with him. Jack took the half-frozen twins into the house, and all the boys took a fatherly interest in seeing that the little brothers were given supper, hot baths, and fresh clothes. The older boys were almost as heartbroken as the youngsters when told the twins could not remain at the Home.

St. Francis had achieved by then a genuine family feeling, for the older boys, as in any large family, had assumed much of the responsibility for the care and direction of the younger boys, and their oversight was very loving, however carefree.

They all knew that Father Bob had promised the town that the perpetrator of any serious offense would be dismissed and returned to the custody of the state, so all the youngsters were very much on their company behavior. Their conduct in and out of school was irreproachable, and the people of Ellsworth were almost ready to think that their earlier opposition to the Home had been mistaken.

The Director himself was beginning to relax. He had been particularly concerned about Jack, but his fears seemed to be groundless. The boy had made friends easily and was doing well at school. Father Bob was delighted above all with his response to the religious program at St. Francis.

One of the first rules of St. Francis was that boys who came to the Home would attend the services of their own church on Sunday, that any who did not claim a religious preference (and they were the majority) would attend the local parish church with Father Bob, and that everyone would attend the daily chapel services, morning and evening. So great was their respect for him that while Father Bob was chaplain, the boys went willingly to the daily Eucharist and daily Evensong, whatever the unfamiliar way of worship meant to them.

Jack was far more than "willing": he was unreservedly eager. The high point of his week was his turn to take Evening Prayer, which then as now was led by the boys. After he had been at St. Francis only a few weeks, a chapel visitor remarked, using the proper term, "My, Jack, you certainly read the service well." Jack was insulted. "Read it, hell!" he snorted. "I knew it by heart."

Then, shortly before Thanksgiving, came "Lucifer"—a boy characterized by Father Bob as "clever as the Devil and about as wicked."

Up to that time the boys had given the impression that they could be trusted anywhere, and so were issued an invitation to attend a two-day Episcopal Youth Organization conference in the nearby town of Hutchinson. The St. Francis group of eight was invited to be the guests of Mr. and Mrs. Dillon, whose chain of grocery stores is known all over Kansas. Their home was spacious and filled with valuable possessions.

On the bus returning to St. Francis after the conference, the boys passed the time by emptying their pockets; and amid chortles of mutual admiration they compared notes to see who had made the biggest haul. They produced knives of all sorts and varieties, fountain pens galore, and enough jewelry to open a shop. The boys boasted of their forty-eight-hour crime wave, and seemed not to realize that the Director would not be able to share their enjoyment.

Late that night Father Bob took the boys aside one by one, and the picture of their extracurricular activities at Hutchinson began to take form. Most of the stolen goods belonged to the

Dillons, and the rest had been harvested at a drugstore and hardware store in the town. Father Bob soon determined that "Lucifer" had been the organizer of the fall from grace and he was dismissed, but during his three weeks at St. Francis he had managed to pry off the top of a perhaps not-too-securely-fastened powder keg.

Father Bob's patience and loyalty toward his boys whatever they had done was sometimes criticized as sentimentality, but the priest never denied bad boys do exist. He knew that no youngster was born a criminal, but he also knew that the reasons behind a boy's delinquency—poor home environment, lack of love and discipline, corrupt associates—did not relieve the offender of responsibility for his actions.

From the moment a boy entered St. Francis, the priest emphasized to him that his wrongdoings mattered, but that something else mattered more—that he was one of God's children, profoundly loved and precious in His sight, regardless of his transgressions. He showed him that he did not have to earn forgiveness, but had only to accept it with a penitent heart. He taught them that the grace of God which makes men healthy and whole comes to them through Jesus Christ by the Holy Spirit—and is found by promise in the Holy Catholic Church. He also taught them that their status before God was the same as all humanity's—not that of the innocent, but of the pardoned. That is why he stressed so much the importance of forgiveness as therapy: it is the way God deals with all of us. "In the act of forgiveness," he said again and again to those who thought him too soft, "we have the most effective instrument for the transformation of character. When you forgive a boy, you deepen his knowledge that he has done wrong, and his penitence grows more sincere."

The Hutchinson aftermath was the first severe test of his theory—and the immediate results would have discouraged a man of lesser faith.

The boys were full of apologies; the stolen goods were returned; the Dillons were understanding. On Father Bob's part, there was ready forgiveness; but because it was not accompanied with stern discipline, the boys' penitence was far from swift. Forgiveness means little if it apparently costs nothing. There was none of the deprivation of privileges which should have followed as the natural consequence of wrongdoing. Allowances were withheld, but the small staff made it impossible to carry through on any real punishment.

Jack put on a good act of contrition—he may have believed it himself—and assured the priest he had learned from the experience. "I guess we all have to learn the hard way"; it was to become his favorite expression, and he repeated it innumerable times during his stay at St. Francis. It was soon obvious that from the Dillon experience he had learned only what he could get away with.

A day later he and Billy rode their bicycles over some nearby section-line roads. They crossed the bridge over the river, and decided to explore a lane which led to a rural farmhouse. Dismounting, they knocked on the door, and when no one answered, they walked in. First they helped themselves to cigarettes lying on the kitchen table; then, poking around, they found money in several drawers. They found the inevitable knives; Father Bob says, "It was always knives, knives, knives" when the boys got into trouble. Jack and Billy also came upon a real prize—they found a gun.

Jack was working again at a pastime he knew well. By the end of that Sunday afternoon, he and his aide had visited and robbed four farmhouses.

Suddenly it seemed that all the barriers were down at St. Francis. "Company behavior" was forgotten; the boys had seen that nothing much would happen to them if they reverted to their old habits.

As Father Bob understood later, "They had lost their vision of goodness and holiness." The round of stealing became continuous.

The heartsick priest began to discover their loot hidden all over the house, and not too carefully. One evening he opened a file drawer to find it brimful with flashlights, tools, and, of course, knives. Jack confessed to the theft and Father Bob, taking solace in the readiness of his confession, immediately forgave him yet again—following the Lord's admonition to forgive "until seventy times seven."

His method of dealing with seemingly incorrigible youngsters appeared to almost everyone to be hopelessly unrealistic, and the priest was harshly criticized for being so gullible; but even while he struggled to find a more effective way to apply the teaching of Christ, his dependable and consistent faith in his Lord and in his boys, regardless of "practicality," would inspire and redeem many of his problem children. Both his ability always to see the boys as they should be and his belief in them however they acted were in themselves therapeutic. In the end, his unqualified faith in the renewing power of forgiveness was fully vindicated.

Father Bob sometimes was easily duped, but he was also often curiously astute. Although he had virtually no clinical experience, he had an ability to get directly to the heart of a boy's problem which a trained psychologist might envy; and he at least was never fooled by excuses. When he found a valuable ring and watch hidden under Johnny's bed, the boy said hopefully, as if exonerated from all blame, "I just didn't think."

"You thought, all right, Johnny," the priest replied sadly, "but it was the wrong kind of thinking, as you very well know." Two weeks of dishwashing may have been inadequate punishment, but the hours spent at the kitchen sink, elbow deep in soapy water full of dirty dishes and greasy pots and pans, at least gave Johnny an opportunity to "think" in the right direction.

Despite the early opposition of some townspeople, store owners in Ellsworth were extraordinarily tolerant and sympathized with the passion of Father Bob to succeed with his boys; they knew that if the pilferings became generally known, the Home wouldn't be able to continue. In the schools only the principal knew the boys' individual backgrounds, in order that the expectations of the teachers and students would not be based on the past. Father

Bob had some success in persuading the merchants to apply the same principle to the boys' current misbehavior, convincing them that if at the end of a few months the boys were to feel isolated and rejected in the community, their new concept of themselves as wanted and worthwhile persons might collapse—perhaps permanently—before they had had a real opportunity to change.

News of that sort is difficult to keep quiet, however, and while the two weekly newspapers were kind in their editorial columns, they were frank in their news reports. The hostile sheriff was the source of most information, and he saw to it that details of every public misdeed of the boys were made known, usually with some dramatic elements added. He said, "I told you so," and attributed to St. Francis every crime and act of violence in the county that he plausibly could.

The frequent thefts were accompanied by a rash of runaways. The boys were not closely supervised, and found it easy to wander off the unfenced property and keep going. The trouble was that a pair of teen-aged legs won't carry its owner far, and the distances between Kansas towns are great. To go AWOL effectively was virtually synonymous with stealing a car.

Father Bob attempted to soften public wrath somewhat by pointing out that the boy didn't want to steal a car, he wanted to steal a ride. The taking of a $3,000 car is not by intention a $3,000 theft, because the boy wants no financial profit from the transaction. His theft seldom lasts longer than the gas. Such an argument was small consolation to the owners of two cars wrecked in one night by three St. Francis boys.

Father Bob had returned late from an all-day speaking trip to Dodge City. He stopped to check with Miss Heidman about how things had gone during his absence. She thought there was cause to worry. She told him of the events of the evening; all the boys had attended a high school musicale at the Memorial Hall. Two of them had left early and returned, not on the St. Francis bus but shortly afterward. The sheriff called at eleven o'clock to see if all the boys were accounted for, because a car had been stolen and wrecked during the evening. He was satisfied to hear that all the boys were present when he called, but Miss Heidman wasn't. The two boys had been missing most of the evening and she was disturbed.

"What boys?" asked Father Bob.

"Harry and Fred."

Harry was the son of cultured and conscientious parents. He had been raised in the well-to-do suburbs of a large city and was a good student and an Eagle Scout, but his craving for excitement had got him into numerous scrapes. Since coming to St. Francis he had acted the perfect gentleman and seemed to be progressing so well that the parents of another boy convicted of car theft in the same community had asked the court to send their son to St. Francis too.

Harry and Fred had been bored at the musicale and had wandered out, planning to return when the event was over. Then they had spotted a particularly tempting parked car. Suddenly they had to take a joy ride. Breaking the car window and using a dime to connect the ignition, they sped away with Harry at the wheel. The car was as good as its advertising, but the road wasn't. Harry skidded around a sharp corner and missed an unexpected bridge. They went over the bank and landed hard in the creek bed. Climbing out of the wreckage, they rushed back toward St. Francis, but they were so late that they decided to try to get away. When they saw a car parked in front of a farmhouse, they released is brakes to get it started. They only succeeded in sending it into another deep ditch. Shaken and frightened, they went home. The owners of the automobiles were not in a forgiving mood; the boys' fathers were each charged several hundred dollars for the cost of repairs.

Father Bob knew that one good break often is all a boy needs to develop into a good citizen instead of a public enemy—and he was determined that at St. Francis a boy would get that chance. Some of the people of Ellsworth were equally concerned that the chance should not be given at their expense. The priest had a vision of errant youth redeemed by decent treatment, by love and by knowing the forgiveness of their Saviour. The public only knew what they saw: St. Francis boys cutting classes, robbing stores, wrecking cars, and acting like the devil.

They could not know and perhaps then would not have been too interested that however unscientific Father Bob's methods and whatever his unfamiliarity with modern techniques, half of his first eight boys would respond to his vision and have no further trouble—an amazing record since sixty to eighty percent of the products of the best-run reformatories today repeat their offenses and must be returned.

Meanwhile, the sheriff stood where he had from the beginning. "You may as well know," he said to Father Bob, "that you haven't got a chance. I'm going to run you and your boys out of town if it's the last thing I do." He very nearly succeeded.

CHAPTER 8

FELONIES, HOMICIDE, AND THERAPY IN CHRIST

A FEW MONTHS after St. Francis opened, a sailor spoke to a priest as they both waited for a train in Ellsworth's Union Pacific railroad station. The sailor related some of the horror stories he had heard about the misdeeds of some St. Francis boys, and commented, "What they need up there is some kind of good leadership." The priest concurred: he was the Home's Director.

If humiliations create humility and open avenues of learning, Father Bob was becoming a humble man, and he was gradually acquiring knowledge.

"These misdemeanors are costing us plenty," he remarked to the County Attorney after a particularly trying week.

"Misdemeanors, my foot," exclaimed the attorney. "They are felonies!" The priest learned the distinction.

One of his most effective teachers was Jack, whose personality and exploits were typical, a mixture of good and bad: "The good known to me," Father Bob says, "and the bad to the public." The boy was host to a mass of conflicting impulses when he came to the Home, and within three months his problems were increased by the handicap of a badly disfigured face.

Often in those first days when the Director was called away from St. Francis he took with him on his journeys the worst troublemakers. They were usually well behaved on such trips, and Miss Heidman's load of responsibility was lightened.

By Christmastide that first year, the staff badly needed a rest. Placements with friends or relatives had been found for all but three of the boys, and Jack was one of them. The way was opened when Father Bob was asked to celebrate Christmas Eucharists at mission churches in the direction of Jack's home in the Oklahoma Panhandle. He could celebrate at three widely scattered altars, and deliver all three boys along the way. Jack would then be able to spend the holidays with his mother and baby sister, to whom he was devoted.

The first stop was for the Christmas Eve midnight Eucharist at McPherson in the heart of Kansas. The next stop was Kingman, where Father Bob's old friend from Associate Mission days, Father Francis, had stayed up after his own midnight Eucharist to wait for the delivery of the boy who was to spend Christmas with him and Mrs. Francis.

Next on the itinerary was Meade, 200 miles to the west, where the Eucharist was scheduled for seven o'clock Christmas morning, and then the party was to drive on to Liberal, only a few miles from the Oklahoma line. The priest and the two boys, Melvin and Jack, never got to Meade.

Snow had fallen all night, and in western Kansas all snows are blizzards. It does not fall vertically from the heavens as in most places, but blows horizontally and never seems to touch the ground. It whips and snarls through the air in icy clusters, and slaps and stings. Highways become slabs of ice. The early hours of that Christmas day were becoming a night so bad, even for Kansas, that no one but physicians or priests would have gone out. Even Father Bob, usually indifferent to hazards of the road, felt the strain. His arms ached from trying to keep the slithering car on the road, and he heartily wished that his charges were safe in their beds back at St. Francis. The only good thing that could be said of their predicament was that traffic was no part of the problem: apparently there wasn't another car in Kansas on the highway that night.

In the snowy darkness of what should have been dawn, Father Bob saw motion in the dim reach of his snow-clogged headlights. A man was frantically waving him to stop; just beyond, blocking the road, was a stalled carful of people. As soon as the priest saw the California license plates, he guessed what the matter was: no antifreeze and a frozen radiator. He carefully eased the Plymouth off the highway onto the shoulder, and rolled his window down a crack to ask how he could help. While the stranded motorist was asking to be pushed to the next town, a glare of headlights appeared suddenly from a dip in the road only 200 yards ahead. Behind the flash was a mammoth cross-country bus, its brakes full on, but still hurtling onward over the icy road. In the instant Father Bob saw it, the bus swerved away from the car on the highway and headed directly toward the Plymouth. With a crash, it rammed the priest's car and tossed it lightly 160 feet back down the roadway.

When the whump of the bouncing had stopped, the priest fell back, holding two pieces of steering wheel, which was broken by the force with which his chest had slammed into it. Never noticing that his left ear was dangling by its lobe, he turned with a sick prayer to his boys. Melvin was moaning; his knees had been smashed by the dashboard. Jack looked more as though his face had been shoved into a meat grinder than into the windshield.

Through his dazed horror, Father Bob found that the bus driver was standing at his side. The three of them were placed gently in the nearly unscratched bus and rushed to the nearest hospital, fifty miles away. As the bus driver explained what had happened, Father Bob saw that, in the brief moment that was his, the man had made the correct moral decision; unable to miss both cars without serious danger to his passengers, he had aimed at the vehicle with fewer people in it. The priest had only compassion for the shaken driver, but he prayed and worried for his broken boys.

Father Bob was released from the hospital before Jack; and his first act was to take the bandaged boy a bag of hard candy and an orange. Jack tried to grin under his swathing, and the priest's eyes filled as the boy said in muffled tones, "Pray for me in the chapel, will you, Father?"

The doctors did their best with the jigsaw puzzle of Jack's face, but they warned the priest that the lines would show. Distressed, Father Bob arranged with the kindly Mr. Gardner of the Boys Industrial School to take the injured boy back for a while so he could have free plastic surgery at the Kansas University Hospital. The priest was there when the bandages were removed. "My heart sank a mile," he says, "when I saw the still-ugly scar from his mouth to his ear, and the other from his mouth to an eye."

When he came back to St. Francis, Jack called himself "Scarface Johnson"—and his behavior matched his appearance. Both Father Bob and the boy knew that the accident had been just that and that no one was responsible, but Jack bore the marks on his face and the priest suffered a lingering guilt in his heart. The Director spent even more time with the boy than he had formerly, enveloped his increasing delinquencies in greater patience and forbearing, and accepted the frequent rebuffs with penitence and kindness. The boy thought he wanted to be left alone, but somewhere deep in his shifting character, love was building a place for him to stand when he would come to himself. The time, however, was not yet.

That summer Bishop Mize offered his Colorado mountain cabin to St. Francis for a few weeks. With some of the other boys, Jack was taken there for a brief vacation, and there he returned to his old work—stealing. He organized his companions for a campaign of robbing cabins and stores of knives, guns, and Indian trinkets. His last day there, he took Ben along to another cabin, where they politely asked a mountain woman if they could take a picture of her rabbits. She did not know that the camera was empty, or that while she conversed cheerfully with the two boys, a third one, Willie, was busily ransacking her house. As their final coup, the three boys were missing at suppertime. They had eased their discomfiture by the old method of running away, and like most fugitive boys failed to consider that after the police picked them up, they would be taken to jail and returned to an industrial school.

If the St. Francis staff has the opportunity, its members will themselves track down a runaway, so that he can face the consequences with the support of the Home life; for at the Home he can be helped to learn from his misdeed; if the police must take over and separate the boy from society in a state institution, his better nature may be locked up as well—sometimes permanently.

Father Bob feels that the moment of crisis in a boy's life is the moment of greatest opportunity, the moment in which one can make or break a youngster. So when the three boys were missed, he started out after them in his car.

He found them some six hours later hiding in the woods. Two of them got in the car meekly enough, but Jack, fighting with himself, was glad to transfer the struggle to the priest—only after a scuffle was he successfully dumped inside; and then the priest could keep him there only by peeling off the boy's trousers and sitting on them.

Jack spoke more truth than he knew when he repeated again and again, "I guess I have to learn the hard way." Sometimes it seemed as though he never would. Father Bob came to realize that some boys must hit rock bottom before their eyes can be opened and they can be saved—and Jack was one of them.

Early Labor Day morning, the Monday before school was to open, Jack, Ben, and Willie disappeared. Monday night came, and still there was no word of them. Tuesday wore on, and Father Bob grew increasingly anxious. Finally on Wednesday a long distance call came from Cherryvale, some 250 miles away, in the Oklahoma-Missouri corner of the state.

"What's the penalty if we come back to St. Francis?" It was Jack's voice. Before the priest could answer, the connection was broken with a click. Knowing very well the boys had not been sitting quietly on a park bench for three days, Father Bob called the Cherryvale police and asked them to hold the boys until he got there. He left at once.

Five hours later the priest was thankful to know that there were no charges against them; evidently they had for once borrowed rides with their thumbs instead of stealing them with crossed wires. The Director interrogated each boy separately, and their stories seemed to jibe. He was stern with the culprits, but was enormously relieved that with Jack in charge, their only crime had been going AWOL.

Upon their return to the Home their punishment was assigned; they had to carry back to the lumberyard downtown the forty-two heavy fence posts left over from a summer fencing job—fourteen fence posts apiece, seven trips with two posts to a trip.

The boys began willingly enough on their assignment and with their usual ingenuity soon devised a sort of stretcher in order to carry more than two posts at a time. For several days after school they made the trek up and down the road to town. Their behavior was excellent, and they appeared honestly sorry that they had caused trouble and worry. Father Bob began to believe that some of the holiness he had tried to teach them at St. Francis had finally taken. He relaxed too soon.

A call came from the sheriff, and the priest's heart sank. A car had been stolen on Labor Day and had just been found abandoned near Cherryvale; the lawman demanded the fingerprints of the boys who had been gone at the time. No fingerprints were necessary: the boys saw that the game was up and readily confessed to the theft.

As usual, they had not intended to steal when they left the Home, but had just started hitchhiking to another town for adventure. They got a lift to Lyons, where to their delight they found a county fair in progress. After doing the fair, they explored the town until nearly midnight, and were thinking about hitchhiking back to St. Francis when Jack spied a car. The Dodge coupe had been parked with the keys in it and the doors unlocked—an invitation the boys could not resist. Jack waved them in and drove until the car ran out of gas.

Jack assumed all the blame, and for once the consequences were bitter to him. To Father Bob's despairing grief, he was sent back to the Industrial School. It was indeed "the hard way," but at last he did learn by it. After a while he was returned to St. Francis for a last-chance attempt to make good, and he succeeded. The story of "Scarface Johnson" would have a happy ending.

Ben and Willie were permitted to stay at the Home, since their previous offenses were unknown to the County Attorney. They became two of the Home's most distinguished "alumni." Fortunately, the theft had not occurred in Ellsworth and the news did not appear in local county papers. If it had, the two boys could not have stayed at St. Francis. Once the community recognized them as car thieves, their chance for rehabilitation might have been lost, for the boys would have found themselves living again in that aura of constant suspicion which in itself can cause a boy to revert; for a boy tends to do what is expected of him—good or bad. It was that sort of atmosphere from which Father Bob had sought in the first place to rescue them when he created the Home.

It was another aspect of the priest's theory of forgiveness which was to prove itself again and again in the coming years: if a felony is forgiven by the victim and handled quietly by the Home, with a wise levying of consequences proper to the individual, a boy can return to normal life. With his merits gradually overcoming his demerits, he moves in little thrusts toward greater self-confidence and lasting rehabilitation. Ben, Willie, and even Jack demonstrated that the principle worked; Mack showed the danger of violating it.

Mack, fifteen and large for his age, came to St. Francis from a turbulent life in Kansas City. He had been in the Industrial School, but had remained in constant trouble—drinking, gambling, and stealing. One evening he came into the priest's tiny study off the central hallway. He was under discipline for some minor offense, and mentioned it briefly; but something far more important was on his mind.

"Father," he said respectfully, "I want to tell you something. It's nothing that happened here. It was two years ago in Kansas City. I had a job in a bowling alley. I got mad at the boss because he wouldn't pay me what he owed me. I went back to the alley at night and climbed through a cellar window. I wanted to make a mess for him, so I put some paper napkins on top of the bowling balls and lit a match to them."

Father Bob had quietly dropped everything when he observed the boy's intense manner. He remained silent as Mack looked at him a moment, backed up against the cold radiator for support, and plunged on.

"The place caught fire," he continued. "I took out through the window and watched from a drugstore across the street. The fire engines came, and firemen went into the building. Ambulances came. When the fire was over, I saw them carry out two people on stretchers. It was the boss and his wife. I didn't know they stayed in the place." There was a pause, and then Mack added, "The woman lived, but the boss died. I've never told anybody before."

Within the hour Father Bob had Mack to his own priest, a Roman Catholic; and by midnight he and Father Bob were on the train to Kansas City. Mack, who knew the meaning of true repentance, had made his confession, received absolution from the Church, and was ready to pay society the penalty.

The following morning he repeated his story to the Juvenile Court judge. A probation officer said that $10,000 had been spent by the state and an insurance company in an attempt to find the guilty party. Mack's confession was the first break in the case, but "John Doe" charges had been filed, and the indictments were arson and homicide.

The judge was impressed by the boy's serious acceptance of responsibility and dealt understandingly with him. Before determining the case, he assigned the boy to the care of the city clinic. After two weeks the clinic psychiatrist recommended that the youngster be returned to St. Francis, where he had already greatly progressed during the preceding months.

Believing that the boy's story was unknown in Ellsworth, Father Bob consented to take the boy back. A Kansas City newspaper had headlined the story, but the boy's name had been withheld, and St. Francis happily had been referred to simply as "a Catholic institution in Kansas," which designation was correct, but would mean *Roman* Catholic to the public. It thus seemed that Mack would return without notoriety.

Unfortunately, he did not. The harm was done the next day in school. With the kindest intentions, his English teacher exclaimed the moment he entered the classroom, "Mack, we heard all about you over the radio, but we want you to know that you are just as welcome here as ever." Perhaps he was, but it did not seem so to him. The hour passed uncomfortably: he saw in every glance the knowledge that he had killed a man. Every extra consideration reminded him that he was separated from his classmates. His spirits sank lower, and he knew that he had lost his chance to live down the past.

His reaction was typical. His behavior had been outstandingly good, but turned increasingly bad. Within the Home he became rebellious and quarrelsome. Outside he was sullen and uncooperative. For the good of the other boys and because Mack himself was not being helped, Father Bob at last told him to pack his things, and promising all possible aid and prayer, he drove him to Kansas City. There Mack promptly stole a truck, and once again found himself in the Industrial School.

His opportunity to find the proper channel for his life while it was still near the shallow headwaters was over. Mack continued to flounder in a backwash of crime. Nevertheless, St. Francis had left its mark: the boy had felt Father Bob's influence—that of a man to whom God and the Spirit are the true realities. Nine years later a letter came from Mack. "I'm sorry, Father, that I can't repay all the kindnesses and the swell memories of the days I spent with you. I will always treasure them—the evenings we spent playing ping-pong together, the times Johnny and I gave you and some others the 'hot seat' with that little generator we found. The times we went hunting, and the time Ben and Willie and I put up the Quonset hut. The time we got the cow and the two hogs, and the hours of sanding I did on the altar for the chapel. And most of all the long, wonderful talks we had together."

The letter was written in the cell of a federal prison.

Some thirty boys passed through St. Francis during the first eighteen months, and the names of all of them were selected from a snowstorm of applications. Most of them were from Kansas City; all of them were from either reformatories or jails; and many of them were so deeply rooted in trouble and so generally intractable that the state was glad to get rid of them by remanding them to the custody of St. Francis. Father Bob, the priest, father, counsellor, general handyman, and director of the Home, was also the sole "evaluating committee," and in his well-meaning inexperience he made many errors in his selection of boys.

Some were let in who needed psychiatric care which the Home was not equipped to give them. St. Francis has never wanted to be a hospital for the mentally or emotionally sick; it serves spiritually bereft boys of normal mentality who are able to keep up in the public school system and have sufficient emotional stability to learn to live as a part of the world to which they will graduate. That is not to say that St. Francis boys are one-time offenders. Like the first ones, the boys today have committed a number and variety of offenses before coming to the Home, and the habits of delinquency are still deeply ingrained. Still, St. Francis can take on only behavior problems, however serious, and must leave treatment of mental and medical ills to others.

Father Bob remarks, "Habits change slowly. God the Holy Ghost works in our lives more often as leaven than as lightning." A stay of at least two years at St. Francis is considered necessary if a boy is to be permanently rehabilitated; two years in which to gain self-confidence, to know himself wanted and accepted by a loving family, to catch a vision of Jesus Christ, and, through the

Sacraments of His Church, to receive His grace. During the first year and a half of the Home's existence, many of the inexpertly selected boys exhibited such uncontrollable criminal tendencies that they had to be returned to the state after only a few weeks. The Home gradually learned why. It teaches its boys to accept responsibility for their acts; but such boys were in fact not responsible because of emotional or mental illness, and could not benefit from the open life pioneered by St. Francis. The difference between a sick boy and a sinful boy is hard to discern, but it is a real and important one. A sick person cannot help himself; he must be kept apart and be given specialized treatment. Most people do wrong of their own free will or because they have never known the right; they are the ones St. Francis can help.

As such hard lessons were being mastered on the campus, Election Day was drawing closer, and the citizens of Ellsworth were eying St. Francis with increasing trepidation.

Just a week before the election, the Home suffered its greatest blow to its prestige. Seven boys, none of whom knew how to drive, ran away and stole a car. Although several of them were new arrivals, and five of them were only thirteen years old, all seven had to be returned to the Industrial School. St. Francis' record for the first eighteen months was hardly impressive; out of thirty boys, nineteen returned to their former ways. On Election Day the town perhaps could not be blamed for voting an overwhelming NO to the county commissioners' proposal to sell the poorhouse to St. Francis.

Father Bob was saddened. He blamed himself and not his boys for what appeared to be the failure of the Home, but as always when he faced adversity, his determination increased rather than diminished. The public record could not shake his faith in his dream because he knew what the townspeople did not know: every St. Francis boy was experiencing longer absences from wrongdoing than he ever had before, and along with the slowly developing habit of rightdoing, he was learning for the first time something of the meaning of holiness. All the boys were coming

88

to know the Presence of the Blessed Christ, if not in their lives at least in their chapel. They were learning what contrition means—sorrow for sin leading to a change of behavior.

Nevertheless, the priest was quite human, and his disappointment at the lopsided verdict was too deep to hide. That evening, after a silent supper, he retreated to his study and sat there alone, with his head in his hands. He caught a deep sigh in mid-escape as he heard his door latch quietly turn. Someone said, "Father?" He made an encouraging sound and looked up to see a young hand which had earned its owner fourteen burglary convictions holding grounds for a fifteenth count—a fat wallet. The sad voice continued, "How can I find out who owns this so I can return it?"

The priest leaped up and threw back the door. "Come, Ed," he cried. "We'll find him together!" With his arm around the startled boy's shoulders and an ear-to-ear grin on his face, Father Bob went down the hall.

CHAPTER **9**

"PADRE, YOU'D BETTER CALL IT QUITS!"

THE NEGATIVE VOTE clouded the future of St. Francis, but it did not put the Home out of business. Father Bob still had the rest of his three-year lease and all his old dedication—which some called stubbornness. Despite the havoc his boys had wreaked on the community, the priest loved them, good and bad, as any parent would, and expected that their charms would become apparent even to their detractors, given sufficient time. Most of Ellsworth thought he was through when his lease ran out; Father Bob thought the air had been cleared and he was just beginning.

"Well, Father—are you about ready to call it quits?" asked an able businessman, one of his staunchest supporters.

"Shucks, no," he quickly replied. "I haven't really started yet!"

To anybody objectively assaying the situation, it seemed that if he really had yet to start, he would be disqualified at the starting line. The Home still had no trained member on the staff, nor did it appear likely that there would be one in the near future. Qualified workers could not be expected to flock to accept subsistence salaries and small, noise-wracked living quarters such as the Director occupied. As matters stood, the Home already was badly overcrowded with twenty-two boys and the tiny staff. The furniture, once shabby, was long broken; there was no money for new, and no improvements could be made until the Home actually belonged to St. Francis.

The first year's expenses had been subscribed in advance; luncheon clubs, church members, society women and a few small organizations had given St. Francis the welcome and necessary financial lift which had been its salvation; but with its apparently poor record and the no-confidence vote of its community, Father Bob couldn't be sure where the next dollar was coming from, or if it was coming at all. In everyone's eyes but his, the great Christian Experiment had failed; but no one, not even those who knew him best, had reckoned with the force of his trust in God. He seemed to have been supernaturally steeled to absorb the Home's problems; and according to his faith, he didn't bear them alone but offered them to God. Each night he and his boys prayed the St. Francis Prayer, whose opening words held his life's petition:

> Lord, make me the instrument of thy peace.
> Where there is hatred, let me sow love;
> Where there is injury, pardon;
> Where there is doubt, Faith.

He knew with a divine certainty that the tide had begun to turn, that if he could only hold on long enough, the town would be convinced.

He was entirely aware that the Home's success was not assured because a boy with a criminal record had returned a wallet, but there were other signs: an increasing number of the runaways which still plagued St. Francis ended with the boys returning voluntarily. Gradually the youngsters were responding to Father Bob's love and trust in them. More and more unruly, rebellious youngsters began to live up to his vision of them as he treated them as he would have them be, rather than as they happened to be.

"Trust a boy," he said again and again, "and he will prove trustworthy." Then he quickly would add, "Anyway, it's worth losing something once in a while for the privilege of trusting someone."

In the beginning the frequency of loss had been distinctly more often than "once in a while," as most of the boys took advantage of someone they thought was an easy mark. Yet their attitude was slowly changing. The leaven of which the priest so often spoke was working.

The first time a kid named Joe popped his tousled head in an Ellsworth grocer's door to sing out, "Hi! I'm from the St. Francis Boys' Home. Father Bob wants me to pay your bill," the storekeeper thought it was a joke. When he learned it wasn't, he figured that Joe must be different from the other no-good hoodlums out there at the county poor farm. He probably just didn't have a family. He couldn't be like the others who had stolen cars and even committed second-degree murder. You couldn't trust young thugs like that to pay your bills.

The grocer was wrong, and a self-effacing, hard-pressed priest of the staid Episcopal Church was proving it. Joe was no different from the other car thieves, burglars, and mugging artists living on the hill. He simply was taking his turn paying off the tradesmen in town, and without misappropriating a penny.

Father Bob also trusted Dick enough to get him a job behind a soda fountain. At the end of the first month his employer said, "Best worker I ever had. Send me another like him."

Father Bob sufficiently trusted one of the worst offenders the Home housed to get him a part-time job at the hardware store: a boy who singlehandedly, and at the risk of his own life, put out a fire in the store which no one else would touch and saved his employer thousands of dollars.

Ellsworth may have voted against the sale of the poorhouse to St. Francis, but the work of the Home was becoming more widely known. Applications poured in, many from far-distant states, far more than could be accepted.

One arrival caused great excitement, for Jim Long had come all the way from Fairbanks, Alaska, to join the family in Kansas. It was not the last excitement Jim caused; his long trip had not exhausted his yearning for travel. Father Bob always had difficulty convincing his new youngsters that truancy is a misdemeanor which lands a boy in jail. Jim seemed not to hear the warning at all.

The first day went well. The good-looking, brown-eyed youngster was excited about his journey, and the boys were eager to hear every detail. He apparently was glad to be at the Home and spent the afternoon playing baseball with the others.

It was very late that night, after everyone should have been long asleep, when the stillness of the house was ruffled by the sound of stifled sobs. Father Bob, who always slept with one ear open, heard. He tiptoed to find Jim's eyes red and his pillow damp. There was no need to ask the trouble. The Director knew that it was the awful malady of homesickness. He touched the boy's shoulder and whispered, "Don't tell anybody, but let's go down and raid the icebox. I'm hungry. How about you?"

The boy covered his feelings as he slipped into his bathrobe, and together priest and boy crept conspiratorially down the stairs.

Over their apple pie and milk, Father Bob joked about how angry Mrs. Kueser would be at the unexpected sampling of tomorrow's dessert (she never minded, as he well knew), and they talked of many things until at last Jim's head began to nod and he was tired enough to sleep. Apple pie and companionship, however, were only temporary help. His battle of homesickness was a long one, and before it was won Jim ran away seven times within the first two months. The first time, Father Bob found him thumbing a ride on the highway to Kansas City, but thereafter he came

93

back each time of his own volition. Someone would see him walking up the Home driveway, downcast and ashamed.

The priest understood, and would welcome him home with a compassion that seemed great enough to take in all the unhappy boys in the world, and yet for each was as personal as if the current offender were the only boy there was.

"I'm alone, too," Father Bob said to Jim as he had to many of his boys. "St. Francis is my only home; but we both have God, so we can't ever be really lonely. Let's work together with Him, and we'll both be happy." Then as an afterthought, "Let's go out and practice a little football. My punting is rusty."

Jim, as did most of the other boys, however tough and hopeless they had been taught they were, responded to the gentle priest who spoke of God and football in the same breath, and prayed, in season, with hands grass-burned from sliding into third base.

Father Bob was not bashful about bringing the boys day by day into God's Presence, nor is St. Francis today. Even serious and faithful churchmen among the visitors must be impressed by how truly religion is not a department of life for the boys, but its center, and how happy and natural a part of the daily routine is worship, which is taken as much for granted as eating, sleeping, playing, and working. Supposedly normal Christian homes, whose members attend Church regularly, often do not find the practice of their religion so easy and natural as do the St. Francis boys, and Father Bob is often asked how he first introduced the Christian Faith to boys who had never heard of Christ, and mostly couldn't care less.

"It's the normal thing for a boy to be a Christian," he replies. "I soon discovered that no matter how low a boy has fallen or how sophisticated he has become in crime, he is old-fashioned enough to regard the normal life as being a Christian life, whatever that means to him. When I spoke to the boys of our Lord, I assumed that I was not telling them of something new, but simply reminding them of something they had once learned and forgotten.

"I can't remember a single time," the priest continues thoughtfully, "that a boy ever was repelled when I took him alone into the chapel upon his admission to St. Francis and explained to him—perhaps the first time he had heard it—the true meaning of the blessed Presence at the altar."

Ray, a brawny, overgrown adolescent who had been four times in and out of Industrial School and most recently in jail for robbery, responded in typical fashion. He arrived at the Home after dark as the family was just sitting down for supper. His mother and father were both drunkards who had given him no religious training, but he obviously considered it the right and expected thing to be a Christian, because as he was spooning up his ice cream, he blurted, "Always expected to be baptized, but never got around to it."

Immediately after the meal, Father Bob led him into the room which served as a chapel. It was in semidarkness, lit only by the flickering flame of the sanctuary lamp. As Father Bob reached to turn on the overhead light, Ray stayed his hand with a gesture. "No, please," he said. "It's nice in here with just the candle." Then the puzzled boy turned to the priest. "How come it's lit, anyway?" he asked.

The priest explained that the candle was kept burning day and night beside the tabernacle, the little cabinet which housed the blessed Sacrament—the Body and Blood of our Lord veiled in the bread and wine. He told how Christ in His love for mankind had made Himself known to people in different ways, how He is present with us unseen wherever we may be, and that He has promised to give us His Life to feed us in the bread and the wine. He further explained that we keep a candle burning before His Presence, to show that He is the Light of the world who shines for all time and for all men, and can never be extinguished in their hearts.

Ray's eyes grew big with wonder and with awe. The next week he stole a car, which inconsistency did not surprise Father Bob, although he often asked plaintively, "How could he carry the cross so beautifully on Sunday, and rob the hardware store on Monday?"

Puzzled or not, the priest was realist enough to recognize that going to chapel twice a day does not immediately transform an experienced offender into a saint. His task was to provide the environment and knowledge of the Christian way, to teach the Word and offer the means of grace, and then to wait for the growing receptiveness in the boy which would enable the Holy Spirit to have His way.

Ray was typical in other ways of the incoming boys at St. Francis: he was without a sense of accomplishment, and happiest when he was on wheels. Father Bob observes, "They all liked anything on wheels, even a lumbering tractor, and they liked balls; but they didn't know what to do with either of them." He recalls the afternoon Miss Heidman looked out the window to see two boys playing catch with one another for the first time. She was greatly pleased, because the pair was one of the most antisocial to come to the Home, and their simple game seemed to her a great victory. Until that afternoon, one of the participants had enjoyed throwing a ball, but the second boy had not been sufficiently cooperative to return it. He preferred instead to throw it through a window!

Ray, like the other newcomers, wanted to make an impression on the older boys. He also would rather circle than tackle the problem of going to a strange school. Father Bob observed that those two factors seemed almost of themselves to reduce to one product—a stolen car. One thing more was needed—a careless car owner to provide temptation by leaving his keys dangling in plain sight. And so it worked out with Ray, who took a car from the courthouse square in the center of town.

That some of his boys sometimes borrowed cars was not so disillusioning to Father Bob as that so-called respectable adults frequently took advantage of the thefts to extort money from the

Home, engaging in a polite form of blackmail. The owner of the car Ray took—and drove for all of fifteen minutes—followed the unwholesome precedent by submitting to St. Francis an enormous bill for unlikely damages. Father Bob angrily paid it rather than risk exaggerated bad publicity for the Home.

"You can train boys," he said with disgust, "but not dishonest adults." The latter, however, never made the ten o'clock news; but St. Francis boys often were on the front pages. The situation could not continue unchanged much longer.

CHAPTER 10

THE SHERIFF OVERPLAYS
HIS HAND

FATHER BOB NEVER DOUBTED that the ultimate success of his boys would prove his revolutionary theory that the Christian Faith was intended to be practiced, however painful or inconvenient the practice might be in a smug and self-satisfied society. He knew that a day-by-day demonstration of Christ's love and forgiveness would result in rehabilitated lives. A belief so costly could not be called mawkish, and it was not sentimentally applied. If in those first years the Home was too lax in discipline and lacked a proper clinical program, the boys nevertheless led busy and well-supervised lives. Eleanor Roosevelt accurately noted in her column, "St. Francis Home knows just where its boys are at all times."

Life at the Home was very different from the sort most of the boys were accustomed to. Before he came there, Sam had thought of it as "that sissy Christian place on the hill," which could not be worse than the jail cell he was otherwise headed for.

Upstairs, Sam found a small but sunny bedroom furnished with two cots, bureau, two straight, unmatched chairs, and a large old-fashioned wardrobe. His eyes went instantly to the window, where gay chintz curtains were blowing in the breeze. Neither home nor jail had featured such niceties.

Joe, from Colorado, was clearing out the two top drawers of the bureau for his new roommate. He nodded toward the wardrobe and said, "Put your things in there. Your half's empty."

Sam started to unpack, pitching in his clothes helter-skelter, but Joe said, "Hey! You'd better hang those things up right. I get graded for how this room looks, too!"

The other boy looked at him and started to snarl (his usual reaction to any directive), thought better of it, and sullenly picked up his clothes and draped them on hangers.

Father Bob hurried up to him at the foot of the stairway a few minutes later. "Let's go out to the barn first," he said excitedly. "The boys and I have something to show you."

On the way, they passed a youngster pursuing four squawking hens. Father Bob grabbed him long enough for him to pant, "Hi!" Sam almost smiled. A little farther on, three boys grinned up from digging sugar beets. "Squares," thought Sam, who had never dug a hole or been so quickly included in a family before.

In the warm shade of the barn, Father Bob pointed into a stall. A wobbly little bull calf, still damp, stood beside his mother. The "midwives," two proud boys only slightly groggy from their all-night vigil, perched on the stall side, looking almost as motherly as the cow.

"Ever see one this young?" whispered the priest.

"I've never seen one at all except in pictures," Sam replied; an elephant would have been no more of a novelty to him.

Father Bob then took him on a short tour of inspection, showing off the Home's eight Holstein cows ("our milk factory"), and the flock of chickens, four of which would supply Sunday dinner if their pursuer did not tire first.

Sam was fascinated in spite of himself, but when the priest pointed out the wide expanse of alfalfa and forage crops raised at the Home, he was considerably less enthusiastic.

"Nobody told me this was a real farm," he mumbled.

Father Bob explained that the boys each worked thirty hours a week during the summer, tending the vegetable garden and the crops and taking care of the animals. Sam's city heart rebelled, until he glimpsed two boys driving the great, lumbering tractor recently donated to St. Francis by the U.S. Government. His eyes glistened. He'd do anything, even farm, if he could do it on wheels.

The priest took Sam in the back door of the house to show him the large, bright kitchen, where cook Helen Kueser gave Sam a large welcoming smile. They walked through the dining room with its two long tables, the chapel, and the recreation room. The large radio and the car magazines recaptured the boy's interest. Father Bob sprawled out in a chair and waved for Sam to do the same. Here it comes, thought the boy. They always put on the friendly act when they want you to do something. Still, the priest didn't seem to be acting, and St. Francis so far was like no institution the youth had known.

The Director talked about life at St. Francis. There were rules, it seemed, but not warnings—it was taken for granted that they'd be followed. Sam had reservations about that. Father Bob explained about school; in the fall, the younger boys walked to the grade school only half a mile away, but Sam would go to the Ellsworth High School in the St. Francis bus. "One of the older boys earned the honor of driving it last term—did a good job, too," remarked the priest. Another chance to get behind a wheel!

"Do you work thirty hours a week in the winter, too?" Sam asked. Father Bob shook his head. "The most important thing then is your school work, so your chores around the Home are cut down to an hour. You'll have your own work to do—everyone is responsible for something—and of course you have your room to keep in order. On Saturdays we take care of what has had to be neglected during the week. We do all our own janitor work around here, you know, and some of the laundry."

The priest mentioned each boy's fifty-cent weekly allowance, and explained that any work over the thirty hours a week in summer, or eight hours during the school year, earned its performer from thirty to forty-five cents an hour. A lot of the youngsters were always broke, but a few managed to save. "One already has over $100 in his savings account," said Father Bob, "and because he wanted money and his school work was good, I'm recommending him for a part-time job in a filling station this coming fall."

Sam was not impressed. Fifty cents a week wouldn't keep him in cigarette money, and he couldn't see killing himself for a measly hundred bucks. He could steal more than that in an hour.

The dinner, Sam reluctantly admitted to himself, was the best he could remember. Hamburgers were his usual fare—how long since he'd had home-cooked chuck roast, let alone as much as he could eat? Afterward, he could only lie leadenly on his bed and listen to the ball game while he read the handbook of rules and regulations Father Bob had given him.

Parts of the manual, he thought, were funnier than a comic book. Go to bed at 9:30, and get up at 6:45? He was used to staying up half the night and sleeping until after noon. And chapel twice a day! Not for him!

It all began to seem more reasonable after his first full day. He had worked six hours under the blazing Kansas sun (he tried taking it easy but no one admired his smartness, so he decided to show them he could do more than anybody) and could hardly wait until 9:30 to get his stiff body into bed. Friday night movies and staying up until ten o'clock did not sound like even the start of a good time, but on the first outing his roommate had to shake him awake when the feature was over. The bus ride to bed was too long.

The first few months were rugged for both Sam and Father Bob. He was loud-mouthed and boastful. He had been given quick acceptance the first week, but spent it as fast as he did his allowance. Soon the other boys didn't like him, or he them. They weren't impressed by his exploits; many of them had better, or worse, records than his. His only claim on the world's attention was useless at St. Francis. He began to wonder why he'd thought it was a sissy place. Take Father Bob: he talked about "God" and "love," but he was no Holy Joe—and he was also the best athlete at the Home. Sam felt a little uncomfortable with the priest because he seemed to know all about him—his thoughts, his fears —and he didn't seem to blame him or to use his weakness against him. It was weird.

Father Bob indeed saw under the garish facade of sophistication, which revealed and did not hide the boy's immaturity and vulnerability. Father Bob saw the swagger, and knew that it covered a deep insecurity. He saw the cockiness, and loved the timid child behind the mask.

Sam complained for months about things he couldn't admit he really didn't mind—chapel, for one thing. Of course Sunday morning church at the Ellsworth parish was long and irksome, but the youth group meeting at night, where he could mingle with the town kids, wasn't half bad. Even Sam, however, could not complain about Mrs. Kueser's cooking and the unheard-of luxury of being able to go back for seconds and thirds. Three meals a day were such an unusual experience for Sam that they may have kept him from looking for more serious trouble than he naturally found. For the first time in his life, an empty stomach was not his partner in crime. He did try to run away once, as much for excitement as anything else, but somehow it wasn't worth the effort when Father Bob didn't get mad or even seem surprised.

Once, when the other boys finally stopped his bragging by telling him to keep his problems to himself, Sam thought he'd show them by grabbing a car in broad Saturday daylight off the crowded courthouse square. That didn't seem to help, either. Three months at St. Francis had set loose inside him an entirely unwelcome conscience. Perhaps to his own surprise, he drove only a few blocks, and then, afraid to risk attempting to find a parking place near the scene of the crime, he headed back toward the Home and parked a couple of blocks away. Fighting against all his habits, he walked straight to the brick Home, up the steps, in the door, down the hall and into Father Bob's study, where, with a look of defiance, he handed over the keys as if he were surrendering his sword. The priest took them gravely, as from an honored friend who only happened for the moment to be on the other side, but he smiled inside and said a silent prayer of thanksgiving.

The act was almost Sam's first experience of deliberate honesty. He could not quickly come to practice the way of life which had won his grudging respect, or tear down the walls he had built against others. He was to get into many other scrapes, and it would take a long time for him to get on good terms with the other fellows, but when he left the Home two years later, he cried.

He had been confirmed a few months before he left St. Francis to take his naval training. From boot camp he wrote Father Bob, "When I first went to St. Francis I hated everybody, but I sure hated to leave. God was just a name to me then, but you made Him seem like a friend. . . . I love Navy life, maybe because in a lot of ways it's a lot like St. Francis. I sure miss you—and if you need anything for the boys and it doesn't cost too much, let me know and I'll send it."

Sam married while he was in the Navy, and brought his first-born to Father Bob to be baptized. It was hard to tell which of the two fathers was prouder of the baby.

Boys still ran away, cars were still being stolen, and knives and flashlights still mysteriously disappeared from downtown stores and reappeared mysteriously at the Home. Nevertheless, it seemed at last that the bad experiences were being outnumbered by the good ones, even if for a time only Father Bob and his staff knew it. The priest was hurt that Ellsworth should read the news in headlines when a St. Francis boy slipped to steal a car but was never informed of the increasing occasions when a repentant boy, shouldering the responsibility for his action, would return the vehicle to its owner within half an hour. The sheriff neglected to pass along such details to the reporters. One of the episodes which hurt Father Bob most concerned Jim.

One rainy night Jim, an associate of Jack in numerous felonies, was missing at chapel. Father Bob searched the Home thoroughly without finding him; and then he thought of the barn.

As he walked in the barn door, he saw the beam of a flashlight play across the rafters, heard boys' voices and muffled laughter—and curiously, the clatter of dishes—all coming from the haymow overhead. He started to climb the ladder, but had stepped only on the first creaky rung when the flashlight and voices were snapped off and he heard in the dark a scurry and the thud of boys' feet in the barnyard outside. Then Jim came slowly down the ladder, alone. Father Bob sent him to his room, but within minutes he was at the door of the priest's study.

"Father," he said hesitantly, "there's something I want to tell you. Those weren't St. Francis boys with me; they were friends from the Industrial School. They called me at noon to say they were running away. When they got here they were hungry and wet, so I took them some food and dry clothes." Jim paused, but went on. "I've got to tell you something, Father. They're going to steal a car. They wanted me along, but I told them no. I think I know where they're going to take it. Maybe we can stop them."

"Let's go," said the priest, reaching for his coat. The two hurried outside, followed by the curious stares of a group standing in the hall. By the time Father Bob and Jim had reached the place, the car was gone.

"They're probably heading south on Highway Forty-five," said Jim. The priest spun the car around and, leaving behind more rubber than the boy would have thought the old vehicle capable of, took out in pursuit. He asked at service stations, hoping they had been seen, but several miles out of town, with neither fugitives nor clues in sight, he turned back. Near the edge of town, however, the car lights picked out three figures in the downpour. Father Bob slowed, stopped, and motioned for Jim to open the door. "Ride?" he asked. The three shivering, soaked boys silently squeezed into the back seat.

One was a stranger to the priest; another was a former St. Francis boy who had been returned to the Industrial School for continued misdeeds; and the third was a St. Francis boy after all, a new arrival who had gone along for the ride. He was the one Father Bob asked to explain what had happened. It seemed that the trio had tried to take the back roads, which had become quagmires of gumbo in the rain. They had worked their car into a mudhole up to its floorboards, had had to abandon it, and had waded back to the highway.

Father Bob turned the tired and fearful youngsters over to Miss Heidman for hot baths and bed; then he enlisted Doyle, the staff's ex-Marine, and a garage owner and his crew to extricate the stolen car and get it back to its owner. It was an all-night job. At one time three other cars were also bogged down.

The next morning, Father Bob called the endlessly understanding Mr. Gardiner at the Industrial School, who asked that St. Francis keep his pair until he could send one of his undermanned staff after them—probably on Monday. That meant three days, during which it was discovered that the young stranger had a fine boy-soprano voice. The priest sent him along to choir rehearsal at Ellsworth's Holy Apostles' Parish Church with the St. Francis boys, and on Sunday, angelic in borrowed black cassock and white cotta, he sang in the Holy Apostles' choir. None of the congregation knew that he was a fugitive from justice.

The story of the car theft made the headlines of the county papers next day, and all credit was given to St. Francis boys—for the steal. There was no mention of the efforts of Father Bob and Jim to prevent the theft or of the Home's labor to return the stolen vehicle. Father Bob wondered if the good done by his boys was to remain his secret forever.

It was not too long afterward that the sheriff overplayed his hand. He charged one of the St. Francis boys with a robbery, but it was later discovered that a youth from one of the town's most prominent families had been the guilty party.

Most Ellsworth people were fair-minded. The revelation that a St. Francis boy was innocent of something and the reminder that the boys were not so very different from their own seemed to make them realize that what they had heard of the Home was decidedly one-sided and came largely from a biased source. Gradually, other matters than runaways and thefts began to register in the town's consciousness. It was remembered that many of the boys were doing well in school, and not a few had distinguished themselves in athletics. The kind townspeople who from the beginning had entertained the youngsters in their homes remarked again on their good manners and gentlemanly behavior, and began to refute more vigorously the idle talk and rumors about "those pampered hoodlums at St. Francis."

On Sunday it was the custom for each St. Francis boy to sit in a pew beside a member of Holy Apostles' Church, of which parish Father Bob then was rector, and for many weeks there had been no episodes of disturbance. Regular churchgoers were touched by Father Bob's devotion to his boys. One woman recalls, "We'd hear of some awful atrocity committed by a boy the day before, and then at church on Sunday Father Bob would refer to it and say we must *love* him into goodness. He and his own example were so persuasive that in spite of ourselves we'd find ourselves doing as he asked. The remarkable thing was that it happened so often as he said."

Two weeks before the next Election Day, new St. Francis statistics were revealed: during the previous twelve months, there had been only four cases of reversion to public acts of unsocial nature resulting in court action.

While the citizens went to the polls that crucial Tuesday, Father Bob went to the chapel. His prayers were answered. The vote was 1,800–1,200 in favor of selling the poorhouse to St. Francis.

The priest rejoiced. He was to rejoice with greater cause in the days to come. Eight weeks later something happened that surely would have thrown the election against him. As it was, it almost closed the Home.

CHAPTER 11

"WHERE THERE IS HATRED,
LET ME SOW LOVE"

FATHER BOB SAYS now that by the time the St. Francis Home was under way he had trained himself to think of women as he did of money, merely as channels to extend the Kingdom. He was too diplomatic to tell them so, however; the channel might suddenly have been blocked. When one of his admirers asked the attractive young priest in some exasperation what he had against marriage, he grinned and said, "Nothing, but no one will have me." It was a half-truth. Plenty were not only willing but anxious to have him, even with all his boys, until they discovered that nothing and no one could successfully compete with his total commitment to St. Francis and the problems of its occupants. The autumn of the second election, Elizabeth learned the lesson that others had learned before her.

That November the priest had double cause for celebration: not only was St. Francis safe on its own land, but a new and more sympathetic sheriff had been elected. In high spirits, Father Bob impulsively invited Elizabeth, presented to him by his indefatigable matchmaker of a sister, to spend a festive Thanksgiving weekend at the Home.

The girl lived twenty-five miles from Ellsworth. "I'm delivering four of my boys to their parents to spend Thanksgiving," the priest explained. "We'll leave St. Francis at six in the morning, and I'll pick you up before eleven." She agreed to the plan with pleasure.

It was after one when he finally arrived, but his sister had warned her about that. On the drive back to St. Francis the talk, as might be supposed, centered about the Boys' Home. The girl's apparently enthralled interest warmed the priest to his subject and he enthusiastically proposed a tour of the grounds before dinner. Whatever he meant by it, his description of the fields, the barns, and the grove of trees by the swimming hole sounded very romantic to her.

Unromantic reality met them at the door. As they walked in, the priest was greeted with news that two boys had been missing since early morning, and that more recently missing was a hunter's car in which were two guns and plenty of ammunition. Father Bob's mind was wiped clean of his guest and Thanksgiving as he realized that his boys were probably guilty of a felony and, if so, were armed as well. Without a word to Elizabeth, he ran to his car and roared away to try to reach the boys before the police found them.

Elizabeth ate her Thanksgiving dinner with Miss Heidman, the boys, and Father Bob's significantly empty chair.

The boys showed her around the property, but she was not so enrapt outside the company of the Director. The younger boys had been put to bed before the weary and downhearted priest returned. Aglow again, Elizabeth suggested a turkey sandwich and a glass of milk. With a weak smile, he sank into a chair and agreed. Just after the girl and Miss Heidman had gone out to the kitchen to prepare the food, the telephone rang. It was a collect call from the culprits to ask if they could return to St. Francis. The priest, worried about the missing firearms, had them held in jail until he could get there. When his guest returned with the tray of food, he was gone.

He brought the pair home well after midnight. Elizabeth's

greeting was not merely lukewarm; it was so icy that Bob felt the chill through his warm concern about the boys and their likely return to Industrial School. "I'm sorry about today," he said a bit sharply to the girl, "but tomorrow will be different."

It wasn't. When she came down to breakfast the next morning, he was already on his way out the door. "Just got word one of the lads I took home yesterday has disappeared," he flung over his shoulder. "They think he's headed for Nebraska."

He was seen no more for three days, but Elizabeth packed her bag and was gone within an hour. She wanted no further "dates" with Father Bob. The priest could not understand her attitude; but as his sister has said, "Bob always was very naive about women."

The troubles of the Thanksgiving weekend were only breezes, but it soon was clear that the calm in which the election had been won was only the eye of the storm. If the first St. Francis boys had blown the town apart, the present ones seemed about to carry away the pieces. Jack "Scarface" Johnson once again was the center of the storm system. Happier weather was indeed in the boy's future, but, as before, only the priest was able so to read the signs just then.

After Jack had been expelled from St. Francis and returned to the Industrial School, the boy had never been far from Father Bob's thoughts or prayers. The Director received frequent reports on the youth's progress or lack of it, and wrote him faithfully. The replies were full of skin-deep penitence offered for effect, but not without sincerity as far as it went; and their invariable conclusion, "Please, Father, just one more chance," kept open in the priest's heart wounds which had healed as badly as the ones on Jack's face.

The youngster's plea finally was granted and not because of good behavior. Rather he was deep in difficulties of his own making when the priest prevailed upon a probate judge to parole Jack once again to St. Francis while he awaited prosecution. "He's one of the most able boys we've ever had," the priest pleaded.

"I'm convinced he wants very much to go straight; if only he can have the stability of a permanent home and the constant assurance that he is loved, I know he will make the grade."

As soon as Jack returned to St. Francis for his second stay, his gratitude went underground. Only a mother, or a Christian trained to see the worthy person who was warped and smothered under the load of misdeeds, could have loved the arrogant, insolent boy. Father Bob did, as he always had. "Poor Jack," remarked Father Bob (only he would have used that adjective), "the only difference in him now seems to be that he is older, and has a new set of temptations." One of his new toys came in bottles.

Before breakfast one morning a few weeks after his return, Jack corralled two other boys doing their chores in the Home's barn. "Got something to show you," he whispered proudly. "Come up in the haymow." They followed him willingly, and looked on admiringly while he dug into a bale and brought out a pint of whiskey. He removed the cap with a flourish, tilted back for a long swallow, and handed the bottle to his guests. When Father Bob came to see why they were not at breakfast, he found the three comfortable in the hay with a nearly empty bottle. All three, the priest thought angrily, were in the same "last-chance" situation, awaiting disposition of their cases by probate judges in their respective counties—but his anger was directed at the event, and not at the boys. Only for extreme cause would St. Francis release any of its boys or see them behind bars, but the boys' act gave the priest no alternative. Sick at heart, he took the bottle, climbed out of the loft, walked back to the house, and called the sheriff.

At noon, someone called, "Father Bob—telephone!" He identified himself and heard the voice of a high-school girl ask, "Aren't Jack and the others supposed to be in jail today?"

"Yes," he answered wearily, "why?"

"I just saw them running down the alley toward the railroad tracks."

Quickly, the priest called the sheriff. Without preliminaries he asked, "How long have Jack and his friends been gone?"

"They aren't gone. I just took them lunch."

"You'd better take another look."

After a pause, the sheriff's voice showed he had run all the way back from the cell block. "You're right! Those scamps got into the empty woman's section, pulled a bar from a bed, and pried a window open in the women's toilet!"

"They were seen near the railroad tracks. You check to the east, and I'll look around in this direction."

The priest did not have to look far. He found the three hiding in the woods of the Boys' Home property. As they had sobered slightly, they decided to come home to St. Francis. At a cost only a parent could appreciate, Father Bob returned them once again to the sheriff. He seemed composed as he left the greatly sobered boys at the jail; it was a lesson he had learned hard. Each time he had to turn one of his charges over to the law, he felt like one who had left a pet lamb at the slaughterhouse, and the necessity of it did not lessen the pain. Behind him, each of the three boys was locked in a separate cell, and the corridor gate was locked as well.

Late that afternoon, St. Francis' phone rang again, and the voice of a hysterical female shot through Father Bob's ear: "Those awful boys of yours have set the jail on fire." Distant fire sirens confirmed the nearer one. The priest arrived downtown almost with the volunteer fire department. Things were not as serious as they appeared. One of the boys had gone to sleep on a cot and dropped his lighted cigarette, or so he claimed. At any rate, the mattress smoldered fiercely and filled the cell block with smoke which boiled impressively out of the windows and into the county offices. Coughing and sputtering, the boys yelled bloody murder. The sheriff ran to investigate, saw the clouds of smoke, dived for his keys, and could not find them. His frantic efforts to call the firemen were delayed; others were doing the same for him. The keys found, the mattress was quickly doused; but the next morning, on the theory that so much smoke could not be wrong, the newspaper headline was ST. FRANCIS BOYS SET FIRE TO JAIL.

The Home had won its election in Jack's absence; it was fortunate that the boy could not unwin the victory, for along with the coffee at Ellsworth breakfast tables that morning there was much regret for votes cast a few weeks before. Heads began once more to shake among citizens who had disapproved Father Bob's freewheeling methods from the start.

"He might better do a little whipping out there than have those kids waste time bending marrow bones pestering the Lord," commented a local lawyer, and he was widely quoted.

Father Bob, of course, saw the matter differently. He deplored what had happened more strongly than did his critics, because he had higher hopes for his boys. Each slip was a surprise and a setback, because he did not look on it as "what you might expect from a hoodlum like that." Neither was chapel to him a mere "bending marrow bones." "If I have to give up the spiritual side of the Home," he said grimly, "I'll give it up altogether." He quite realized that a way to implant stronger discipline had to be found, and soon. St. Francis was operating under a temporary state license which would never become permanent if the boys' troubles continued to be taken out on the community, but the Home would be just another waiting room on the way to bad or indifferent ends if ever the emphasis on forgiveness were lessened.

"Don't demand penitence first," the priest said again and again; "forgive first, as our Lord did, and repentance will follow."

Psychologists know that guilt eats out the will; a chief work of psychiatrists is to free the person from nameless guilts of the past which still nibble at the present. Father Bob's aim was the same, but some of his boys' guilts had names found in lawbooks, and his methods were found in the New Testament. A boy who lashes out at society expresses his inner turmoil, but he does not thereby relieve himself much; however good or bad his surroundings, he must first come to terms with himself before he can help himself or accept help. St. Francis' first task was to put its boys at ease. Only after their emotional reactions had become less explosive and pent-up feelings of guilt had been expressed could any rehabilitation begin. To admit guilt is itself a great release (even when the sense of guilt is mistaken; most people feel guilty for many things that are not their fault), and to receive glad forgiveness is reassuring; but St. Francis was able to offer more. Through the Church, it offered not only personal forgiveness and acceptance, but the authority of absolution, the putting away of past sin and guilt forever. Where that power was accepted, boys' lives and characters were transformed almost unbelievably. Father Bob saw it happen scores of times, not least in the boy he called "Lefty of the circus."

Lefty was an orphaned Irish boy with a ferocious temper which often sent him running in blind rage. He had no way to support himself but to steal. Four good sets of foster parents had been found for him; he had picked fights with each and fled. While hitchhiking across the nation, his path had crossed that of the Ringling Brothers-Barnum and Bailey Circus; he got on as a roustabout and worked himself into the elephant act in center ring, for which he wore a crimson and blue uniform which he thought was beautiful. "It had a big golden X across the front of it," he said, "and it made me feel like a general."

For the first time in his life, Lefty was content; his uniform flashed and glistened under the lights in a happy round of eastern and southern cities. Then summer was over and the circus retired to its winter quarters in Florida. Lefty no longer was a general living on applause and glamour, but just another unkempt boy watering the elephants. He ran away.

He ran into a Mississippi jail and was long in getting out. He went straight to a Gulf port and stowed away on a freighter to Cuba. He didn't like the sunny island: "They don't speak English there," he complained, and found a way back to the States. He followed the Mississippi to St. Louis and thumbed rides to Kansas City. There once again he was discovered practicing his trade of petty thievery and was taken to jail. They asked his age. He was fifteen.

He came to St. Francis and, with the easy adaptability common to young transients who make their way by being likable, found himself right at home. To acquaint the boy with the practice of honesty, Father Bob soon began to give him a turn at paying the merchants in town. Happy and well-fed, Lefty brushed aside any temptations to steal and run; his self-confidence increased, and Father Bob bragged, "He grew in wisdom and stature and in favor with God and man."

One morning, posts and shabby walls around the town blossomed with tigers and clowns; bright new posters announced that The Greatest Show on Earth was coming to Salina, only thirty-five miles away. The posters were not necessary; when Lefty got the word, he jumped and shouted and ran to tell everybody that the circus—his circus—was coming. Father Bob was among the first to know; Lefty was sure that, when the Big Top learned he was near, he'd be invited to take his old place in the center ring with the elephants. The priest was almost as excited as the boy, and promised that if it could be arranged, Lefty could return to the circus for a one-night stand.

Lefty's cup was full; indeed, it was overflowing in all directions like a fountain. He had a home and friends for the first time in his life. His new-found honesty had won him the approval and acceptance he craved. Then, as a reward and a climax, he would be able to don that gorgeous uniform with its big gold cross and strut in glory before all who knew him. He would have to build new and bigger barns to hold the harvest of admiration. As he helped a St. Francis newcomer unpack the night before the Big Top arrived, he was so happy that it seemed only right to lift sixteen dollars from a suitcase and, out of the generosity of his Irish heart, expansively to share the windfall with three of his cronies.

Father Bob, who seemed never to need sleep, was still in his study at two o'clock in the morning when one of the boys, barefoot and in nightclothes, walked softly in and handed over his part of the misappropriated funds with a short explanation. The priest thought a moment; then, mindful of the Home's need for discipline, he walked sadly to Lefty's room. The boy lay at peace, his coarse red hair almost black in the moonlight, a smile on his face. Quietly, not to awaken his roommate who breathed regularly in a dark corner, Father Bob shook Lefty's shoulder.

The pale eyes blinked sleepily, then saw the priest and froze. Father Bob thought that was how the red-haired fisherman named Peter must have looked when he heard the rooster crow. "I know about the money," he told the boy.

"I—I'll give it back," blurted the worried would-be elephant trainer.

"Of course you will," said Father Bob gently, "but you'll have to take your medicine, too. I had to tell you right away—there can't be any circus for you tomorrow."

Father Bob was ready to quiet any tears, or even curses, before Lefty made a disturbance that might be embarrassing to him later; but the priest was utterly unprepared for the scream of rage and disappointment that tore from the boy and ripped through the slumbering house, leaving behind a face broken into something animal-like. Yowling profanities with an energy that made variety unnecessary, the youth bolted from bed, bowling the athletic priest over backward across the cot of the suddenly wide-eyed and upright roommate.

Kicking furiously into a pair of levis, Lefty informed the priest and several surrounding counties that he was leaving the blankety-blank place forever. Half into his pants, he grabbed a suitcase (his roommate's), wrenched it open, and started to throw things into it. It wasn't enough. Soon he was just throwing things: a handful of books went through the windowpane, a chair slammed against the wall, and the desk tumbled across the room. The priest had found his feet and dived for the boy's flailing arms. His chunky form once again was tossed aside as Lefty, with a berserk roar, hurtled into the gathering crowd at the door and ran down the stairs, scattering boys and staff members as he flew.

Father Bob close behind him, Lefty dodged into the dining

room and in one motion swept up the table, as long as a church pew, raised it, and with enough force to shatter it, sent it smashing into the wall. "The kid's crazy," a staff member exclaimed. "I'm calling the sheriff!"

Father Bob grabbed the man's arm and spun him around. "Wait," he said urgently, "a crisis can make or break a boy, and we're not sending Lefty to the jail or the pen or the hospital. We'll handle this ourselves." Leaving his helper undecided, the priest dashed to the front door after the fleeing youngster. By then, no one was standing in their way. "Everybody go to bed," ordered the Director as he disappeared into the dark.

In the shadows of the front porch, the panting Lefty just had strength left to kick the old davenport about a yard. It sat down on one end as two of its feet crumpled under it. Then his anger gave way to wailing sobs almost as loud as his previous shouts, and he collapsed on the tilting sofa. Father Bob walked over to him.

"I walked very gingerly," the priest confessed later. "I didn't know what might be hurled my way." He sat down near the weeping boy, who withdrew slightly and stifled his sobs a bit. The priest let him cry.

After a while the sniffles came less frequently. Father Bob eased an arm over the back of the davenport toward the boy, who did not move. The priest said quietly, "Look, Lefty—I hate to see you go, but if that's what you want, all right. Maybe we can get those charges dropped in Kansas City; we'll try. I have one good suitcase; you can have it. We'll get together some things for you, the best we have so you'll have everything nice, and I'll give you some money. Maybe you can go with the circus, or get a job somewhere else. If you ever should want to come back, just write and let us know." The priest swallowed. "But, Lefty," he choked, "this is the only home I have and it's the only one you have. I do wish you'd stay."

The boy melted. Taking a great gulp of air, he threw his arms around the priest and sobbed, slipping half off the sofa onto his knees. "Father," he gasped, "you know I don't have no place to go. I wanna stay here."

The priest squeezed his shoulder reassuringly and gave his sudden smile. "Good. Let's go to bed." Holding each other, the two walked into the house. "Tomorrow," said Father Bob, "you'll pay back the money you took, and you'll be confined to the campus without privileges for a month." The boy was silent, but he nodded his head. The priest patted his shoulder lightly. "One more thing, Lefty. I was wrong before; we won't cancel your privileges until the day *after* tomorrow. Tomorrow we're all going to the circus."

From some deep reservoir not yet drained, a new gush of tears flooded down Lefty's cheeks; laughing, crying, and hiccuping, he ran into his room and buried his face in his pillow. Father Bob motioned his doubtful roommate toward bed. "Thanks for picking up in here, Al. Everything's all right now. Get some sleep; we'll fix things in the morning." Flicking off the light and closing the door, the Director realized that he was being watched. "Go to bed, all of you!" he shouted, and doors shut hastily all down the hall. Suddenly, the order seemed like good advice, even for the priest who never slept.

Lefty appeared the following afternoon and evening with the Ringling Brothers-Barnum and Bailey Circus, had his picture in the papers and, despite his minor part in the act, was as big a hit as he had imagined he would be. More than stories of glory carried him through the following thirty days, however; thereafter he knew with serene certainty that no matter what he did, he was wanted. Something in the former roustabout had changed. He seemed to have cast out all his anger and resentment in one binge of destruction, and thereafter his dark red hair was a sign only of his ancestry and not of a lighted fuse. Father Bob knew the battle was won the day Lefty confided in him, "Jack was riding me about something this morning, but instead of busting him one, I went to my room and prayed. Things worked out a lot better."

People commented in months after that Lefty had "become a different person." Father Bob and the staff taught by him disagreed. They saw in the polite, temperate young man who left

St. Francis the same worthwhile person who had entered, however obscured he had been under a mask of bravado and bent beneath a load of guilt, suspicion, and bad habits too heavy for his years. They had accepted the boy with all his disagreeable faults, but they had spoken and appealed only to the responsible, lovable self hidden within. What the St. Francis staff saw in him, Lefty began to see and live up to; at last, that better person worked forward and took command.

Father Bob says, "Our method, such as it is, is only to deal with recalcitrant mankind as our Lord deals with it. His love for even despised tax collectors and women taken in adultery showed them who they actually were and should be. They began to grow into His vision of them, and became the St. Matthews and St. Mary Magdalenes of the Gospel."

Neither was the priest's decision to let Lefty have his moment in the circus the result of an attack of gooey-heartedness. It was a return to a sounder principle forgotten in the press of distractions. Father Bob had long before discovered the wisdom of beginning penalties only after pending plans had been completed. To make correction wait its turn emphasized forgiveness and made the culprit more likely to accept the punishment willingly and without resentment. A youngster's sense of justice almost demands retribution in good time, but it also expects promises to be kept, no matter what. The faith of a child is a tender plant easily crushed by disappointment.

Forgiveness did not always come hard. Twelve-year-old Bobby, after a few weeks at St. Francis, presented Father Bob with a beautiful gold watch. The priest accepted the thought with all his heart, but the gift itself with misgivings. That afternoon the Ellsworth jeweler called.

"I hate to bother you, Father," he began, "but one of your boys was in the shop this morning——"

"The watch isn't hurt a bit," the priest interrupted. "We'll be right in."

Father Bob found the curly-haired child, the son of pickpockets, and questioned him gently. "I just wanted to give you something so you'd know how much I love you," cried the youngster.

"I know," said the priest. "It's the same with us and God; we love Him and all we have to give Him is our sins. The watch was a good present, and a good thought, but now we have to make it right." The two went together to the jeweler, who listened to the boy's story, understood, and said nothing more about it.

The town as a whole was growing more understanding, at least during those periods when the St. Francis boys were content to make their news on the sports pages instead of the police columns and their appearances in church rather than in court. Of great help were the newly elected sheriff, county attorney, and public school superintendent, who were eager to minimize such troubles as did occur. They knew that society has only the choice between making a place for the delinquent boy and destroying him. The Home and the town profited by their leadership.

It seemed that the hard lesson was being learned; that the person and his acts are not the same, and that the person can be loved and accepted whose every action and attitude are unlovable. To lavish the compassion of Christ on the young sinner was the heart of Father Bob's method of rehabilitation; but only a hard head made the soft heart effective. The priest knew his boys better than did anybody else, which is why his love and forgiveness meant something.

The Reverend Clifford Nobes remembers the night Father Bob called him at his Kansas City parish to say that a boy had run away and probably was in his area.

"You'll be seeing him soon, I expect. He'll give you a heart-rending story and ask for money—a loan, of course. Give him up to twenty-five dollars, but only a little at a time—enough for a room and meals. If you give him more, he'll just make off with it. I'll pay you back."

The boy was at the door of the rectory almost immediately, and he did indeed have a story to tell. He told it so well that Father

Nobes says, "I fell for it like a ton of bricks. I handed him the whole twenty-five dollars and wished I had more to give him." As Father Bob had predicted, that was the last his benefactor saw of the boy or the money.

Father Bob had quickly learned that he could not be responsible for the St. Francis Home and also continue his mission ministry. It was a full-time job to counsel the boys, handle all the administrative and personnel work, and strive constantly to pay the bills. For a twenty-hour day every day, the Director received a salary of $25 a week. No other staff member could or would work for so little.

Father Bob admitted that his first budget estimate was "a wild pipe dream," but his business advisors had not been much more realistic. Costs continued to rise. St. Francis was never intended to be a free home; no boy has been turned away for lack of funds, but the policy has always been that the parents should pay what they could and the court what they would. In those early days, the average payment per boy was $35 a month and the cost of keeping him was $100 a month. Since neither Church nor State provided a subsidy, the difference was met by private donations. It still is.

Much early help was given by the Episcopal Youth Organizations of the national Church which made St. Francis their project for two years; later such diverse groups as the Eagles, the Elks, and the American Legion joined the Daughters of the American Revolution and a number of women's guilds of Episcopal parishes to contribute money, furniture, food, and finally building improvements.

The large boxes of clothing which arrived periodically at the Home were particularly appreciated. The boys wore their own clothes and not uniforms, but those they came with soon wore out and often could not be replaced by their parents. Every box was shopping day: the boys picked out what they needed and would fit them, and when they were through, Father Bob would take anything left that he could get into. He would buy nothing for himself but vestments to wear at the altar.

For a man who had so wholeheartedly embraced personal poverty, the priest spent a disproportionate amount of time asking for money (and still does, as Bishop of Damaraland). Raising funds was a never-ending job and one Father Bob despised. His prayers for support were answered by speaking engagements, however, and dutifully he would climb into the old Plymouth and rattle away to tell about the Home's needs and hope for the best.

Although boys no longer traveled with him often, he always invited someone to go along "for company." Whether or not he planned it so, his "company" soon discovered that their chief function was to pay the bills. The priest was so delightful a companion that his invitations seldom were refused, and were accepted again and again even after disastrous trips on which the ancient car ran out of gas or broke down, often far off a main road while Father Bob was lost on one of his infamous short cuts.

The Director always was as short on pocket money as the car was on fuel and stamina. He helped others, and took it for granted that others would help him as gladly and unquestioningly. He seldom was disappointed.

"The Lord took care of Bob," is the explanation of his old Kansas City friends, Mr. and Mrs. Peter Bowers—even though he didn't take care of himself. Mrs. Bowers has not forgotten one outing with him. He stopped by the house one day to ask if she'd like to ride back to Ellsworth with him and a youngster he had just enrolled for St. Francis. She grabbed her hat and an overnight bag immediately; she had friends in the little city she had been wanting to visit.

Somewhere in the middle of Kansas, twenty-five miles past the last inhabited house, the Plymouth coughed to a stop. Father Bob got out cheerfully and, charging the youngster to take care of Mrs. Bowers, hurried off to the nearest gas station. Neither he nor his passengers had any idea where that might be.

"I was worried sick about him," she remembers. "I could see

him walking miles before he found a service station, and then having to walk back carrying a five-gallon can." She was almost put out when he returned less than an hour later, and not even carrying the gas. Four young men were taking turns doing it for him, serving him happily, as nearly everyone did. "I could hear them all the way up the road, saying, 'Father Bob' this, and 'Father Bob' that." The gas wasn't paid for: she paid for it and the rest of the tankful when they reached the crossroads station; but the anecdote, told now for over ten years, was worth it.

Sale of the county poorhouse to St. Francis, delayed once by the necessity of an election, was held up again when the new county attorney discovered that a statute forbade the sale of property offered by the electorate to a stipulated buyer, which meant that the transaction would have to be conducted by sealed bids. The attorney thought the matter would be a mere formality and that no one would bid against the priest.

He did not reckon with the curious wave of fear which chilled some Ellsworth citizens when it seemed that the Boys' Home would at last become an established fact. Sympathetic officials had given St. Francis a better press in recent weeks, but no one could have put a bushel over the smoke which had billowed out of the county jail the afternoon of Jack's party, and that incident recalled others.

Father Bob had never said, "There's no such thing as a bad boy," although he distinguished carefully between the bad and the boy, but the old saying was a favorite of some local wits. Two days before the bids were to be opened, someone remarked to the priest, "Those juvenile robbers and arsonists of yours may not be bad, but they're the most mischievous bunch of kids I ever hope to see." A laugh followed, but the bite and sarcasm in the words sent the Director to see the banker on the Home's Board.

"Yes, Father," said his friend sadly, "there are people in this town who don't intend to have St. Francis stay here. Business ethics won't permit me to give you any details, but I have heard that there will be rival bidders. The money you've saved to buy the Home will never do it now, that's for sure."

The priest's knuckles went white on the edge of the desk as his neck and face turned scarlet. "Can't they understand . . ." he began tightly, but his eyes and mouth snapped shut and he crossed himself as he always did when his quick temper started to explode. He took a deep breath, flexed his fingers, and said quietly, "Our blessed Lord has brought us this far. He'll take us the rest of the way."

He did, but it took a miracle.

CHAPTER **12**

MORE PROBLEMS, BUT THE GIRLS GET THEIR SHIPWRECK

AT NINE O'CLOCK the following morning, two hours after he had celebrated the Holy Eucharist with special intention for the Home, Father Bob sat in his tiny room thinking and praying. At the same hour, scores of Ellsworth churchwomen were also praying. Their support had been recruited by Tillie O'Donnell, a parishioner whose Irish family had pioneered Kansas and later lent its name to O'Donnell Hall, St. Francis' first activities building.

The Home's bid had been submitted to the county commissioners days before. Sealed or not, all Ellsworth and any rival bidders knew that $10,000 was every cent Father Bob had. The priest faced the situation clearly: when the bids were opened at 1:30 the next afternoon, an offer that was a hundred dollars or even ten dollars higher would mean that St. Francis was lost. No human help was in sight. He prayed.

He paid little attention when the telephone rang, but Jack's voice called out, "Long distance, Padre, from Oklahoma City." As he went to the phone, he wondered how long it had been since the instrument had brought any good news.

"Hello?" he said hesitatingly.

A gruff and unfamiliar voice announced, "My name is Carlock. I just read about your Home in *Time* magazine. I wasn't exactly an angel when I was a kid, and I have a little conscience money saved up. Is there anything you particularly need right now?"

Father Bob was speechless for a moment, then he laughed. "If you weren't an angel before, Mr. Carlock, you are now. When can I see you? It's urgent."

Less than six hours later, the priest walked into Red Carlock's office, 250 miles south of Ellsworth. He was not alone; an innocent-faced blue-eyed youngster had accompanied him. Father Bob had chosen his traveling companion with care; Jimmy had the sort of personality that could turn rock hearts to mush, and he had stolen cars from Seattle to Laramie.

After introductions, Red Carlock heard the priest's story in silence and responded with only occasional grunts; his eyes were on the boy. When Father Bob had outlined the Home's situation, the man did not look around. He said, "So your name is Jimmy. Tell me about yourself."

The boy did not hesitate: he recited the long list of his misdeeds, told about his experiences in jail and his two years at St. Francis, and related his plans to work his way through college. When he had finished, Mr. Carlock's big hand reached across his desk for a checkbook. He filled in the blanks and handed the form to the priest. "Here," he said; "don't use it unless you have to, but if any so-and-so bids against your boys, hit him with that."

Father Bob was still looking at the check; it was for $3,551.00.

Father Bob walked into the county commissioners' office just in time to hear Tillie O'Donnell heatedly tongue-lash a dour-mouthed stranger. "How dare you bid against those darling boys at the Home!" she exclaimed with fire in her eye, but the man stolidly submitted his envelope. The priest could not hold back a smile. It vanished when he saw with alarm that the table held not one bid but two beside his own. He reached over the table and reclaimed the envelope which held the St. Francis offer. He ripped it open, hastily changed the original entry, and replaced it on the table.

With a toss of her head at the other two bidders, Tillie plumped down beside the priest, but the pat of her hand on his arm went unacknowledged. Five minutes dragged by before the three bids were opened and read. As Father Bob listened and prayed, the palms of his clasped hands were slick with sweat and he could feel his heart pound.

The first bid was $11,000 and was submitted by the owner of an Ellsworth filling station. He was the secret bidder Father Bob had been warned about. The second bid, submitted by the stranger Tillie had scolded, was $12,000. The priest's sigh of relief could be heard around the room: St. Francis' bid was $13,000. It was so announced and accepted. Tillie's shriek of joy proclaimed the miracle: St. Francis was the owner of its own home.

Father Bob paused just once in his dash to tell his waiting boys the good news. He stopped at the service station owned by the local man who had bid against him. "I was so bitter toward that man," he said later, "that I had to buy a tankful of gas from him. It was as close as I could come to obeying St. Paul when he said, '. . . if thine enemy hunger, feed him,' and 'overcome evil with good.'" The priest did not mention that St. Paul observes in the same place, ". . . in so doing thou shalt heap coals of fire on his head."

When the boys heard the report, they cheered louder than Tillie had. That night in chapel the Director and his boys offered their prayers of thanksgiving. Even the youngsters who had been frequent runaways seemed grateful that St. Francis would continue to be there to come back to.

Jack went around until bedtime telling everyone who would listen, "It's a miracle, nothing else but!" The boy was a fervent believer in miracles; but the Director was glad that of late Jack had stopped waiting for a miracle to change his character and was making a good attempt to mend his own ways.

The Bavaria Home was the former county poor house.

"Lord, make me the instrument of Thy peace."

As many as twelve St. Francis boys graduate from Salina and Ellsworth High Schools every year.

The first boys at Bavaria—1948.

O'Donnell Hall ground-breaking, 1956.

*. . . where the Church
welcomes boys who are
unwelcome elsewhere.*

*K.P. is no different,
no matter where the location.*

Every boy wants a dog.

Bishop Mize confirming in Africa.

The simple—
and impressive—interior.

St. Francis had its start under
Bishop Nichols, head of the Church
Missionary District of Salina.

St. Onesimus
Chapel

*Father Bob
and his boys.*

The Ellsworth Home and the Activities Building addition.

*An "old boy" returns
to visit his priest.*

St. Francis sign also says "Welcome!"

The following day, business continued as usual. Since St. Francis at last owned its property, long-deferred repairs would have to be made quickly. Father Bob had to be off on a prearranged fund-raising tour. He asked Jack to drive with him to the Hutchinson railroad station and then to return the car to Ellsworth alone. The priest believed that the boy's past weeks of well-doing and his pride at being tapped would outweigh any temptation, and that successful completion of the assignment would give him new self-confidence.

On the way to Hutchinson the car's motor died for no apparent reason, and Father Bob was unable to restart it before the vehicle rolled to a halt right on the highway. It was an old story; the priest was as inept with machines as he was intuitive about boys, and he expected cars to run with as little care as he gave himself. Jack's eyes cut pityingly at the driver, but then they widened in wonder: just a few yards ahead, over an unmarked crossing obscured by a hedge of Osage orange trees, a fast Missouri Pacific train suddenly shot by. Both priest and boy stared at it dumfounded; neither had noticed the tracks.

"Golly," said Jack, "what if we had stopped on the tracks?" Then he thought again. "*What if we hadn't stopped at all?*" He turned to the priest. "Father, you know what? It's another miracle, just a plain *miracle!*" Father Bob agreed soberly. As soon as the train had passed, the car started without difficulty and they went on. Both breathed a prayer of thanksgiving, and Jack wondered if perhaps St. Raphael himself was their guardian angel.

After putting the priest on the train, Jack started back to the Home, but did not go straight back. He stopped to visit his many friends at the Industrial School at Hutchinson. He had stories to tell them, and it wasn't his fault if they somehow got the idea that their buddy Jack was official chauffeur for St. Francis, the right-hand man of the Director, and almost sole keeper of the car keys. The boy left in good time "on an important mission" and guided the old Plymouth home as though it were a limousine. He completed his picture of himself as a Very Responsible Person by actually pulling up to the door at the specified hour. Father Bob laughed later, "When I phoned that night to find that he had not only returned but on time as well, I called it Jack's third miracle in twenty-four hours and praised God mightily!"

Jack was not the only youngster who was improving little by little. Just as he slowly responded to the only authority he had ever respected, the Church, whose voice for him was Father Bob, so others who had been thought equally incorrigible began to respond in the same way.

Ralph was paroled to St. Francis after he had been convicted on several counts of burglary and one count of armed robbery; during his last escapade he had been surprised and had slashed his victim with a knife. Early in his days at the Home, something in the chapel caught him, heart and soul. When the priest would turn from the altar during the daily celebration of the Holy Eucharist, he would glimpse the boy's eyes under their dark brows fixed on the cross with burning intensity. Ralph had a reputation for violence, but when a nearby parish church requested a St. Francis boy to be an acolyte at its early Sunday Communion, he maintained a spotless record for many weeks in order to claim the job.

All that winter Ralph got up every Sunday morning in the dark and walked several miles in the bitter cold, often through deep wind-driven Kansas snow, to keep his sacred appointment. He never had to be prodded, nor was he ever late. During those icy, lonely walks, the boy had time to think seriously. Perhaps it was then more than afterward in seminary that he acquired the quiet, solid manner that was to make him such an effective priest of the Church.

Long before St. Francis had actually taken title to its Ellsworth property, Father Bob had planned to expand the Home.

"When Father Bob first mentioned another unit," said Mr. Barofsky, one of the original Board members, "I thought he was insane. As a banker I would never dream of expanding before I was sure the first deal would work." The difference, of course, was that Father Bob had known from the beginning that the Home would work. Events, disheartening as they were at times, proved him right.

New reasons to expand came daily. Word of St. Francis had spread like reports of a new wonder drug, and applications poured in from every part of the country. Pleas came from parents of boys in trouble, from ministers of all Christian groups, and from welfare authorities who were clamoring for more noninstitutional rehabilitation centers.

Where or how a second unit could be managed, Father Bob did not know; he was sure only that the Ellsworth home could not be further enlarged. To put more than twenty-five or so boys under one roof would destroy the homelike atmosphere, and with it the very purpose of St. Francis. Expansion had to be through additional and separate units, rather than the building of any larger single one.

The Bishop of Salina opened the way.

Bishop Nichols was almost as interested in the boys as was his young priest, and his reasonable caution complemented Father Bob's reckless faith and idealism. The Bishop had feared that the Ellsworth sale might fall through, and therefore had bid all the money he had, $8,000, on the former old people's home in Bavaria, seven miles west of his see city. He claimed to have acted in self-defense: "Knowing Bob," he said, "I was afraid that if he lost the Ellsworth place he would move into the Bishop's residence—it was the only other house in the district large enough to hold his boys!"

The Bishop was outbid by a farmer's $30,000. The man planned to use the forty acres for a chicken farm and the building for an investment. When he learned that the only other interested party was the least wealthy Church body in the area, the big old structure began to look more like a white elephant than an investment and he withdrew his bid. Bishop Nichols was informed that the property was for sale again and that $9,000 would claim it. He relayed the information to Father Bob when the priest stopped by on his way to a speaking engagement in Kansas City.

The following day, Mrs. Peter Bowers found Father Bob on her doorstep at mealtime. As he ate, he remarked, "If I could only get my hands on a thousand dollars, we could have that Home in Bavaria."

"You'll have it in ten days," she responded. As soon as he was gone, she telephoned one of the members of the University Cotillion Club of which she was then a sponsor. It was a group of Kansas City college students from many different Christian bodies which, thanks to Mrs. Bowers' early interest, had supported St. Francis from the start. A masquerade ball was planned for the following Friday night, and despite the haste the affair was a success. Three days before the closing of the bids, she handed the bishop a check for $1,008. So it was that within a few weeks St. Francis came to possess two properties which together would have cost $250,000 to replace. Father Bob did not savor his riches, but just gave thanks that one Home was rooted and bearing fruit, and another was on the way.

The Bavaria Home was well located, only thirty-five miles from Ellsworth and Father Bob, yet far enough away so that its boys would go to other schools and become parts of a different community. The priest loved his boys, but knew that no one town could absorb very many of them into its life. A second Home in a separate locality offered another advantage: if a boy did not make good in one place, he could be given a fresh start in the other.

However urgently the second unit was needed, its development had to proceed slowly. Around Bavaria and Salina were heard such mutterings as, "Why can't Father Mize keep his hoods in Ellsworth and not push them off on us?" Delay would have been necessary even had the priest not learned to consider the fact that others did not always share his vision and hope for delinquent boys. He never understood their attitude. The Ellsworth Home was eating all the funds budgeted to it while asking for more, and the Bavaria house would be uninhabitable until it could be renovated completely.

Although the second building was larger than the first and built in a grander style, it had been too long vacant. Most of the window glass was broken; there was no furnace; plumbing fixtures were lacking; and the roof leaked like a rotten umbrella. Father Bob counted his resources at the time, and decided he had only one: "An endless supply of boys—nothing but boys and still more boys, from every state in the Union, of assorted colors, creeds, and lack of creed."

Once again, the Lord seemed to provide; there stepped forward Mr. and Mrs. Davis, a farmer-mechanic and his wife who were able to begin to fix up the place. Father Bob gave them a meager allowance and four extra hands—two boys from overcrowded Ellsworth.

Ronnie and Ralph were heartily welcomed by the boys at the Bavaria High School. There were only seven of them and they all played on the basketball team—five starters and two substitutes. The squad was at the bottom of the Salina County League and any help was appreciated. The St. Francis boys were even better appreciated by the girls of the school, two dozen strong. "Those girls were like the ones on the remote South Atlantic isle of Tristan da Cunha," observed Father Bob; "they had only one prayer— 'Lord, send us a good shipwreck!'" Ronnie and Ralph were the first arrivals of a raft of boys who would follow when the Bavaria unit officially was opened the following year.

While the town's girls anticipated the plenty to come, Father Bob struggled with a problem of scarcity. For two years he had tried to find capable workers to augment his tiny staff, but had had little success even though he had no plans for anything that could be called a clinical program, and made no attempt to bring in trained specialists. His only "specialist" was Nannie, the Home's much-loved "mammy," who had come to wash and stayed to cook. She was always saying, "You-all's gotta use psychology on these boys like I does." In later years, Father Bob affectionately referred to her as St. Francis' first psychologist; for a long time, she was as close to one as they had.

When the Homes later did seek so-called scientific help, they discovered that their founder's early ignorance very probably had been a good thing. St. Francis turned out to need a specialized sort of specialist indeed. Before it had worked out its own genius, it could not have survived much of the unrealistic and callous-minded philosophy it found to motivate some "social workers."

The priest's whole philosophy for his work was summed up in his phrase, "therapy in Christ." St. Francis today uses the same method, but supplements it with scientific aids to rehabilitation. "Therapy in Christ" is the creation of an environment in which each boy has before him the example of adults who know and serve God in His Church, as well as the constant support and encourage-ment of being cared for, hoped for, understood, and loved no matter what he does. By being around people who treat him as Jesus told His followers to treat each other, the boy learns to know the Christ and to recognize His unseen companionship. In short, the St. Francis Homes heal simply by being what every local unit of the Church is supposed to be: a community of love in which each person has a secure place, not because of his own achieve-ment or virtue but because God loves him. Much has been learned about the human mind in recent years, and St. Francis is happy to use that knowledge to help its boys lower the mental barriers they have put up against the assaults of a cruel world. But while psychology takes down walls, a thoroughly realistic and unsenti-mental Christian community builds up foundations.

Each day at St. Francis starts and ends with God in the chapel; there every boy can daily admit his failures, consider the impor-tance of every wrong step, and accept his responsibilities, both personal and corporate. In the words of its worship, the Church in chapel offers forgiveness through Christ as the first step toward restoration within a community which accepts with love and hope even the individual's rejection of it. The chapel provides a place where the new life of the young Christian is maintained and nourished through the visible and tangible sacraments of Christ's Church. Even boys who are not Christians or who come from other Christian traditions must be touched and lifted by so consistent an appeal to them as responsible, free, and worthwhile persons.

Father Bob and Albert Schweitzer are of one mind in at least one idea: example is not the main thing which influences others; it is the only thing. It was not easy to assemble a staff which would itself live and act on the principles which alone undergirded Father Bob's vision for St. Francis; at times it had been impossible. Any sort of workers, competent or otherwise, were reluctant to take on a backbreaking and heartbreaking job for so little pay.

People therefore came and went. Most of them were run-of-the-mill folk, both good and bad, who somehow found themselves at St. Francis for reasons other than Father Bob's "total abandonment to the needs of God's straying children." Such employees worked at the Home only until something better came along; but Father Bob mused, "You know, those men and women lived the best part of their lives at St. Francis." A few lived the worst part there, and had to be sent packing.

The constantly changing staff did not include many of the sort of people the Director really wanted—people whose faith was a natural, unforced thing because they knew themselves and their God. There were a few happy exceptions.

Manetta Heidman of Wayne University was one. She was as able as she was conscientious, the sort of person whose presence makes everyone happier, who knows when to be quiet and when to organize a picnic. During the Home's first two years, she often bore all the responsibility when Father Bob was away. Her constant loyalty to her Lord and her never-failing worship at all chapel services set a high standard for all the boys to follow. She left something of herself in the little room with its altar, and seven years later came back to reclaim it, when she took another leave of absence from her university in order to help out St. Francis again.

Miss Heidman's right hand was Helen Kueser, the jolly cook, who had a shoulder no boy was ashamed to cry on and a heart big enough to take in youngsters only a mother could love and a few whose mothers did not. The Home also had the frequent help of Raymond Lewis, a captain in the Church Army, an evangelistic and missionary society of Episcopal laymen. Captain Lewis used many of his vacations to work at Ellsworth, and with his colleague, Captain John Hunt, exercised inestimable influence on the boys.

When Captain Ray was around, Father Bob could imagine that St. Francis himself was paying a visit—the young saint had been quite a troubadour, and Ray had the same overflowing spirit of holy joy which spilled out in happy song. Captain Ray was as careless of discipline as he was of dignity, but many of the boys wanted only to be "like Cap." Dick was one of them; after two years at St. Francis and a hitch in the Navy, he decided, "The Church Army is for me because it serves God and man in a special way." He learned one of the special ways the day that Captain Ray crawled through scorched acres of dusty brown wheat stalks to find him after he had run away and to bring him home with gentleness and understanding.

Most valuable in the parade of help were Mr. and Mrs. Harry Welch and their three teen-aged children, former parishioners of Father Bob. During the Welches' months at St. Francis, not a single case of disorder occurred among the boys. "Those three children," the priest said, "showed my boys what youth should be."

Sixteen-year-old Don and fifteen-year-old Bobby were popular, but it was their fourteen-year-old sister Dorothy who had the electric effect on the Home. She was a naturally attractive girl,

and boys who would not have been good to earn a visit from a
certified Santa Claus behaved impeccably so that Dorothy could
stay.

The night before she and her family arrived at the crowded
house, Father Bob had spoken to his youngsters. "You're about to
become the luckiest lads of any boys' home in the nation, but
remember one thing. Dorothy remains here only as long as every
single one of you abides by the rule that you must never touch
her in any circumstance—not in fun, not in affection, not by accident. If anyone so much as brushes her arm at the dining table,
she will be gone before the next meal." A week later, any boy
responsible for her departure probably would have been lynched
by twenty-five enraged foster brothers. There were many cases
of puppy love and at least one real crush, but Dorothy conducted
herself always with impressive poise and restraint. Once two holes
mysteriously were burned in a piece of her lingerie as it dried in
the laundry, but the thing was spirited away quickly, and the girl
was able to say some years later, "While I lived at St. Francis, no
one was rude or crude to me in any way."

Before many months, the Welches were forced to move by the
impossibility of providing for their children's proper medical care
or future education on the little money St. Francis could pay. They
had wanted to stay indefinitely, and no one remembers what the
weather was when they left: in every important respect, the day
was dark and wet.

The Welches gone, Father Bob staggered for the first time under
the weight of his combined jobs. The boys themselves never tired
him; their youth refreshed him and their problems he offered to
God. It was the constant and frustrating detail work of running
the Home which irritated him, all the more since he had been free
of it for a while; and even his great energy was spent by the unend-
ing travel and struggle to raise funds.

The Bishop's concern deepened as Father Bob appeared more
and more exhausted, but he could find no way to relieve his bone-
weary priest. It seemed to be an answer to prayer, therefore, that

one day a middle-aged and cultured man appeared at the Episcopal residence in Salina.

The tall, bearded man introduced himself. "I am Father Rien. I am a priest of that part of the Russian Orthodox Church which is still challenging atheistic communism. Our bishops have been banished, and even in America the communists find ways to persecute us."

Bishop Nichols listened with interest as the priest told how he had been a prisoner in Russia and how he managed to escape, but the Bishop came to attention when Father Rien mentioned in passing some experience in boys' institutions in other countries. "I have a job for you if you'll take it," he told the man.

While letters of verification and confirmation were awaited, Father Rien was sent to St. Francis. Father Bob was as impressed as his Bishop had been. The Russian knew medicine and theology, and seemed to be able to read every boy's thoughts. Before any mischief could be committed, Father Rien had stopped it. He seemed to know what made a delinquent boy tick.

After a month during which St. Francis was supervised with extraordinary efficiency, Father Rien was invited by the Chamber of Commerce to speak on Soviet Russia. Father Bob courteously accompanied him, but he was appalled at what he heard. "It was a violent, bloodcurdling talk," the Director later reported. "The man was filled with hatred and obviously knew nothing of loving one's enemy or of overcoming evil with good." Father Bob went home worried.

He remembered that Father Rien still had no references, never received any mail, and would permit no picture of himself to be taken. He began to notice that the discipline which was settling over the Home was not a happy one. Then one afternoon he heard sounds of a struggle in the basement.

He was down the stairs in three leaps, heaved a flailing Lefty off the battered form of Father Rien, and banged the cursing boy's head on the concrete floor to subdue him. Suddenly he let Lefty go. His anger broken, the boy was crying, not like someone ashamed, but like a child betrayed. Father Bob whispered to him, "I'm sorry, Lefty; forgive me. Go get cleaned up; you can tell me what happened later." Sending the boy up the stairs, the Director turned to the Russian, who was battered but seemed inhumanly composed. "Let's go to my office," he said grimly.

Their talk was inconclusive. Father Bob found the man impossible to pin down; his answers were crisp but unsatisfying. "Will you take a psychological examination?" the Director asked finally, and was surprised when the Russian priest agreed without protest.

Matters then moved quickly. In the same mail a few days later came the report on the test and a letter from the Prior of the Anglican Benedictine community in northern Indiana (now at Three Rivers, Michigan). Father Bob ripped open the psychologist's envelope first. It said that Father Rien appeared to be a psychopath, a person with no sense of right or wrong or social restraint, and added that quite likely he was an impostor. His mind spinning, the Director turned to the letter from the Prior; it also concerned the Russian.

The writer had heard about the priest who was assisting at St. Francis, and was struck by the close resemblance of his name to that of a man who had spent several weeks at the monastery. He also had presented himself as a Russian priest, and a teaching job had been secured for him at a well-known military school in the Midwest. From there and with no apparent reason, he had disappeared. The Benedictine monks had turned detective, traced his movements, and uncovered his background.

When they found him again, he was acting as a Roman priest in a Roman Catholic monastery, and they were able to tell his superior there that he had a long record of crimes and impostures. He had posed as an Anglican priest in England, where he had claimed to have been shot down over Dunkirk and to have lost all his records in a bombing. He once had posed as a physician, and had earned the attention of the F.B.I. in Iowa when he posed as an officer in the U.S. Army. He had been in prisons all over the United States. The Roman superior had investigated and dis-

covered that the man already had established a friendly relationship with their Bishop of Wichita, who evidently was to be the next
victim. That plan spoiled, the imposter vanished again. Could
he be the same one now at St. Francis?

Father Bob had no doubt that he was, and lost no time in arranging his dismissal from the Home. The situation was delicate, however, and needed to be handled so that the boys' routine and any
loyalty they had given to the man would be upset as little as possible. Separating any staff member who has become a part of the
lives of easily disturbed children is a problem dreaded by every
director of a home or institution. Every possible kindness must be
shown, and Father Bob would have had it so in any event.

Father Rien, whoever he was, was taken to Salina to see the
Bishop. There he was given the reasons for his dismissal and sent
on to live with a priest in a Colorado town where he could seek
help. He was not permitted to return to St. Francis, but his clothing, few possessions, and pay were forwarded to his new address.
The priest who took him in was fully informed and therefore was
not surprised one morning to find that his guest had disappeared
as thoroughly as last week's dream.

Despite all troubles, the Home was doing well. A few evenings
after Father Rien's departure, Father Bob was able to give thanks
in chapel that for one whole year no St. Francis boy had been lost
to the law or to a secular institution. That was the important
thing, beside which the imminent opening of the Bavaria unit and
the resultant doubling of staff problems was insignificant.

The Director's mind was quiet on one matter. He knew whom he
wanted to head the new Home: the enthusiastic young Father
Francis who had served with him in the old Associate Mission.
Bishop Nichols was unconvinced, however; where Father Bob
saw potential, the Bishop saw youth and inexperience. He delayed his approval so long that the new Home opened without its
priest.

On the first of August, 1948, six boys were transferred from

Ellsworth to Bavaria to join Ronnie and Ralph and so increase the young male population of the town by a total of eight. The day was the Feast of St. Peter's Chains and commemorated the Apostle's miraculous release from prison, but to the high school girls it meant instead release from an almost manless world: they were delighted with the "shipwreck" which had brought such eligible survivors to their shores.

On the first of September, the Bishop's reluctant approval at last in hand, the Reverend Peter Francis arrived at Bavaria to begin the work in which he continues today. As he and his wife settled their two baby boys into their new quarters, they braced themselves for difficult days ahead. The storm was not long in breaking, and if the young dean of Bavaria was to wonder often why he had taken the job, Father Bob was to wonder at times why he ever had selected him. His service would be neither smooth nor uninterrupted.

So it was that the second Home was established, and what someone has called "The Chain Store Plan of Rehabilitation" was under way.

CHAPTER 13

A WEDDING, A DEATH, AND EASTER

WHEN FATHER FRANCIS walked in the door of the St. Francis Home in Bavaria, the boys knew that in him they would have a real friend and an authority worthy of respect. Since their move the month before, they had been running wild and had formed bad habits they would not easily give up, but something about their new priest reassured them. The man was six feet tall and built like a wrestler, and while all two hundred pounds of him radiated kindness, it was plain that he intended to take no nonsense from anybody.

The first nonsense he found was in the Home's financial records. Although the Bavaria unit had almost nothing to spend, the same housemother who had grossly failed to supervise the boys for four weeks had also let the budget get out of control. Father Francis quickly dismissed her, only to find when the canceled checks were returned at the end of the month that she had written herself a severance check for a full year's salary. The young priest was undismayed by the irregularities in both the books and the boys' lives, and the Bishop was encouraged by the way he seemed to be redeeming a situation near catastrophe.

With order somewhat established in his office, Father Francis gathered his eight boys around him to consider some ways to make their Home look and feel like home. The Bavaria building was a substantial one, but makeshift repairs had made it only livable and its yard was barren, desolate, and forbidding. Of the six trees around the house, five were dead and one was dying. The morning half the Home's chickens were discovered strangled, the young priest reflected that the two boys responsible couldn't be blamed too much for acting like characters in a horror movie when their residence looked like a setting for one. Some simple landscaping was planned.

After the Home was abruptly reduced in importance as a chicken farm, attention was turned to the surrounding acres. Mr. Davis, who had proved himself a good repairman the summer before, turned out to be an even better farmer. Under his direction, the boys made a success of agriculture and it was their chief occupation for several years.

Father Francis also quickly helped the boys to lay out a baseball diamond and a basketball court in order to provide a better place than the chicken yard to work off hostility. The priest himself played both games expertly. After a few hot and fast scrimmages under the basketball hoop, the boys forgot the formal and slightly awed way they had said "Father Francis," and walked arm in sweaty arm to the house with a laughing "Father Pete."

That autumn, the Bavaria grade school basketball team, fortified with three St. Francis boys as regulars, won the county championship; and the high school team rose from its former home at the bottom of the league to a happy third place. In the spring, seven of the nine starters on the high school baseball team were from St. Francis. Such facts were reason enough in the sports-minded plains for school and civic authorities to overlook the early extracurricular activities of some of the new boys.

One like Sherman took a lot of overlooking. The boy was only sixteen when he came to the Home, but his record listed a long series of truck thefts and purse snatchings. His immediate offense

had been to bump an untended road grader off a mountain highway just to see it bounce.

Despite his past, Sherman's prospects looked good. He had
learned to love the Church from a parish priest who recognized
undeveloped talents in the lad and who had persuaded the juvenile court judge to be a godfather when Sherman was baptized
the year before. His priest stayed close to the boy during the year
they waited for a vacancy at St. Francis. Sherman was one of
Father Pete's first wards, and also one of the first to participate in
Father Bob's "membership plan," a merit system of promotion
within the Homes which worked so well that it is unchanged
today.

A new arrival at St. Francis is called a "supervised boy." He
may not leave the grounds for thirty days without the company
of a staff member, which rules out vacations, trips to town, or outside jobs. After a month, a newcomer may be elected to "membership" if he has kept the simple rules of the Home. Even a simple
rule is not easy to a St. Francis boy, who is there because he has
considered regulations things to be broken. Twice-daily attendance in chapel and a satisfactory grade average at school are essential, but so is his relationship with the other boys. After the staff
approves a candidate, their vote is his final obstacle to membership, and the election is no rubber-stamp affair.

As he was intended to, Sherman chafed under the restrictions
of his first weeks at the Home. He saw that members got double
his "supervised" allowance and held after-school jobs which
financed dates, new clothes and other luxuries. Members could go
home for Christmas; they had a voice in the Home's affairs; and
best of all, they could go to town alone. They had to get permission and first file a "flight plan" which told exactly where they
were going, but it was better than having someone breathing
down their necks all the time. Some of the kids told gripers that
they had met similar regulations in their boarding school days.

Sherman longed to be a member; but he scarcely thought about
"honor membership," that status achieved as yet by nobody, which
would grant to its holders complete control of their finances and

mail, and all the freedom of college students. Even to apply for such privileges, he would have to survive for a year as a member, and that modest position was remaining tantalizingly beyond his grasp.

The confused and belligerent boy was not popular among his fellows. He caused trouble for them all by picking fights, and he worked harder at mischief than at keeping up his grades. To celebrate the end of his first month at St. Francis, he kicked out the slats of a supply closet at the high school. Not only was he unready for membership, but his continuing at the Home was in doubt. His last act of violence, however, seemed to get most of the rebellion out of his system, and the kind but firm guidance of Father Pete began to show in the boy. It was then that his love of the Church came forward and gave him a reason to do well: he earnestly wanted to assist in the evening chapel services, but continued demerits denied him that privilege.

The boys are permitted to work off part of their demerits—fifteen minutes of work for each demerit. Sherman was an energetic boy, and he really did not mind sweeping the porch or washing the windows after school. Furthermore, he liked the outdoors; although he could not admit it, he almost enjoyed pulling weeds or cutting grass on weekends. What he definitely did not like was to have to walk off demerits, and that was the only way to cancel them when there was no work to be done. Father Pete watched any walking boy with sympathy, for he could remember the bitterness of the same sort of discipline from his school days, and how he hated that walking, that endless walking, with everybody watching. One Saturday Sherman found that he had accumulated thirty-two demerits, a number beyond expunging by work or walking: he would have to become a "scribe." Any boy who earned more than thirty demerits in a week had to copy in legible handwriting the entire St. Francis Boys' Home handbook. Some boys had done so twenty times, but once was enough for Sherman: the laborious task kept him indoors all weekend, and that was the worst punishment of all to him.

From then on he settled down. He was elected a member and

a year later became an honor member at St. Francis. He distinguished himself in school as a student and athlete. With the help of Kansas University correspondence courses, he completed three years of senior high school in two years and two summers to catch up with his class. After he left St. Francis, he worked his way through four years of college and went on to three years of seminary. Today Sherman has two admiring families—his own wife and children, and the people of the large city parish whose priest he is. He also has three proud fathers—Father Pete, Father Bob, and the priest who sent him to St. Francis in the beginning.

William King, the clinical psychologist at St. Francis since 1952, affirms that young people not only *need* but *like* authority, because it gives them a sense of security. Again and again the Homes hear from released boys who complain that their parents do not discipline them upon their return home. Father Pete did not have to learn the principle from psychology, however; he saw it demonstrated during his first year at Bavaria by fifteen-year-old Dave. The boy's family had insisted that their son be released after he had been at St. Francis only a few months.

Father Pete was eating breakfast when he heard a car in the driveway; looking out, he saw Dave, who was supposed to have been at home with his family for several weeks past. The boy climbed out of a relatively new Ford and sauntered up to the front door with knapsack in hand.

The priest had little hope that the boy and the car were keeping company legally, but he held out his hand in warm greeting. "Hi, Dave. This is a surprise! How are things going?" Then, pointing to the car, he said, "Nice job. Yours?"

The reply was only stuttering and stammering. Father Pete brushed Dave's confusion aside, grabbed up his pack, and invited him to come into the study to visit a little.

Dave had indeed stolen the car—from the priest in his home town. He had driven seven hundred miles back to Bavaria, pausing only to siphon gas.

"I want to stay here," he said to Father Francis, "where some-

148

one is over me and tells me the right thing to do. I can do it then. I don't have the willpower myself. When you told me what to do, I did it and was proud of myself. Nobody at home tells me anything, and I just feel lost."

Experience proved that Father Bob was correct from the start when he set the time that a boy should remain at St. Francis at two years or so. It takes that long for him to develop enough self-confidence and foresight to make it on his own. The boys who achieve sufficient self-control at the Homes to become members do exceptionally well when they are released. In fact, the records show that no boy who has done well at the Homes ever returned to careless ways.

Shortly after Bavaria opened, a thoughtful and well-to-do Kansas City businessman offered to finance a "Boy of the Month" plan. Father Bob accepted the suggestion, and the prospect of a weekend in the big city long was a strong incentive to good behavior. Nowadays, the Boy of the Month no longer receives a whole weekend, but has his choice of a dinner in town or the equivalent in money. Only impatient creditors or a special savings project can induce most youngsters to forego the party. Once six months went by when no boy's conduct warranted the title Boy of the Month; but other times so many were eligible that it was hard to make a choice.

On the whole, Bavaria's first boys established a good record in both Home and community. The Bavaria and Salina townspeople were delighted and surprised that "those hoods" had not torn their community apart as they had Ellsworth. Once Father Bob let slip in public that he was thinking of sending some of the Bavaria boys to Brookville, a rival high school. The remark raced around the community and brought quick response. "We want all the boys," said the principal of Bavaria High. "St. Francis belongs to *us!*"

Father Bob and Father Francis were pleased but they kept their fingers crossed, for they both knew that eleven St. Francis boys could be too many from one family. "After all," said the

Director, "the Homes want to supplement the environment, not create it."

Father Bob might have picked Father Pete out of a magnifying mirror—the younger man dwarfed the older, but both were stocky and heavy set, and at least once they had been mistaken for brothers. However much they were alike physically, their temperaments were as unlike as day and night. Their ideas later were to clash on the operation of the Homes and the guidance of the boys, but for the moment Father Bob was able to relax in the happy opinion that the first dean of Bavaria was all he had hoped for.

The day before the second unit opened, a stranger had asked Father Bob if he had any children. He answered gleefully, "Sure, twenty-six. Tomorrow I'll have fifty. All boys!" She was relieved when he explained.

The sudden increase in an already large family added greatly to the heavy burden on Father Bob, even though he did have the capable assistance of Father Pete. St. Francis was not a plan or an organization; it was simply Father Bob. Others could analyze his methods, but he could only love his boys and work twenty hours a day. He did not know how to delegate authority. As Director of the Homes, he not only oversaw Bavaria, he also felt it necessary to spend much time there. Moreover, the need for money had doubled.

Although both units were in operation, they had at least ten times as many applications as they could accept, and it bothered Father Bob to reject boys for whom there was room in the Homes but not in the budget. He therefore courted collapse by scheduling even more speaking engagements to try to bring home extra money. Worn out by travel and administrative details for two Homes, he also had to deal with day-to-day problems, such as the delegation of Bavaria parents who had to be reassured that their daughters could date his boys safely.

He was able to report that never in the Homes' existence had their boys caused any incident with the local girls. The concerned parents were to learn that their girls would be safer with St. Francis youngsters than with any others. Father Bob heard more than one parent say, "They're the best-behaved youngsters ever to date my daughter. When they are with those boys, we always know just where our girls are, and exactly what time they'll be home."

Father Bob made certain that a boy was driven by a staff member to pick up his date, then driven on to the movies or dance or wherever they were going, and that the couple was called for at a specified time. The boy's date was let out at her home and the staff member waited discreetly in the car while the boy accompanied her to the front door to say good-night. The same system is in effect today.

The present Director, who has daughters of his own, says, "Many townspeople are still apprehensive about their girls, and so contribute to the loneliness of our boys. The overly cautious father always says 'No' to a date; the father who is relaxed and friendly but still careful will allow his daughter to go. It seems to me that the daughters of the latter sort are happier and better able to handle themselves than the others."

To the surprise of the youngsters themselves, the close chaperoning seems to be no drag but rather to increase their enjoyment. The local girls are as anxious to date the St. Francis boys as the boys are to date them.

The first wedding at St. Francis was that of Lefty, the circus boy with the quick temper, and Helen, the daughter of a local store-owner. Nobody in town or at the Home will forget either the proposal or the marriage ceremony.

Some months after his tussle with "Father Rien," Lefty knocked on Father Bob's door one evening. "Padre," he said, "I got a letter today from my sister in New York saying her baby is sick. Could I go visit them for a few days? I could use the money in my savings."

Lefty's recent record was good, so the priest told him to go.

Father Bob studied the schedule and said, "You can go tomorrow on the noon bus and come back here Wednesday night on the 10:02. We'll meet you at the bus station."

Father Bob went to the station Wednesday, but Lefty did not get off the bus. Two weeks later he walked into St. Francis at suppertime. He was wearing the uniform of a U.S. soldier.

Lefty had gone to the recruiting office, lied about his age, and somehow failed to mention that he was at St. Francis on parole from the Industrial School.

Father Bob conferred the next morning with the juvenile court judge. They both felt the boy was not yet ready for the exacting discipline of Army life, but that since he had placed his own neck in the noose, it should be left there. Whatever the outcome, they thought, it would be a maturing experience. So it was.

From the beginning, the boy sent a portion of his monthly pay to the Home: part to go in his savings account and part to be used for the support of some other boy at St. Francis. Much of the remainder went for long distance calls to Father Bob. Invariably he began the conversation by saying, "I think I'm going to be shipped out tomorrow, so I called to say good-bye." After a few such openings, it became apparent that the boy was only homesick. Eventually he was shipped out—to the Aleutian Islands. In place of telephone calls came letters, scores of them, and most of them illegible.

One came at last that Father Bob could read; it had been written with great care. "Dear Padre," it said. "I want you to do me a favor. I want you to take fifty dollars out of our joint account and go down to the jewelry store and buy an engagement ring. Get Nannie to help pick it out. Then invite Helen to dinner, propose for me, and put the ring on her finger."

For a second Father Bob was alarmed: the sum was all of Lefty's savings, and proposals were not in his priestly line; but nevertheless he carried out the private's orders.

The priest liked Helen. Lefty had met her while working part-time in her father's store and she had come often to St. Francis parties. The boy had introduced her to his new-found Church, and Father Bob had baptized her. She had become a member of the Holy Apostles' choir, and was taking instruction there for Confirmation.

It should be a good match, Father Bob reflected. Lefty would be twenty-two when he returned to Kansas from his Army stint. That would be plenty old enough to marry, and until then it would give him stability and a sense of security to know that Helen was waiting.

When Father Bob told the boys about the letter, they were equally as pleased—and excited. Helen was invited to dinner the following Saturday night, and Nannie, the cook, found that the menu had become state business: it was planned by a special meeting of members.

Next day Father Bob took Nannie to the jewelry store to choose the ring. "Lefty obviously didn't trust my taste," said the priest, smiling. Both he and Nannie felt somewhat relieved that all twenty-six boys, after each had examined it minutely, approved the selection which they had been two hours in choosing.

Saturday night, Nannie did her best, and the dinner was a great success. After the last spoonful of ice cream had been eaten, Father Bob got to his feet and in Lefty's name made a formal if somewhat halting proposal. Helen accepted with a smile; and Father Bob slipped the ring on her finger. As he started to sit down, twenty-six young voices yelled almost in unison, "Kiss her, kiss her!" Weekly movies had taught them that no proposal is complete without a kiss. Father Bob's face turned scarlet, but he did as they demanded. There were loud cheers from the youngsters, and Father Bob could think of nothing to do but to revert from suitor to priest, and he ended the evening with a short talk on the sanctity of marriage.

Not four years but only two months later, Lefty walked in the door of St. Francis and asked Father Bob to solemnize the marriage. The priest at first refused: the boy was only eighteen, and the circumstances were at least unusual. (Whether Lefty had

known that he would return so soon, he never revealed.) When
Lefty declared that if his own priest would not marry him he
would find someone who would, Father Bob gave in and agreed
to have the wedding in St. Francis' chapel.

The boys vowed that it would be the best wedding ever, and
insisted that everything be done by the storybook. They scrubbed
and polished the Home until it glistened. Nannie baked a huge
cake, and flowers donated by the local florist decorated every
room in the Home.

On the big day, the boys and staff trooped into the little chapel
a few minutes before ten. The chapel seated only twenty, but
it did allow for some standing room. It was fragrant with flowers
and aglow with candles. At precisely ten o'clock Helen, lovely
in her white dress, walked down the aisle on her father's arm
as the young congregation sang "Praise My Soul, the King of
Heaven" (number 282 in *The Hymnal* of the Episcopal Church, the
same hymn to which Princess Elizabeth had entered Westminster
Abbey for her marriage to Prince Philip). The boys' voices almost
rattled the windows, although some were a bit choked with the
glory of it all.

A fifteen-year-old St. Francis boy was best man, the fifteen-
year-old sister of the bride was the maid of honor, and a twelve-
year-old lad was the acolyte. The ceremony and Nuptial Eucharist were almost over when the best man fainted! Father Bob
looked at the young server, who seemed about to lend a hand
when he too suddenly fell down in a dead faint. The priest glanced
at the maid of honor and saw that she was as white as a sheet;
just as she began to reel, her father hastily grabbed her and half
carried her out of the chapel.

"The chapel was so hot and crowded that I was lucky to get
Lefty and Helen married while they were still on their feet,"
remembers Father Bob, and he still breaks up when he thinks
of the reception afterward. "The dear housemother had listened
to Princess Elizabeth's wedding on the radio, and had told the
boys all about it: I had to do everything just as the Archbishop of

Canterbury had. Then, while we were eating our cake, she said over and over, 'Lefty's wedding was every bit as lovely as Princess Elizabeth's, until Willie fainted.'"

The marriage was a happy success. The first four children were so close in age that they looked like quadruplets, and Father Bob baptized them all. Lefty now manages what he calls the back-end of a store. He claims to have no ability to deal with figures or the public, but the front office says it couldn't get along without him.

Early in 1950 the Board of Directors decided that a more efficient organization was needed since the administrative work of the Home had doubled. An office was rented in Salina to serve as headquarters for the administrative staff, which then included Father Bob, his secretary, and the Homes' first business manager, Harold Kinsley.

Father Bob had told the boys that St. Francis was his only home; he might more truly have said that St. Francis was his only world. He had created it and in turn it had supported him. He left the Ellsworth Home with the same reluctance that a fish leaves its bowl, and with much the same result. Separated from his family of boys, he flopped about on dry and unfamiliar ground.

At their invitation, he moved in with the Kinsleys, but the arrangement was not satisfactory. His business manager and host found that Father Bob never seemed to sleep. Night after night the priest would shake him at two or three o'clock and enthusiastically exclaim, "Listen! I've got a whale of a good idea for the Homes!" Even during the few hours Father Bob would lie down, his mind would not rest.

The priest subsequently moved to an attic room in another house, an accommodation recommended only by its cheapness. It was draughty and cold in winter and unbearably hot in summer. The priest fell into his old habit of sleeping in his car. One summer night he was greatly embarrassed when a policeman discovered and was about to arrest him. When he explained that the car was his own, the puzzled officer was sympathetic, but strongly suggested that in the future Father Bob should find somewhere else to sleep than in an auto parked on a main city street.

The present Director of the Homes has said that each unit's Dean of Boys is the most important member of its staff, for he is the father of the Home in function as well as respectful title, and is immediately in charge of the youngsters. It was a long time before someone suitable could be found to replace Father Bob as dean of the Ellsworth Home. The man first selected to take his place was responsible for the first and only death at St. Francis. He came highly recommended, and no one suspected that he was a heavy and secret drinker.

One afternoon he took a group of boys to swim in the nearby Smoky Hill River. His canteen was not filled with water and in concentrating on it he failed to notice that a boy who could not swim had floated around the bend on an inner tube. Once he was missed, some older boys quickly found his inner tube—empty. Father Bob was grief-stricken when he learned of the tragedy, but insisted on accompanying the body to Colorado for the burial.

Along with the year's heartaches, there was also unexpected joy for the Director.

First, there was the boys' Lenten offering, which amounted to over half the district's missionary giving for 1950. By sacrificing Coke money and saving here and there, they had filled their dining room mite boxes to the total of $99.45. (It was to be used to assist their friend Captain Lewis in his Church Army Missions in desert towns of New Mexico.) While the amount of money was something to be pleased about, what really mattered was that the boys were at last learning the meaning of the words they said each night in prayer: "O divine Master, grant that we may not so much seek to be consoled as to console . . . to be loved, as to love; for it is in giving that we receive."

There was also the Passion Sunday dust storm. As the Ellsworth boys had gradually won over their community by various public-spirited deeds, so on that day the boys at Bavaria showed their fellow citizens the stuff they were made of.

Prolonged drought conditions had brought on a series of dust storms. The sky was a dirty red when the boys started for the Salina Cathedral Parish where they attended church on Sunday. They had taped all the windows tightly and carefully closed the door before going out into the eerie light of the morning.

When they emerged from the church an hour and a half later, the usual stiff Kansas wind had become a tornadic gale which staggered them. They were almost blinded by the barrier of dust that had buried the day in a dark brown night. The boys formed a chain and, led by Father Pete, groped their way to the car and started on a cautious seven-mile drive back to Bavaria.

Not even the taillights of a car ahead were visible until collision was imminent; they inched along at two and three miles an hour and hoped other motorists were doing the same. The storm was truly a blizzard of dirt, and time after time they bumped gently into drifts of shifting soil which crisscrossed the road unseen in the unnatural, howling, umber darkness. After nearly three hours of crawling along the highway, they heaved sighs of relief as they realized they were approaching the turnoff to the Home. Seconds before they reached it, they heard sounds like successive cannon shots above the roaring wind. The storm had whipped up with renewed fury and a line of blinded cars had smashed into each other, crash after crash, until seventeen lay about the highway like pieces of a giant snake chopped and battered into segments. The St. Francis boys, handkerchiefs already tied over their faces, jumped out of their cars, leaned themselves against the wind, and went to work. For hours they labored to right overturned vehicles, to free people trapped by twisted metal, and to give first aid to the injured. Their own eyes soon were gritty from the dust and their bodies painfully bruised from being hurled by solid blows of wind against the sides of standing cars. After all that could be done had been accomplished, the boys still had no clear idea of what had happened and were too weary to ask further. They made it back to the Home, and later learned that three people had been killed in the highway pileup.

The next day, a man who had not been silent in his opposition to the Bavaria unit spoke for others when he said, "I sure have to eat my words. If it hadn't been for those heroic kids, more than three people would have died." In the darkness and wreckage of the preceding day, the boys themselves had feared that the toll would be higher.

Finally, on the Tuesday after Easter, the boys who had made the grade were admitted to membership through the first enactment of a ritual which was to become part and parcel of the St. Francis tradition.

The choir stalls of Christ Cathedral Church in Salina were filled that night with fifty St. Francis boys. Sitting near the altar the Bishop of Salina admitted twenty-one boys to be members of St. Francis; and three were admitted to be honor members, and Sherman was one of that first trio.

Two boys, one from Ellsworth and one from Bavaria, said Evening Prayer before admission. No rehearsal had been necessary; their clear young voices carried throughout the cathedral building as easily as they did in their small chapels at the Homes.

Father Bob presented the candidates to the Bishop by saying, "I present unto you these persons to be received as Members in the fellowship and fraternity of the St. Francis Boys' Homes." One by one, they came: Joe, the formerly expert car stealer; Frank, the ex-arsonist; Tim, the sometime robber.

In firm tones the Bishop asked, "Do you promise to endeavor to follow in your personal and daily life the standards taught us and the examples given unto us by our Lord and Saviour Jesus Christ?"

Father Bob listened as each young voice made its response, "I do." He watched the solemn-faced youngsters kneel while the Bishop placed around their necks St. Francis medals which he had blessed, and said, "Receive this medal as a token and pledge of your willingness to accept the responsibilities and to respect the privileges of membership in the St. Francis Boys' Homes. And may God strengthen you in your purpose and resolve."

Father Bob had laughed and cried easily in happier days, but as he watched boys he loved with all his being come to the altar rail where they left the road to crime one more turn behind, he wept unashamedly. For the moment tears washed away the ache of his then uncertain function within the Homes, his longing to know the new boys as he had known the ones kneeling there before the Bishop, and the unhealed pain of the Colorado boy's unncessary death. Red cassocks, brass crosses, shining candles, and bright hangings all melted into splotches of color as he wiped his streaming eyes, caught his breath, and said the *Te Deum* over and over in his heart.

CHAPTER 14

COLORADO—
CALM BEFORE THE STORM

THE CAR PACKED with half a dozen exuberant kids came to a stop before the cabin, and Father Bob was the first out. He drew a long, deep breath of the cool Colorado mountain air. What a difference from the baking-hot Kansas prairies! Once again he blessed his father for the cottage.

Summers right at St. Francis are always fun. Boys can picnic, fish, and swim in the Smoky Hill River, and ride the farm horses in the open pasture. They can walk just across the road from the Ellsworth unit to the Ellsworth Country Club, where the boys are invited to play golf whenever they wish. Nevertheless, the best part of the summer is the mountain vacation which is given to the youngsters who have earned it by good behavior.

Bishop Mize started the custom of lending his cabin to Father Bob and a few deserving boys for a couple of weeks each summer. Soon afterward other townspeople who owned summer homes did the same, and now there is always some place available to the lads for a change of air and scenery.

Father Bob looked forward to the annual mountain holiday as

eagerly as did his youngsters—and the day they arrived in Colorado, the six boys in the car were scarcely less relaxed and happy than their priest. At the moment, the Director did not even have cause to worry about the boys left back at Ellsworth. For once, the staff was entirely adequate. Two men training in the Church Army were spending the summer on the premises, and a young seminarian was assisting at the Home as part of his clinical training. Father Bob's heart was still buoyed by the memory of the recent service of admission at the cathedral church: twenty-one new members and three honor members; and the Homes had had no reversions for two whole years.

The boys piled noisily out of the car at the priest's heels, and trooped up to the front door of the cabin. There a welcoming committee awaited them: Father Bob's sister, her husband, their two children, and Maria, the little Mexican housemaid whose warm smile made up for her halting English.

As the priest introduced his boys, his almost paternal regard for them was plain to see. "Here's Tim, the captain of his school basketball team; Dave, the highest ranking boy in his class; Phil, who was elected president at the last Episcopal Youth Conference." He thought how different they were from the first group he had taken to the Mize cabin, the ones who had spent their time frisking the neighbors' cottages. He was more than ordinarily thankful for the difference, because two of the present boys had taken part in that escapade!

The newcomers unpacked neatly, St. Francis style, and refueled on cookies and milk. Led by two knowledgeable guides the boys went out to explore the area.

Father Bob settled down in the big living room chair, stretched his legs luxuriously, and prepared to chat with his sister. In the middle of the first sentence, he winced. Leaning over, he untied his shoe and slipped it off.

"Sorry, Marge," he said, ruefully rubbing his foot. "Guess I got the wrong size out of the box this time. They sure pinch!"

Marge gave him a smile. Her brother was always having trouble with his shoes. He would not take time to have them fitted or spend money to get ones which would last. In any event, the tops always wore out before the soles: mute evidence of the time he spent on his knees. She remembered how Mr. Bowers, his friend in Kansas City, had noticed one evening the badly scuffed toes, and insisted on taking him to a shoe store to buy him a new pair. The priest had started home with the package under his arm, but on the way to his car he passed a drunk staggering down the street in a torn pair of moccasins. Because he was shoe-conscious at the moment, Father Bob hailed the fellow, unwrapped his new shoes, and handed them to the derelict to try on. They fit perfectly. The priest said, "Keep them," and walked on.

Father Bob never cared how he looked personally, but before the altar he was more concerned about his appearance out of respect to his priestly office in the Church, the Body of Christ. Marge vividly recalled an occasion when her brother stopped by their father's house for a brief visit on his way to a parish in another town where he was to have a service. Sitting in her living room, the young priest had crossed his legs and exclaimed in dismay as he noticed a hole the size of a fifty-cent piece in the sole of his shoe.

"I'll be terribly embarrassed to kneel at that beautiful altar with holes in my shoes," he said to his father. "How about borrowing a pair of yours?" Bishop Mize agreed, but made his son promise faithfully that he would keep them for himself or return them.

Years of experience had accustomed but not reconciled the Bishop to his son's habits. Time after time, he or his daughter would give Father Bob new things to wear, and three days later they would see him dressed in the same old clothes. He never noticed their loving annoyance. He would explain blithely, "Jim was applying for a job this week, and simply had to look decent," or, "Harry needed a new suit to wear to the dance last night." There was never any reason given why the Jims and Harrys had not returned the clothes when their special need was past.

The Bishop was puzzled continually by his son's way of life, and once remarked to Marge, "Bob never has a cent in his pocket, and his clothes never fit. The last time he was here he brought in three of his boys just in time for dinner, and he does the same thing everywhere he goes. When he left, he charged all his gasoline to me. The Mize family does not do things that way!"

On that first night of the Colorado holiday, Father Bob's bubbling good spirits made supper a festive affair for everyone. His delight in his sister's company and his pleasure in his boys' happy behavior inspired wit and laughter in everybody at the party. Marge herself was impressed by the easy good manners of the St. Francis youngsters, and remarked later that evening, "They actually are better behaved than my own children."

The St. Francis boys usually came to the Home from antisociety as well as antisocial backgrounds, but they found Father Bob more ready to forgive theft than a breach of etiquette. He was himself the product of good breeding and culture, and his gentlemanliness seemed to rub off on the boys even more quickly than did his goodness. The first thing he taught his bashful and socially backward lads was to introduce themselves clearly and politely to visitors, and the visitors were always favorably impressed.

Acting on his observation that the first step toward becoming a gentleman is to act like one, Father Bob insisted that his boys practice good table manners from their first day at the Homes. One section of the Boys' Handbook is devoted to the proper way to eat: how to grasp a knife and fork, how to clear a table, and the like. ("Do not stack the dishes!") Father Bob grinned quietly as he noticed that his boys might have been consciously dramatizing that part of the handbook as they sat around his sister's table. There was Tim meticulously breaking his bread bite by bite ("Bread is broken and each portion buttered as eaten"), and Dave swallowing carefully before answering a question ("One does not talk with food in the mouth"), and Dick making little lunges forward as he repeatedly remembered just in time not to lean on his elbow ("Elbows are never placed on the table until the completion of a meal"). The priest's broad smile was about to break into chuckles when someone glanced his way and he hastily tried to control his face. It was too late. No one could have been serious that night.

Even Evening Prayer dissolved into "a joyful noise unto the Lord." Father Bob, his arm around the little Spanish girl, led the entire group into the small chapel, which had been started by his father and finished by the St. Francis group only the summer before. Maria sat wonderingly beside Marge, and the priest began the Office. Only the opening sentences were done properly: as the congregation was about to make its first response, a pack of coyotes ran yap-yap-yapping across the yard exactly as though it were answering the reader. The boys giggled.

With forced dignity, Father Bob began again. Once more, the coyotes joined in on the first response. Both Marge and the boys bent over to smother their chuckles, and Maria fled convulsed from the chapel. The priest stubbornly began to read the responses himself, but when the yipping outside interrupted for the third time in the same place, his hard-won sternness collapsed into laughter. When he could catch his breath, he skipped to the final blessing to complete the shortest version of Evening Prayer on record, then gasped, "Let's go out and just listen to Brother Coyote praise the Lord tonight!"

The next day two of the boys came to the priest to ask if they could borrow some rifles to go hunting. Father Bob pondered the matter: should he, dare he, place such temptation in their hands? The youngsters seemed well on the road to rehabilitation, but . . . He quickly remembered his own philosophy, "trust a boy and he becomes trustworthy," and said, "Sure, go ahead." The pair went off with a hunting dog and guns conveniently borrowed from a neighbor.

They came back a few hours later, without game or incident, but in love with the dog.

"Padre," said Phil, "I wish we could have a dog at St. Francis." The others shouted their support.

A few months later they all had their wish, and a little more of the spirit of St. Francis of Assisi, lover of man and beast, walked through the Homes that year. In fact, when Father Bob later made his annual pilgrimage through the buildings to bless each boy's room, Gary, who along with others was waiting for him after chapel, wondered if it would be irreligious to ask that Blacky, his foundling cocker spaniel, also receive a blessing. "Of course not," said the priest. After Blacky was duly blessed, the procession went to all the other dogs in the kennel, and then on to the barn to bless the horses.

Dick was more enthralled with the Colorado outing than anyone else. He was a fourteen-year-old colored boy from a big city. He had never before seen mountains in his life, and had seen open country only since coming to St. Francis. Each evening after chapel he stood alone for a few minutes to look up at the stars which appeared close enough to touch. When he would lower his great, dark eyes, they seemed to hold lingering reflections of the stars' brilliance.

The color of a boy's skin is no more considered at St. Francis than his religious (if any) or social background; colored boys have come to the Homes and Negroes have been members of the Board of Directors from the beginning.

Only once was there any complaint. Shortly after the Ellsworth unit opened, two fourteen-year-old Negro youngsters cornered Father Bob during their second week. "Father," the spokesman said, "we hate it here. The other boys are real nice and friendly, but the trouble is, we've never lived with whites before and we don't like it!"

Father Bob was unhappy and helpless. He found any distinction between races to be simply incomprehensible. Years later, his sister was in Africa for her brother's consecration to be Bishop of Damaraland. She cherishes the moment that an Anglo-Saxon dignitary of the Church was presented to him. Standing slightly behind the V.I.P. was a very small and very black African boy. The new Bishop greeted the English prelate, then reached for the child's hand and said pleasantly, "And this, I suppose, is your son?"

"When I teased my brother about the matter afterward," she said, "he didn't know what I was talking about. After I explained, he only said, 'Oh, was the child colored? I didn't notice.'"

As the blessedly peaceful and uneventful vacation drew to a close, the youngsters pleaded to stay in Colorado a few days longer. Father Bob explained patiently that he had a series of speaking engagements arranged, and he had no choice but to take the boys home on schedule and then to be on his way. However, when his brother-in-law learned that the first talk was in Wyoming, he saw another possibility.

"Look, Bob," he said, "why don't you leave the boys here, go make your speech, and pick them up on your way back to Kansas? It will save retracing your steps later, and give the boys a little extra time here. Marge and I will keep our eyes on them, and we'll all get alone fine." The idea was overheard by some of the boys, who set up a lusty chorus of *"Please,* Padre!" The priest nodded happily; the plan seemed to be a good one.

When he was in his car and ready to leave three days later, Marge asked what had long since been a routine question: "Are you absolutely sure you have everything?" Father Bob nodded absently, and reached down to turn the key in the ignition; but Marge took no chances. She knew her brother. After his every visit she had gone through the house to pick up all the things he'd forgotten. "Wait, Bob," she said, and turned to one of the boys standing by. "Tim," she asked, "run upstairs and take a quick look around his room, please." Within a minute he was back. "Bare as Mother Hubbard's cupboard," he reported. Father Bob grinned smugly at his sister. "Told you so," he said, and was away.

Half an hour later Marge was attending to upstairs chores and, humming softly while she swept, opened the door of the closet in her brother's room. Horrified, she saw all his clothes hanging neatly on their hangers. Obviously he had nothing with him to wear except what he had on his back—a faded sports shirt and a frayed pair of trousers. She was frantic: he wouldn't arrive at the Wyoming parish until night, the Sunday Eucharist would be at eleven tomorrow morning, and he'd surely be invited out afterward. Helplessly she resigned herself to the fact that there was no earthly way she could get his clothes to him before that time, and she prayed only that he would be able to borrow something decent to put on.

When Father Bob returned on Monday to pick up his charges, however, even Marge who was used to him was aghast at the ill-fitting, cheap-looking suit he wore.

"Where on earth did you get that thing?" she blurted out.

"Well," came the offhand answer, "it was nearly midnight when I drove into town and suddenly realized I'd forgotten my clothes; but, golly, wasn't I lucky? I found a pawnshop open and bought this. Only three dollars, too!" It looked it, thought Marge, but he sounded so pleased with himself that she had to smile. That brother of hers!

The boys were as nearly ready to go as youngsters ever are; they had not admitted to themselves that the holiday was ending and had left their packing until the last minute. Tim was slightly flushed and glanced around guiltily as he overcasually brought down Father Bob's overlooked clothes and stuffed them in the car as though they were something else and someone else were doing it. The youngsters finished loading the car while Father Bob had a quick cup of coffee. At last they were set, all closets and drawers checked twice by everybody; with every window full of waving arms, they headed back to St. Francis.

Refreshed by two weeks of companionship among his boys and happy in the beginning of a third year's spotless record at St. Francis, Father Bob plunged confidently back into his work. When his speaking tour took him one rainy morning to St. John's Church in Wichita, he cast so rare a spell of charm under the high, dark beams of the mellow old building that no one gave any mind to the distant rolls of thunder or the persistent ringing of a telephone in the undercroft. At last the thing was answered, but it had signaled the cracking of foundations under the Homes which would continue until the founder's dream would seem to have crumbled into ashes and dust.

In the sacristy Father Bob was given the message. He was to call Ellsworth: three new arrivals had been missing for hours, a trail of farmhouse robberies led across the western part of the state, and a car stolen at Ellsworth had been wrecked while fleeing from the hot pursuit of police near Liberal, a Kansas town on the border of the Oklahoma Panhandle. The vehicle had run off a sandbank into the Cimarron River and its three occupants had disappeared across the river into the willow thicket. They were presumed to be the St. Francis runaways.

The distressed and fearful priest ran down the high steps of the church to the parish office in the white frame house behind. He knew the Liberal area; it was dangerous with quicksand. While he placed his call, someone turned on a radio. As neatly as in a motion picture, the instrument warmed up on an announcer's matter-of-fact voice reading the noon news. The receiver lay forgotten in the Director's hand as he heard, "One of the boys who escaped Liberal police earlier today has been captured. The wet and shivering youth surrendered without a fight near the stolen car he and his companions wrecked and abandoned in the Cimarron River after a high-speed chase. He told arresting officers that the two boys still at large possess firearms taken in a series of farm burglaries last night. Police believe the pair to be surrounded in a wooded area. They were traced there from a burning building which the fugitives may have set afire in an attempt to warm themselves and dry their clothes. The Seward County sheriff has warned his volunteer posse that the youths are armed and should be considered dangerous. The boy in custody told Liberal authorities that the three had run away from the St. Francis Boys' Home at Ellsworth in order to celebrate his fourteenth birthday."

The color drained from Father Bob's face. Boys under *his* care and protection were being hunted like animals. The oldest was fifteen. For a moment he staggered against the desk. Then he thrust emotion aside and responded to the situation with the cool efficiency which over the several years had become almost a reflex.

He immediately telephoned a friend in Ellsworth who owned a private plane, told him the story, and asked the flyer to meet him at Hays. He knew that a train was leaving Wichita in fifteen minutes, and he was on it. When he arrived at Hays, the aviator had disconcerting news. "Sorry, Father," he said. "We can't fly; the cloud ceiling is too low. We'll have to drive."

They both ran to his car and drove at breakneck speed toward Liberal.

They ground to a stop before the ranch house near the river, fourteen miles northeast of town, hoping for some information. Their knock was answered by guns bristling in the crack of the partly opened door. Three bearded men reported that the armed bandits had not yet been found. As Father Bob and his friend dashed back to the car, a pickup truck pulled into the driveway.

"No, haven't seen the bandits," the ranch woman inside said before the question was even asked. "All I seen was two young boys duck into a draw about two miles down the section line."

In a spray of gravel the priest and his companion were headed down the designated road. Before they had gone a hundred yards, they spied two bedraggled, frightened little fugitives.

"All Maurice and Jimmy wanted was to be with friends again," said Father Bob. "They were scared to death and were hungry. Before we took them to the Liberal jail, we stopped off at another ranch house and begged a meal from a kind farm woman."

The following morning, the priest got clearances to return the three boys to the sheriff at Ellsworth; but when he stopped by the Liberal jail to pick them up, he found only Maurice, lying on a bunk in his cell.

"Where are Jimmy and Floyd?" he asked.

"They're gone," came the disinterested reply. "The sheriff left a door unlocked last night and they just walked out."

"Why didn't you go too, Maurice?"

"Me? I've got a headache."

Later that day two boys flagged down a tourist on Highway 54 in the Oklahoma Panhandle.

"Can you take us back to Liberal, Kansas?" asked one. "We're supposed to be in jail," added the other. Jimmy and Floyd were tired of being fugitives from justice.

Before Father Bob had done what he could for the trio, three Bavaria boys ran away and dispersed in Wichita. One returned on his own, one was returned to the Home from a small town jail in Illinois, and one was located later in the Detention Center at St. Louis. A year later, the last youngster was elected vice-president of the Episcopal Young People in the District of Salina.

With those two episodes, the Homes began a nerve-wracking revival of runaways and car thefts. Father Bob realized that something drastic would have to be done.

St. Francis was then barely five years old and had grown like Topsy. Each day's needs had been met as they came along, without plan or system. The priest saw clearly that not only was a stronger structure of discipline necessary, but some sort of master plan would have to be devised as well.

The Homes were overcrowded and badly in need of improvements. Each unit, for example, still had only one shower on the second floor. The only supplementary building which had been procured was an old farmhouse on 120 acres next to the Ellsworth unit; some Kansas City businessmen had provided over half the money for it. Ellsworth still had no suitable Dean of Boys. Furthermore, the budget provided an annual expenditure of only one thousand dollars per boy; but even that almost criminally inadequate financial goal had never been fully met. Father Bob had tried the year before to organize a continuing and stable financial campaign, but the effort had not succeeded. In the eyes of too many people the Homes had not entirely proved themselves. That they had been able to function for five years with some good result was testimony that the priest had a genius both for raising boys and for raising money; but there was a limit to how much one man could do alone in either endeavor.

Father Bob once heard someone call him a "consecrated boob." He agreed with the opinion at the time; now the moment had come to do something about it. To learn how St. Francis achieved its undoubted benefits and how the Homes could continue, he set the wheels in motion for a professional analysis of St. Francis. He would not believe that the results of such a survey would threaten the very existence of the Homes and his own career in the priesthood.

CHAPTER 15

THE EVENT WHICH NEARLY DOOMED THE HOMES

FATHER BOB had hoped that the Christian Social Relations Department of the Episcopal Church's National Council would make the survey, but it felt unable to spare staff members for such an investigation. The priest finally arranged for the Child Welfare League of America to do the job.

"How much will it cost?" was his first question, and he quailed at the answer: $1,600. However, when the Christian Social Relations Department and the Home Missions Department of the national Church each offered to pay a third of the cost, St. Francis could manage the remaining five hundred dollars. The go-ahead was given.

In May of 1950, Mr. John Dula of the Welfare League stepped off the train at Salina into a blinding dust storm; and he could hardly have arrived at a less favorable time to begin his survey of the Homes. The day before, the old plumbing system of the Bavaria unit had gurgled its last and collapsed. When Mr. Dula, choking from the dust, walked into the Home to be greeted by a weary Father Francis, he choked for another reason: the kitchen and pantry were awash with sewer water which had backed up as far as the dining room. Someone had suggested to Father Pete that the plumbing be repaired, at least temporarily. "Get it fixed?" he had countered. "That wouldn't be honest. Let Mr. Dula see us as we are."

The surveyor did. For two weeks he stopped, looked, and listened to everybody and everything. When he returned to New York, his report, one hundred and sixteen pages of it, commended little about St. Francis except the motive for its existence. Before he revisited Kansas to submit his recommendations to the board of directors, he considerately wrote Father Bob and Bishop Nichols to forewarn them. They were braced for the jolt, but the board listened to the survey results in shocked unbelief.

Mr. Dula's opinions were not gentle ones—he stated that either costly changes (so costly that the Homes could not hope to make them) must be made, or the St. Francis Home for Boys must be closed. The survey found that virtually everything at St. Francis was wrong: wrong location (it should be in a city where clinical and other resources would be available), wrong leadership, wrong staff, wrong program, wrong boys.

Father Bob knew well the deficiencies of the Homes and his own inadequacies as Director—that was the reason he had asked for a survey—but he was stunned by the unsympathetic tone of the paper. It was some time before he realized that the survey had not judged the Homes themselves, but had condemned them for not being the sort of institution they had never intended to be. For the moment the priest could only blame himself: he had neither training nor previous experience for his job. He had only the conviction that God could use so-called misfits, and a certainty that God's purpose was to establish the St. Francis Homes. He had no method but his therapy-in-Christ and his only technique was that of an old-fashioned missionary; yet it could not be coincidence alone that St. Francis had reclaimed so many lives.

The priest had no money, but had begged pennies, furniture, clothing and daily bread. He had no property and had begun by renting a poorhouse for twenty-five dollars a month. He had no trained staff, but had taken whatever help he could find. Was it merely chance that the Homes had pulled through, met their bills, acquired their property, added a second unit, and sent out an unusually large proportion of their boys to lead responsible lives dedicated to Christ and His Church?

To such questions no answer was available, for the survey had not attempted a scientific measure of results. To have studied the number of rehabilitations would have required a second survey. The first one was concerned only with procedures.

Whether or not the report was sound, St. Francis had to heed it. The state legislature had recently taken Kansas institutional licensing procedures out of a nebulous arrangement between Health and Welfare authorities, and had concentrated them in the State Board of Health. The chief licenser from that department, a medical doctor, had visited the Homes with Mr. Dula during the research for the survey. The physician was affable but unyielding: he, too, squarely told the board to follow the recommendations or shut down.

Gradually Father Bob and his advisors realized that the recommendations were an ultimatum, not an either/or proposition but a death sentence. Father Bob wanted to see the Homes improved by any means, but the recommended drastic changes were financially impossible for any private institution and would force St. Francis to close its doors.

Father Bob prepared himself to battle for his Homes. Pride in his creation and director's office had no part in the struggle; he was fighting in the Name of Christ for the lives of his boys—the Johnnys and Eddies and Jacks in the Homes and yet to come. Upset by it all, he was most infuriated by the implication in the report that the Homes were inimical to children.

"Do you consider that St. Francis has been 'inimical' to John W.?" he heatedly demanded of the surveyor. He recapitulated John's history: after repeated car thefts and robbery, the boy had been sent to the Homes by the psychological clinic of Purdue University; he had become an honor member at St. Francis, and was elected a youth commissioner of the District of Salina; he later went to college and graduated with honors; his new relationship with Christ completed his reformation. John was only one of many, but Father Bob's outburst won him neither answer nor change of verdict.

According to the Welfare League, if the Homes were to remain open they would first have to move into the city. The League approved some of St. Francis' procedures, but the boys' program would have to be complete within St. Francis itself. If such recommendations were followed, the boys would not need to leave their own campus to use neighborhood facilities. The budget for staff salaries would have to be increased to amount to more than half the operating expenses. One provision was more irking and puzzling than any other, however, because it seemed to undermine the very reason for the Homes' existence: in the future, no disturbed boys were to be taken by St. Francis.

At lunch with a representative of the Welfare League, the Director and Bishop Nichols attempted to clarify that stipulation.

"What exactly do you mean by 'disturbed' boys?" asked Bishop Nichols.

"Anyone who has ever been in trouble with the courts," came the straight-faced reply.

The Bishop and Father Bob looked at each other in baffled disbelief. How could a Home for juvenile delinquents be operated if a boy's first admission requirement was that he had never been in trouble with the law? In fact, the League's recommendations would turn St. Francis into just another urban secular detention center. The Bishop and the priest ate hurriedly and walked out.

The next day Bishop Nichols went to Topeka to talk to the Kansas state psychologist, who worked one day a week at St. Francis, on loan to the Homes from the State Department of Health.

"I want you to know," the psychologist said, "that my heart is with you in this thing. I've seen with my own eyes what the Christian ideals of St. Francis mean to the boys you handle." He looked hard at the Bishop, and added, "Tell Father Bob that I believe he has builded better than he knows."

Such expressions of professional support were few as the Director began his two-front battle: first, to keep St. Francis open, and second, to keep it from being secularized. The recommendations would have the Homes' religious aspect de-emphasized almost out of existence. Father Bob had founded St. Francis on the historical Christian teaching and not on a nebulous nonsectarian humanism. He was convinced that a boy could not come to permanent rehabilitation without an active awareness of Christ and His redeeming grace. To win the one battle without the other would not be even a Pyrrhic victory; it would be a total defeat.

More and more Father Bob realized that the true nature of the Homes was invisible to those to whom he had given near powers of life and death. A welfare worker one day said to the priest, "Look, your Homes are overcrowded, so why not use the chapel space for something really useful? If you feel you must have religious services, have them in the parlors." Father Bob turned red and started to retort, but instead he bit his lip, made a hasty sign of the cross, turned on his heel, and walked off. His temper was getting short under the weight of worry and constant harassment. Until then he had kept his patience with the boys as always, but as he struggled to love even such unfeeling stupidity, he ran into two youngsters misbehaving slightly, and his pent-up anger overran his self-control. For the first time he took his feelings out on his boys. They stood dumfounded as the priest who believed in forgiveness lashed them with violent words.

That night, filled with remorse, he said to Bishop Nichols, "I never lost my temper before with the boys. It's not their fault that I'm in this mess. In blowing up like that, I've undone all the good I've tried to do for those kids." As the Bishop comforted his distraught priest, he understood at what cost Father Bob had kept the appearance of hope and patience since the survey proceedings had begun.

Those were the darkest days in Father Bob's life, but he was strengthened by the steady support of his Bishop and the board of directors, and was gratified that the townspeople rallied to the defense of St. Francis. Not one "I told you so" was heard.

The Board next turned to the Advisory Council of St. Francis, a group which included several of the important children's agencies in Kansas. It originally had been formed to give supplementary expert counsel to the Bishop and the board. The board asked it and especially its Topeka members for help. The St. Francis body pointed out that the Homes, a small-town organization, had been faced with the big-city recommendations. What to do? The group's help proved invaluable; because of its calibre, both the New York and Kansas welfare authorities who worked with it as a part of their survey committee listened with respect to its suggestions.

First, the Advisory Council gave Father Bob a vote of confidence by retaining him as Director of the Homes.

"Perhaps," Father Bob said ruefully, "they felt that my mistakes were a type of training which made up for some of my classroom deficiencies in social work."

Second, the Council recommended moderate changes in the St. Francis procedures which quieted the excessive demands of the Welfare League. A few of their suggestions were that Father Bob immediately appoint a program director trained in youth therapy, that a part-time psychologist on the scene replace the visiting state psychologist, that no boy be admitted to the Home whose delinquency was caused or accompanied by mental illness, and that greater care be exercised in the selection of the staff.

The changes seemed reasonable and possible, but when Father Bob attempted to carry them out, only turmoil resulted. He gave the program directorship's weighty authority to someone already on the staff who seemed qualified, and it was the wrong move. It occasioned the resignation of Father Francis, whose abrupt departure was a calamity for the Homes and a severe personal blow to the Director. The young priest had demonstrated great facility for dealing with the boys in his care and he also was Father Bob's right-hand man, the one who had his confidence above all others.

Father Francis' decision to resign was not made suddenly. It was his final attempt to call attention to a situation which had been building for months. The young priest thought he had seen a conspiracy forming and the new program director was a part of it. He believed that the two staff members, one of whom served also on the Board of Directors (a circumstance which the survey had deplored and which was rectified as soon as possible), were attempting to wrest control of the Homes from Father Bob. He had tried repeatedly to warn the Director, but his fears had been brushed aside.

"At last," said Father Francis, "I simply couldn't sit still and watch any longer without doing something to stop it." His action, however, did not make his point. The Director was worn down with worry, and interpreted his associate's leaving to mean only one thing: disloyalty, both to him and to St. Francis. Father Bob sadly and bitterly accepted the resignation and would hear no further explanation.

The older priest's greatest weakness was also his greatest strength: he would never see fault in anyone. He did not understand people who sought power for power's sake. So dedicated and unsuspicious was he, that when it was suggested to him that "it might be a good idea if everyone in contact with the boys had a psychological test. How about your taking some tests next week?" he gladly agreed for the sake of the Homes—even though the suggestion came from one of the staff members he had been warned against.

What he didn't know was that a nefarious rumor had already been circulated to the effect that his relationship with the boys was poor, that they had lost respect for him, and that the staff and boys had come to think more and more harshly and uncomfortably of him.

The findings of the tests horrified Father Bob. According to the supposedly scientific evaluation, he was emotionally unstable and temperamentally unfit to participate in a rehabilitation program for boys, much less to direct it. Still the priest was not suspicious; he was dazed by the succession of unsympathetic and unloving blows. His long-held dream, realized five years before, had become a nightmare. As the human love he needed as much as sleep or food seemed to fail, he held desperately to the love of God. For a while the prayer of his heart was more often the *Kyrie*—Lord have mercy—than the *Te Deum*—we praise Thee, O God. In something very close to despair, the priest went to his Bishop.

Bishop Nichols was not too surprised at the story he heard. A man not only of profound wisdom but of astute perception, he had more than a little idea of what had been going on within St. Francis ever since Father Bob, in an effort to streamline the organization, had delegated much of his authority to two of his co-workers. To the Bishop, the circumstances of pseudoscientific testing were highly suspect, and the alleged findings only confirmed his suspicions. He at once made arrangements with a well-known psychiatrist in Kansas City to re-examine his priest.

The following week Father Bob underwent a true psychiatric examination, submitting to a battery of properly conducted tests which were then professionally analyzed. The results were very different from conclusions of the earlier and more shocking report. The priest was vindicated and given a clean bill of emotional health.

Bishop Nichols was aware of the weeks of pressure which had been exerted on the board to believe the worst. He asked the psychiatrist therefore to attend the next board meeting to make a full report. Afterward, the Bishop's eyes glistened with satisfaction as he said, "Bob's enemies were laid out flat, as they should have been."

The priest felt no sense of triumph. The Homes' situation was still chaotic and promised only further chaos as the staff struggled to justify their existence under state law. The boys' behavior, which had precipitated the crisis, had grown worse during the general turmoil of the year. Bewildered and shaken by the experience which had threatened his dream and jeopardized his ministry, Father Bob requested a leave of absence.

The ebullient good spirits and confidence which had built the Homes against such odds were gone. When someone requested the priest's opinion on a problem and received no answer, he asked testily, "Well, you're the Director, aren't you?" The priest just shook his head. "I honestly don't know, any more," he said dully.

The Prayer Book had taught him that "in returning and rest we shall be saved, in quietness and confidence shall be our strength." On June sixth Father Bob headed for his old retreat in the wilderness, the Mize cabin in Colorado. Like the fisherman Apostle Peter, he felt as if he had toiled all night and had caught nothing.

CHAPTER **16**

CONSPIRACY AND CHAOS

FATHER BOB never acknowledged that anyone had conspired against him, but the events which followed his leaving for Colorado that spring of 1951 left no doubt about the matter in the mind of Bishop Nichols or of most of the board members.

Before the priest had been away a month, the board received a lengthy statement from one of the staff members left in temporary charge of St. Francis. In it, the Director was politely torn limb from limb.

The "serious weakness of the Homes' leadership" under Father Bob was detailed at great length. His competence was not merely questioned; it was scathingly impugned. The chairman of the board was excoriated for having said that the priest should continue his directorship for no reason other than that "he founded St. Francis at great sacrifice."

The writer even assailed Father Bob's previously unquestioned ability as a fund raiser. The writer echoed the opinions of the discredited psychological examination: he felt there was no place whatever in the organization for the founder. (It was a strange coincidence that some of the followers of St. Francis of Assisi had come to feel the same way about their supposedly impractical

181

founder.) The statement concluded with the recommendation that a new leader be found for St. Francis while Father Bob was away, and it left no reasonable doubt about who the writer believed the choice should be.

At the next board meeting, it was obvious to everyone present to whom Bishop Nichols directed his opening remark.

"I prefer," he said coolly, "to take whatever chances there may be in having Father Bob at the head of St. Francis, rather than to take the risk of placing any other presently available person at the helm."

The Bishop did not deny that St. Francis greatly needed reconstruction, but he quietly wrecked the charge that Father Bob alone was responsible for the confusion which had followed in the survey. "The confusion," he stated in firm tones, "in great part is owing to an uncertainty among some of us as to the One who is actually the Head of the Homes."

He went on to point out that blame for the past year's lamentably rapid turnover in staff (thirty-four persons had come and gone) could not justly be laid at Father Bob's door, because the priest had had no part in handling the staff at either of the units during that time. He had been forced to delegate that responsibility to another. The room was very quiet. That man was the same one who had submitted the report which accused the Director of incompetence.

"The Director has weaknesses like all the rest of us," the Bishop continued, "but he also has gifts far greater than most—and certainly far greater than any possessed by those who have assumed the temporary leadership of the Homes during his absence."

The Bishop knew that, with the exception of the member who had written the report, the board had all its old confidence in Father Bob's leadership. His first five years had demonstrated that if by nature he was unfitted for administrative work, by grace he had been a channel through which miracles had been worked in the lives of disturbed boys. One of the board members had dryly commented, "If Father Bob had taken a psychological test to determine his aptitude for directing an institution in the beginning, he would have flunked it and the Homes would never have been created." The board had always approved the priest's concept of a wholesome, familylike Christian home for erring boys, in which they would find the loving influence of Jesus Christ. To be sure, too much had depended on one man and his limited vitality, and less intuitive methods would have to supplement the original program; but the board members were almost as concerned as the Director that the clinical emphasis recommended by the welfare agencies not crowd out the love and forgiveness of Christ from the lives of the boys. Were that permitted to happen, St. Francis would break faith with its boys and with its multitude of loyal supporters.

The Bishop concluded, "Among the personnel of St. Francis, I see no one but Father Bob who is determined and able to keep the Christian emphasis at the heart of the Homes. We need his policies maintained; we need the example of his life close enough to the staff and to the boys to let his living faith and loyalty to Christ do its work in their hearts." Bishop Nichols paused. "I cannot too strongly recommend," he said at last, "that Father Bob be recalled on September first to continue to be Director of St. Francis."

One member of the board rose and walked out of the room. The vote they took was unanimous—with one member abstaining.

Father Bob, physically rested and spiritually renewed, strode into his office on the first day of September. He was ready once more to do battle, and battle it was to be.

His first concern was to check the quality of the religious life at the Homes. He made a quick trip to both Bavaria and Ellsworth, asked some sharp questions, and saw clearly that the secularization which had threatened St. Francis before he left was no longer a threat but an accomplished fact. His policies had been so largely disregarded and the chapel worship so greatly curtailed that no difference could be discovered between St. Francis and any secular institution. He was not surprised to learn that also in the three months he had been away, the boys had gone out of control, with runaways and car thefts by the score.

By the end of his first afternoon back, he had ordered all chapel services reinstated. He then began to reinstate the religious policies upon which St. Francis had been founded and upon which it had to continue in order to have any reason to exist. He turned to the problem of the staff.

The temporary program director's trial period was at an end, and Father Bob dismissed him. The experiment had failed in every way; it had produced bedlam among the boys and strife among the staff. Next, the priest dismissed the Dean of Boys at the Bavaria unit. He was a man with no religious convictions who had been appointed shortly before by the program director.

The boys in his charge were so badly out of hand that Father Bob transferred to Bavaria the competent and experienced John Heiden, Dean of the Ellsworth unit, so that he could stabilize the situation there; a new man was engaged to head the Ellsworth Home. The move lost one good man; Mr. Heiden resigned almost immediately because of Bavaria's inadequate housing for his family.

Nevertheless, the search continued for a program director with enough clinical training to meet the demands of the surveyors and sufficient awareness of spiritual reality to meet the Director's requirements. The search began to look hopeless; no such combination appeared to exist. The priest was no nearer finding such a person weeks later than when he had first begun.

One morning as he sat at his desk wondering which way to turn, there was a knock on the door, and in response to his invitation a personable man and woman entered to introduce themselves. As he listened to what they had to say, and then glanced over the credentials they handed him, it seemed to him that another St. Francis miracle had come to pass!

"This is an answer to prayer if I ever saw one," he thought to himself exuberantly. As he silently framed the words, however, his mind flashed back to the day a lifetime ago that "Father" Rien had as suddenly appeared out of nowhere. He questioned the couple closely, and decided that the situation at hand could hold no such mistake. The man was a deacon in the Episcopal Church and would soon be ordained to the priesthood. He was a convert from another denomination who had been a professional social worker; his wife was a highly trained clinical psychologist who had earned degrees from both American and European universities.

Father Bob relaxed and offered a heartfelt prayer of thanksgiving. The couple was exactly what the Child Welfare League had ordered, but of overriding importance to the priest was the hope that the pair would be the saving of St. Francis as a religious institution. After their references were carefully investigated, the husband was put to work as the Homes' social worker and his wife became program director. Working with a Salina psychiatrist, the pair appeared to be the long-sought ideal therapeutic team; they were not.

The woman program director was the one who hired and fired. To fill the vacancy at Bavaria, she hired two men whose applications Father Bob had previously rejected, even though the battery of references and correspondence in the files indicated that they were anything but competent. One of the two, qualified by academic degrees to be supervisor in residence at Bavaria, was afraid of the boys. He left after one week. The second had a vicious temper and was discovered to be dishonest. He lasted a month. Gambling desperately, the program director then made the cook head of the staff in residence. "He seemed to have a command over youth," she said when questioned. The responsibility sent the poor man back to the bottle he had been fighting when hired for the kitchen, and he soon was discharged. She then brought in an inexperienced subordinate from the Ellsworth unit, and the Dean of Ellsworth resigned.

The welfare surveyors were beginning to admit that a program director separate from and over the Deans of Boys was not working well.

In fact, it was a long, costly and almost fatal experiment. Within a few months, the authority for the program direction of each unit was returned to the respective Deans of Boys, who have exercised it ever since; but while the damage was being repaired, the Homes had never been in worse shape. The psychologist and social worker who had seemed equipped to save St. Francis instead had almost destroyed it and had been released, and both the Bavaria and Ellsworth units were leaderless.

As harassing as those problems were, Father Bob had a thornier one than staff vacancies: his heart's concern was the continually threatened Christian influence at St. Francis. Both the first program director and the therapeutic team were irreligious. The woman psychologist, although the wife of a deacon, never attended church during her stay at the Homes. The religious emphasis at St. Francis had been in constant jeopardy. The love and forgiveness of God which were the very essence of the priest's therapy-in-Christ had no part in the thinking of most of the psychiatrists and social workers who had charge of the clinical program during much of the period. Father Bob had demonstrated with his boys over the years that love is indeed "a more excellent way." He saw what was happening to his youngsters as a result, and he found the situation as it stood to be intolerable.

The claim of the Christian faith on which Father Bob based all his hope is not that it is practical but that it is true. That it is both is indicated strongly by the history of Tommy Winters.

Tommy first came to St. Francis in 1950 when he was fifteen years old. A year later, he had made a fine record at the Home and distinguished himself in school, and so was returned to his family. Six months later he got into trouble again, and was allowed by the court at his own request to return to St. Francis, but he was warned that if St. Francis should decline to keep him, he would have to go to jail.

For months Tommy's behavior at the Home was above reproach; then he slipped and committed a misdemeanor. Under the new routine, the boy was examined by the clinical team headed by a psychiatrist. They routinely determined that he should be released from St. Francis.

Father Bob was appalled at their decision; it would mean jail for the lad, after which he would be put out in public life without assistance, therapeutic or otherwise. Only three weeks of school remained and dismissal would mean the loss of the boy's credit for the year. Moreover, he had come voluntarily to St. Francis in search of security and something to trust.

Father Bob asked that the clinical team meet with him and Tommy's Dean to explain first-hand the need for any act which would have such extreme consequences. Neither the priest nor Tommy's Dean of Boys was able to change the clinicists' decision: Tommy must leave St. Francis. The priest and his staff were sick at heart, but according to their agreement under the Welfare League's recommendation that the Homes turn full authority over to the clinical team, the youngster was returned to jail, social segregation, and the almost inevitable degrading of his young personality.

For days Father Bob was so bothered in conscience that he couldn't sleep. Finally, at two o'clock one morning he wrote a memorandum to the board which detailed Tommy's history. Then he added the following:

"What am I to answer before God to a mother's question, 'Why, after the struggle I've made and the trust Tommy had in you, couldn't he have finished his third year of high school?'

"What am I to answer when high school officials ask the same question?

"What am I to answer when the boys of Tom's unit ask, 'Why should I stay here? St. Francis threw Tommy in jail.'

"What am I to say to the State Board of Health when it tells me, 'Your philosophy doesn't fit in with that of a clinical team; St. Francis must either close or have a different Director.'

"All I can say is that, in obedience to God and conscience, it will be necessary to seek other sorts of psychiatrists and supplementary clinicists to co-ordinate the St. Francis program in the Christian way. The only alternative is to submit my resignation as

Executive Director. In such an alternative, I would be glad, if the board desires, to assist St. Francis as a full-time worker in whatever way I could, if it were clearly understood that I would not be able to be a spokesman for a clinical setup not based on sound Christian principles."

The board agreed with Father Bob that a different clinical setup was needed which would not supersede but would complement the Homes' religious values. Again, it refused to consider the alternative of his resignation.

Matters turned out for Tommy as they had for many other St. Francis boys; the priest's trust in him was justified. The sheriff pulled strings and bent rules to secure the youngster's release from jail after only a few weeks. Tom returned to school and graduated with no further incident. Today he is happily married and doing well in public life.

Shortly after the episode with Tommy, the Homes decided not to have a psychiatrist on the therapeutic team and their decision was supported by the Welfare League. The reason was twofold.

First, St. Francis had come to believe admission best limited to boys who were not likely to need the specialized help of a psychiatrist. One such boy was accepted during the time a psychiatrist was at hand, a boy who claimed to have pushed another lad off a seventeen-story building and who plainly needed the care of a psychiatric institution rather than that of a fraternity whose members are part and parcel of the surrounding community. He was a psychotic youngster, one of those persons who are unable to respond to love and cannot safely live in public life, even under the guidance and influence of St. Francis.

Second, a psychiatrist by virtue of his training is necessarily the head of any therapeutic team of which he is a part, and as in the case of Tommy, he, not the Director, assumes the ultimate authority. Time and again the situation proved untenable because St. Francis existed to work out the problems of young men within a community based on the Christian view of the human situation; the training of the psychiatrist and the training of a priest are not necessarily in conflict—indeed each has much help to offer the other—but they are different, and for St. Francis to be St. Francis, the Christian authority had to be the final one. When the experimental period ended, the therapists were made directly responsible and subordinate to the head of the Homes.

Thus, through many trials and much error, the policy and staff setup came into being that is in effect today. Father Bob may have never agreed entirely that the therapy-in-Christ program needed to be supplemented by supposedly modern psychological methods; but the combination of Christian and clinical therapy has won the Homes their present recognition by welfare authorities as among the finest in the United States. No one can deny, however, that St. Francis is what it is today only because of the priest's determination to remain true to his original vision, no matter what the cost. Perhaps the Homes, as good teachers must nowadays, have simply done what was necessary to be certified for their job, and then gone ahead and done it by love.

Father Bob has said, "Psychotherapy is an aid, yes; but it is an *adjunct* to—not the *core* of—the St. Francis program, which centers at all times in God and in Christ's Mystical Body, the Church. Our Lord is the center of all healing and rehabilitation."

Slowly Father Bob was able to gather about him a staff which would live and work with the same conviction. In addition to the Director, it consists of a psychiatric social worker, a group worker, a clinical psychologist, the priests who are deans of each of the two units, and the business manager. The men work together with a common mind and purpose: the welfare of the boys in their care.

Things were not so well ordered in 1952, however. St. Francis then was in turmoil. The period of experimentation had extended into two years: two years in which the Home was not a home permeated by God's love and forgiveness and trust, but a prison of locked doors and vandalism and hostility. It was a period in which a priest's dream of a household of God, in which Jesus Christ Himself would be the cornerstone, had been at times almost obliterated.

On an oppressively hot September night, Father Bob tossed

and turned in bed, the problems of St. Francis competing with the heat to keep him from sleep. Once more both the Ellsworth and Bavaria units were without leadership, and once more a program director was proving highly unsatisfactory and would have to be dismissed. What was the answer to it all? Where and how had he failed? As such questions beat in his brain, he suddenly seemed to hear with startling clarity the words spoken at his ordination to the priesthood nearly twenty years before.

". . . therefore ye ought and have need, to pray earnestly for his Holy Spirit . . . seeing that ye cannot by any other means compass the doing of so weighty a work. . . ."

Never had the weight seemed heavier nor the need for guidance greater. As his heart pleaded with desperate urgency, "Lord, speak, for thy servant heareth," his room suddenly was illuminated by the headlights of a passing car. In that fleeting second, Bob Mize caught sight of the tablet of paper in its customary place on the bedtable. Almost of itself, his hand reached out. He switched on the light above his head, propped the pad against his knees, and began to write.

"Dear Pete: I hate to ask you, knowing how happy and well-set you are, but St. Francis is having a whale of a lot of trouble. We need you like sixty. Is there a chance?"

Lest his mind change before morning, the priest quickly slipped into bathrobe and slippers; he scurried out of the house and across the dark street to drop the penciled note into the mailbox.

CHAPTER 17

DAWN

ONE OF THE BRIGHTEST DAYS in all St. Francis' history was late in 1952, when Father Pete returned in response to the Director's plea to be Dean of the mother Home at Ellsworth. He was an anchor which could stabilize the Homes, then still floundering in uncertainty and confusion after the survey, and he has held them to their mooring ever since.

Father Pete is superbly fitted to his task by background and temperament. He was born in New York's Hell's Kitchen and raised in Greenwich Village; upon his mother's death, he was placed at the age of six in an Episcopal Home for four years, good years.

"I loved it and didn't want to leave. It even had a wall," he recollects happily, "but I never minded it in the least."

He attended an Episcopal boys' school in New Jersey, but drove to Kansas one summer with a friend, and remained in Salina to finish school at St. John's Military Academy. There he learned the discipline which was to serve him well with his St. Francis charges. At college in Wisconsin he met Phyllis, the pretty brown-eyed girl who became his wife and the mother of his two sons.

"The St. Francis boys may call you 'Father,'" she told her

mountainous husband, "but I'm not the mother of any twenty-six boys. Peter and Michael are enough for me!"

Peter and Michael are both strapping youngsters in their middle teens who threaten to rival their father in size. The Francis family no longer lives in the old farmhouse which was its first home at the Ellsworth unit, but in a charming modern dwelling on the edge of the golf links, just across the street from the Home.

Pete and Mike are good friends with all the St. Francis boys. They go to school with them, double-date, and are more often to be found at the Home than around their own place. The new activities building, O'Donnell Hall, provides much to do and many buddies to do it with; it boasts a large and well-equipped gym, a handball court, a complete workshop, and a snack bar. The St. Francis boys know, however, that Father Pete's home is off limits: the priest's sons do all their visiting at the Home, lest any feelings of partiality develop.

Father Francis and Mrs. Francis have never had any trouble with the Ellsworth boys. "When Peter and Michael were little," Mrs. Francis says, "it was wonderful to have a houseful of baby sitters across the way, and they always took fine care of our youngsters."

Father Pete once feared that as his children grew older, the St. Francis lads might feel resentful of the privileges his own youngsters enjoy. Peter now is allowed to drive a car while the St. Francis boys may not. No such difficulties have arisen. The boys at the Home seem without exception to take things as they are for granted.

Father Pete was particularly pleased when he recently overheard a new boy ask some of the oldsters who Peter and Michael were. They told him and commented, "Peter's a real brain, and both of them are real good guys."

Father Pete's second term at St. Francis is now over ten years along. During that decade, he has established a superb record of reclamations at Ellsworth. His enthusiasm for his work and his open affection for the well-groomed boys at the Home leave no doubt about where his heart and talents lie, yet his decision to return to St. Francis had been far from easy to make. He reached it only after much prayer and many hours of discussion with Phyllis.

On the surface, the reasons to refuse seemed to predominate. He and his family were nicely settled in Iola, Kansas, where he was the rector of St. Peter's Parish. Phyllis loved their pleasant house, a welcome change from the poor and crowded living conditions they had endured for two years at Bavaria. The young priest was teeming with ideas and enjoyed the free hand he had in the conduct of parish affairs, unhampered by the interference and conflict that had marred his first stay at St. Francis.

From the beginning of his stay at Bavaria, the younger priest had had differences of opinion with his Director about the management of the boys. Both were dedicated, both were emotional, and both had strong personalities of opposing types. One was a realist, practical to the core, who believed in the merits of firm discipline. The other was an idealist with a great vision, whose concept of discipline was an outpouring of love and an always-ready forgiveness.

Their qualities actually complemented one another, but they resulted inevitably in conflicts. Had the two men not known how to forgive each other seventy times seventy times and how to begin each day afresh, St. Francis would have been the poorer.

"I was young and impetuous when I started at the Homes," Father Pete says, "but I gradually came to realize the greatness of Bob. When he wanted me back, I couldn't refuse."

Each man came to learn from the other and to respect the different gifts God had given each. Father Pete as long-time Dean of the Ellsworth unit has made his own unique contribution to St. Francis while following the sound and basic pattern established by the founder. The vision of "therapy in Christ" is no longer tarnished: it is kept shining.

After the survey and against his will and desire, Father Bob had become increasingly an administrator. In his enforced capacity of promotional director, he found himself mostly removed from the company of his boys. He was not suited by temperament or desire to be a swivel-chair official. His satisfaction was in working with boys, not with papers; his genius was at restoring lost souls, not in managing an organization. His continuing frustration was reflected in his attitude toward the staff.

A saint is simply a Christian who has caught a glimpse of the Reality which supports this world and has fallen in love with Him who made it. As he pursues the love affair, he begins to reflect that Reality and to become an individual cut to a unique pattern, a person sure of his Beloved. The temptations at such a point are to turn from being an individual to being an individualist, a mere eccentric, and to fall from being certain of God to mistaking one's own taste or ideas for the will of God. Few persons who travel the Christian way escape being misled by those temptations at some time or in some degree. Like the founder of many great religious works and very like his patron saint, Father Bob had a curious combination of humility and arrogance: things had to be done his way, in accordance with his vision. He was not easy to work for.

Father Pete was fully aware of the lay of the land when he agreed to return to St. Francis, and he went back with the stipulation that he be given the Ellsworth and not the Bavaria unit. A cottage for the Director was then being built at Bavaria, and the younger priest did not have to strain his imagination to foresee the conflict of authority which would result if Father Bob and he both were to live at the same unit. Any uncertainty about who was really in charge would be unsettling to the boys, and hand them a weapon as dangerous as a gun. As would any youngsters in such a situation, they would play one priest against the other, and the result would be breakdown in discipline.

Once more Father Pete proved a good prophet. Because of the location of the Director's cottage, Bavaria was in constant trouble. The present Director does not live at the cottage, and is so careful not to interfere with the Deans at either Home that he never visits either unit without calling first, but to this day Bavaria is less stable than Ellsworth. It has had six deans, and every change is an upsetting experience for the boys.

From the beginning, Father Pete considered some practices at the Homes unwise. For instance, Father Bob permitted the boys to drive cars when they had achieved membership and reached the age of sixteen.

The younger priest contended that to let a boy loose in a car was to tempt him to take the car and disappear. Father Bob's principle was that to allow a boy to drive would get the yearning for cars out of his system and remove the temptation to steal one. The Director remembered Jack's success at returning his car alone long after several other boys had failed similar tests and simply kept going after, or even before, their errand was done. Several vehicles and runaways later, the older priest had to agree that his young associate was right again.

There was the same plausibility in the Director's scheme of having the boys do all the construction work around the Homes, but Father Pete discovered that the practice did not often work out. The youngsters could do simple jobs, such as laying out a patio at Ellsworth, or building an altar and pews for the chapel, but they were not competent to do any complicated construction work, and no member of the staff could teach them. Father Bob admitted the difficulty, but salvaged his dream by insisting that the boys should help on any building projects.

"I well remember," says Father Pete, "the time Bob told me how busy the boys were building the fireplace in his cottage. He was so pleased with them that I dropped in to see how they were doing. I found them sitting around in a circle playing cards while a mason skillfully placed the bricks. He was quite happy to have the boys out of his way."

Father Pete, who is not the full-time ascetic that Father Bob is, was often irritated by the Director's lack of regard for what the younger priest considered the necessities of a household. He remembers, "I didn't think he should expect the kids to live out of suitcases, and it was a constant struggle to get decent furniture for their rooms. He thought a packing case made a fine bureau. I didn't."

The most fundamental and serious difference between the two priests concerned the religious program at the Homes. Soon after Father Pete's return to St. Francis, the matter had to be faced. He felt that Father Bob viewed the chapel services, as he did many things, through Father-Bob-colored glasses and did not truly understand that the effects of so rigid a program were not all good.

The younger priest was able to see, as Father Bob could not, that compulsory attendance at the daily Eucharist was not accomplishing its purpose. Many of the boys accepted confirmation only to get in well with the staff. Father Pete began to notice that several confirmed boys did not often come to the altar rail to make their communions. He took one aside after celebration to ask, "Is something wrong, Charlie?"

The mumbled answer was, "I never wanted to be confirmed in the first place."

"Then why were you?" asked the priest.

"Because I knew Father Bob wanted me to be," came the expected reply.

The Founder was a long time in understanding that the force of his personality made the boys take his wishes for commands. Father Bob's only desire was to bring lonely boys to knowledge of the love and closeness of God; he wanted to welcome lost and troubled youngsters into the shelter of the Church, where they could find the nourishment of God's grace and the support of belonging to a happy human fellowship. He never intended to coerce them to enter the Church, but he blithely expected that none would refuse. Few did, but not a few bitterly resented the violation of their freedom to choose, even though consciously they were as little aware as the priest of just how it had happened.

When Father Bob was a very small boy his sister overheard him tell a playmate, "You have to be an Episcopalian, because Jesus is one!"

Obviously, as an adult, the priest's God is not that small; yet he has never lost his passionate love for the Church or his desire to bring everyone within her sheltering embrace. If his Anglican emphasis was in any way a weakness, it was at the same time a strength. If he was in any way blinded to his own mistakes, it was only because he thought of himself very little at all.

Father Pete, supported by the present Director, is responsible for the modified religious program in effect at the Homes today. No boy is urged, although he is given every opportunity, to become a member of the Episcopal Church. Chapel twice a day is compulsory, but no youngster is required to participate in the services—only to remain quiet so as not to disturb others.

"It is interesting," says Father Craig, the present Director, "to see the difference between the beginning and end of each year. In September when the boys are new, only a fraction participate in the worship. By June, nearly every boy is taking part."

Confirmation instruction is strictly voluntary, and if any youngster seems to be attending classes merely to win the favor of the staff, he is asked to examine his motives more carefully. The procedure impresses the boys—a thing has to be good if it can be trusted to sell itself—and whatever Father Bob secretly thinks about such a diffident approach to evangelism, the results are sufficient to gladden even his zealous heart. While they are at St. Francis, about fifty per cent of the boys are confirmed by the Bishop of Western Kansas (the name of the district was changed in 1960); and the Ellsworth unit supplies eighty-five per cent of the confirmands of the Church of the Holy Apostles.

No boy has to go to Sunday School, but nearly all do for one reason or another. Father Pete points out realistically, "There are girls there!"

The boys are now required to be present at the celebration of the Holy Eucharist only once a week and not daily as before. A majority of those who have not been confirmed, and thus may not receive Communion, go of their own volition to be blessed at the altar rail.

The former chapel services actually were as little planned as the rest of the St. Francis program. Father Bob has said, "The truth is, I never intended to institute such an intensive schedule of worship as we had earlier at St. Francis when we had a shortened form of Morning Prayer before the Eucharist each day. The first Johnny was the one who really established the tradition, not I. After he had lived with me at WaKeeney, he just assumed that we would continue the daily offices as well as the Eucharist, and I never thought about doing otherwise."

The Sacrament of Penance is available to all churchmen who wish it and is carefully explained to the lads at St. Francis, since many of them do not understand that confession is not to the priest as a man but as a duly commissioned representative of Christ's Body, the Church, or that the priest dares to declare sins to be forgiven only because of the authority Christ gave to his Church the evening of the first Easter (St. John 20:23). The psychiatric social workers approve the voluntary use of the Sacrament by the many boys who seek it because of its great psychological benefits. The priests are glad for the help it gives the boys in their spiritual growth. Both recognize that nothing else removes the burden and handicap of guilt for past sins in quite the same way.

Not many boys come to St. Francis with any kind of religious training. Those who do have religious convictions of their own are sent to their own churches on Sunday. Youngsters from Roman Catholic families must first secure their priest's permission to enter the Home, and it has always been forthcoming. When boys come from other Christian groups, the parents' wishes are followed exactly. One youngster was brought to St. Francis by his Baptist mother who somehow had the notion that it was a Baptist Home. They arrived just at suppertime and the woman was appalled to see all the boys in the dining room cross themselves after the grace, including her own son, who obviously intended to be one of the gang from the start.

She gasped, jerked the boy away from the table, and hustled him out of the room. Father Pete caught her at the door, calmed her a bit, and promised that the boy would not be encouraged in any religious decisions without her knowledge and consent. A year later, the youngster did ask the priest to be baptized and enrolled in the confirmation class. Father Pete had the boy discuss the matter at length with his mother. She refused her consent, and the boy was still a Baptist when he left St. Francis three years later. Father Pete hears that he has joined his mother's church and is doing right well there.

When Father Pete returned to be Dean of the St. Francis Home at Ellsworth, he soon wished he could know again the peace of his Iola parish. The disorder he found when he first came to Bavaria was nothing compared with the bedlam which greeted him at the demoralized mother Home.

Moving arrangements for the Francis family were made by the woman whose deficiencies in the post at last persuaded the Welfare Board to abolish the program director's office. Instead of hiring professional movers, she sent some boys from the Bavaria unit to Iola to load the Francises' seven rooms of furniture into two small rented trucks. The boys, whose previous experience must have been trash-hauling, dumped rather than loaded the furniture into the vehicles and careened back to the farmhouse at the Ellsworth unit where the Francises were to live.

The unloading was even more helter-skelter than the loading. When the exhausted Francises arrived at eleven o'clock that night, they found the piano in the kitchen, the refrigerator in one of the bedrooms, and the beds stacked along the living room wall. Something told Father Pete that the Ellsworth home must be in a bigger mess than his furniture. He quickly arranged some mattresses on the floor to make do for the night, then strode over to the Home to check his suspicions. He discovered a program of "permissive behavior" in full cry a few minutes before midnight.

A nine-year-old boy with a cigarette in his hand greeted him at the door. Before the priest could say a word, the lad burst out belligerently, "She says I can smoke if I want to and to call her if

I have any trouble with you," and ducked into the lounge where the television was blaring at full volume, two hours after even the oldest boys were supposed to be in bed.

Upstairs, Father Pete discovered a bed bending under in a violent wrestling match. At the priest's quiet suggestion that a bed was not a proper sort of prize ring, one boy stopped, but the other defiantly continued his attack. After several orders to break it up were ignored, Father Pete picked up a handy ruler from a desk and cracked the culprit across the knuckles with it.

"You can't do that!" screamed the boy. "I'll call Mrs. P. the way she told me to!"

The priest was beginning to see what sort of briefing the boys had been given before his arrival. The woman had underestimated her opponent. The TV was off, the boys were in bed, and their lights were out in a few minutes. In a few days, to the youngsters' secret relief, order was restored in the Home and the last program director had departed. Nevertheless, the boys' inner confusion took long to heal and so did the differences of mind between the Dean and his Director.

It was a harassing time. "Those were the days," Father Pete says wearily, "when I thought I must have been crazy even to have thought about returning to St. Francis." Whatever his feelings, he took hold and the Homes began to move ahead. Father Bob was often on speaking tours, but with Father Francis in charge, he no longer had to glue the situation back together upon every return. He trusted and loved the younger priest. Their disagreements were frequent and sharp, but the disputes never touched the bonds of affection and common faith which held the men and the work together.

Soon afterward, they were joined by a third able helper, the Rev. Eldred Murdoch, who came to Bavaria to be Dean of Boys, and St. Francis seemed to sail more smoothly than it had for a long time. Administrative conflict had come to an end when Father Bob once again was in charge as Executive Director. The revised demands of the children's welfare agencies had been met in clinical and other areas without compromising or diluting the founder's therapy-in-Christ method.

Father Bob turned ably to his administrative duties with a quiet if not happy mind. He looked back with no little longing on the days when he himself had been in the midst of the boys' lives and problems; he regretfully learned to do without the comradeship he had needed almost as much as they. Whenever he was in Salina he made himself accessible to the youngsters, but the involvement was gone. He was away too much to know the new boys well, and he had to be careful not to undercut the authority of the deans, although he often wished he could intercede on a boy's behalf.

Occasionally he could, for sometimes a boy in personal distress wanted only Father Bob, as Tommy did the night his father died.

The priest was busy unpacking after several weeks away when he heard a knock at the door. Opening it, he saw the youngster standing there, his face wet with tears. Father Bob's mind flew back over the years to the night when another young boy had stood shivering outside another door and spoken the words, "Father, help me."

For over an hour the priest listened to the youngster pour out his grief. Finally the boy pleaded, "Please, Father, I want to go home for the funeral. I know it will cost a lot of money, but I'll pay you back. Just let me go."

Father Bob knew the boy's record at the Homes. He had never been cooperative; he had never kept a trust; and neither the staff nor other boys had yet considered him ready for membership. Without hesitation, the priest picked up the telephone and made the necessary arrangements.

"Go on, Tommy," he said. "Stay with your mother for a couple of weeks—she'll need you. Never mind the money."

Kindness and understanding again had found the man lost in a boy. Tommy returned to St. Francis after the funeral exactly on schedule but mysteriously changed. Within a few months he had become a member, and when he left the Homes, he went on to a constructive life. He is happily married today, the father of two children, and still affectionately keeps in touch with Father Bob.

In those days, however, Father Bob's Tommys were few and far between. His priesthood was being spent not in a humble ministering to spiritually bereft boys, but in supersalesmanship; his life was being dedicated to raising dollars instead of guiding souls. Good priests occasionally become famous, but they are never quite comfortable in the public eye. Father Bob was continually torn between knowing that his boys had to eat and feeling that he was being presumptuous in asking for the wherewithal to feed them.

"I guess my fear of presumption handicaps the Homes more than anything else," he said one day after hesitating to accept a contribution from a donor in New York, "but I can't forget that some place in New York may need the money even more than we do."

He needed many people around him; he numbered his friends in the hundreds and yet he was a lonely man. His aloneness cut deeply because his life was in the Homes, but it was being lived apart from them. He shunned money for himself, but he was spending his life in its pursuit; and he discovered with horror that when he spoke, the unthinking people would afterward praise him for an achievement he attributed to God alone. They always seemed more interested in him than in his boys.

He was cited for "Distinguished Service to Mankind" by the University of Kansas: he accepted for the sake of the Homes, but the award almost burned his hands.

However his life had changed, his habits had not. The night after he received the citation in Lawrence, Kansas, he was scheduled to address several hundred people at eight o'clock. Every seat was filled by seven thirty. A rainstorm arrived before Father Bob did, two hours late. He was drenched to the skin, and someone from the audience had to rush home and bring him some dry clothing before he could begin to speak.

Not all the time was frustrating: as Christmas approached, he knew great joy. The building program at the Homes was going ahead rapidly and soon ground was scheduled to be broken for the new chapel at Bavaria. The priest could see it before a spade had been turned, and he already had named it. It was to be dedicated to St. Onesimus, the slave boy who had run away with some of his master's possessions, but had met Christ when he was imprisoned with St. Paul. The letter from St. Paul to Philemon is written about the lad, who later became Bishop of Ephesus. He probably was one of the collectors of St. Paul's letters, and thus an editor of the New Testament.

Christmas is a busy time for priests, and Father Bob usually arranged to visit his sister and brother-in-law for a few days afterward, during Epiphany. That year, however, he was asked to celebrate the Christmas Eucharist for a church near the Braden home. He called Marge long distance to tell her, and was quickly invited to spend Christmas with her family.

He left on December twentieth with a high heart and four St. Francis kids who had nowhere to go for the holidays.

CHAPTER 18

HIGHLIGHTS AND HANDOUTS

MARGE HAD A HOUSEFUL of guests for Christmas, so she was momentarily dismayed to see four people climb out of her brother's car in addition to the one she had invited. Of course, she chided herself, she should have remembered Father Bob's old habit of taking a few boys with him wherever he went, but in the confusion of the holidays, she had forgotten. She managed a cordial welcome for the unexpected youngsters; then she drew her brother aside and whispered frantically, "Where on earth can I put them? There's not an empty bed in the house!"

"Don't you worry," he whispered back. "They'll bed down in their sleeping bags on the living room floor. They'll just be happy to be in a home."

They were indeed, and that night when the Braden boy and his sister invited the St. Francis lads to go with them to a Christmas party, their cup of happiness was full. Eyes alight, they eagerly accepted—all except Ed. He was the oldest of the group and so painfully shy that Marge's heart had gone out to him the moment he had walked into the house. She suffered for him as the others tumbled over each other to get ready—he plainly longed to go, but was just too bashful.

He was an attractive boy, the son of estranged parents who had never given their son any reason to believe they cared whether he lived or died. His mother had brought him to St. Francis the year before on the advice of a priest in her home state, but the staff had been distressed by her callous attitude. She had refused their offer to show her the Homes, and said that she could not take time even to see the room which was to be her son's. During his stay at St. Francis, Ed had not had a postcard from her, much less a gift.

During his first few months at Ellsworth, the boy's grades had been poor. No one could understand why; he had a high IQ and worked hard at his lessons. Finally he was discovered to have a hearing deficiency, and the Homes provided a hearing aid. His grades had begun to improve immediately; he had become an excellent student. But he had not lost his excruciating shyness.

Marge was not the only one who had noticed Ed's difficulty. She was pleased to hear her daughter say, "Instead of going to the party, let's you and me go to the movies. I'd rather anyway."

To go somewhere with such a warm, friendly girl was not much easier than to face a crowd of strangers at a party. Ed's face reddened, but he managed to say, only a trifle hesitantly, "Sure. I guess that'd be fine." While the others went on a round of neighborhood parties during the rest of the holidays, young Barbara Braden kept Ed under her protective wing, and no one had a better time than he.

The day before Christmas, Marge dashed out to buy something for each of the St. Francis boys. When Christmas morning came, everyone had a present. Sitting on the floor by the tree, the boys tore through the wrappings and ribbons as quickly as possible—again, all except Ed. He sat as if mesmerized, gazing at the gaily wrapped box which had been handed him. The other youngsters were too caught up in their own excitement to notice, but Father Bob and Marge were watching. After a few minutes, the priest said, "Well, Ed, aren't you going to open yours?" The boy looked up and murmured, "I never got anything this pretty before." Then he picked up the package very carefully, as though afraid it might disintegrate under his touch, and carried it, unopened, upstairs.

Half an hour later, Father Bob called him down to breakfast. Eyes shining, the boy thanked Marge for his billfold; then he said shyly, "Here. I have a present for you, too." Into her hand he thrust a picture of himself taken at school.

"I think I was the only person he ever had had to give his picture to," Marge said.

Father Bob's Christmas gift from his family was a handsome new overcoat and hat. Marge and her husband were particularly glad they had decided to give him those when they learned that he was planning to attend a conference in New York City two days after Christmas. His old coat was worn out, and he had no hat at all.

He returned to the Bradens after the conference with neither hat nor coat.

"Where's your coat?" was Marge's sharp greeting as her brother walked in. He looked embarrassed, and then half-apologetically explained, "Oh, Marge, you know, it was snowing in New York, and I saw an old man on the street. He had no coat at all, only an old sweater, and he was freezing. I had to give him mine. What else could I do?"

Marge shook her head and smiled. The same old story! Give to Father Bob and give to the whole wide world!

"And your hat?" she asked wryly.

For a second the priest looked startled. "I haven't the slightest idea," he said impatiently. "I must have left it somewhere, I guess."

When Father Bob and the boys returned to St. Francis a few days later, another Christmas surprise was waiting for them. From his North Dakota vacation Father Murdoch had brought back a new horse for the youngsters at the Bavaria unit. It was the eighth horse in the new barn, and the boys were very proud of their "stables," which even included a grandson of Man-O-War. The thoroughbred was a gift from Mr. Carlock, who, since having made possible the purchase of the Ellsworth property, had kept a sharp eye on the needs and progress of the Homes.

The youngsters also took pride in the saddles they had bought with their own earnings and a little help from their unit's chicken business—which had become a thriving concern after athletics had replaced chicken strangling as a pastime. New saddles cost from fifty dollars up and good ones hardly less than one hundred and fifty; but the boys had been able to purchase battered old ones for only five dollars each. They painstakingly refurbished them until they were worthy of the finest horseflesh. All the boys of the Bavaria unit felt personally honored when Father Murdoch was elected president of the local riding club. They had high respect for the Dean's ability to keep his seat on Man-O-War's progeny; the animal was far too spirited for any of them to handle!

The staff at St. Francis was becoming as well acquainted with the Director's compulsion to give away gifts as was his family. Every year on his birthday they had presented him with something carefully selected, and every year the present had mysteriously disappeared within the week. When birthday time approached again, they decided to arrange something he could not give away: a surprise party!

It took a lot of planning to make it a real surprise. The main problem was to find a pretext which would get him to the Brookville Hotel for dinner without arousing his suspicion. Father Bob himself unwittingly provided the solution when he announced that he was taking a late train for Florida the night the party was planned.

"How about having dinner with us at the hotel before you go to the depot?" Mr. White, the business manager, asked casually.

"That's a mighty fine idea," came the preoccupied response, so offhandedly that the next worry was whether or not he would remember to show up at all. The staff took the chance and Father Pete reserved the room for the dinner. He planned the menu to include everything the Director liked best and topped it off by ordering a large decorated birthday cake.

The staff gathered at the hotel on the appointed night, and anxiously watched the door for the unpredictable guest of honor to appear. They were considerably relieved when he came rushing in only half an hour late.

He had his luggage in hand and, most uncharacteristically, he was wearing a hat. Mr. White had to smile. Earlier that day Father Bob and he had gone through a box of clothing which had been sent to the Homes. Crushed at the very bottom of the carton lay an old brown hat. The business manager had picked it up to throw it away, but the priest had grabbed it, jammed it on his head, and said, "I'm wearing this hat. It's just the thing for my trip." His associate had said nothing, supposing the thing would be quickly misplaced, but there it was. With a smug glance in his direction, the priest placed the disreputable-looking headgear carefully on a chair next to his suitcase.

When the Director saw the entire staff assembled, he apparently assumed the dinner was a business affair which he had forgotten, because throughout the meal he led a discussion of various problems at the Homes. When the table finally was cleared, everyone darted quick glances toward the kitchen, from which the cake would appear to reveal the purpose of the party.

Father Bob saw it first. As the lights suddenly were lowered and the waitress carried the cake around the table, her way lighted by the flaming candles, he began in lusty tones to sing "Happy Birthday!" When he came to "Happy Birthday, dear——" he turned, startled, to the man beside him and whispered, "Say, whose birthday is it, anyway?" At that moment the waitress set the cake in front of him and his mouth fell open. He was flabbergasted, and very touched, as he was at any demonstration of affection: his need to receive love was second only to his ability to give it.

The "business dinner" quickly became a real celebration, but a short one. Trains were one of the few things which would not wait on Father Bob and he knew it. In midsentence he caught a glimpse of his watch, grabbed for his luggage and hat, announced to his immediate company, "That was a mighty fine birthday party, the best I ever had. Thanks!" and was gone.

After the staff had lingered for a short while to savor their successful effort, Mr. White looked around for the expensive hat he had purchased only three days before. It was not to be found, but in its place was the Director's old brown one.

Within two days Mr. White had a note from the priest en route. It apologized for the misappropriation of the hat, and pledged that it would be returned immediately. Days later came another card: "Awfully sorry—someone stole your hat out of the car. Please buy yourself another, and charge it to my account."

Mr. White had long since bought himself another and charged it to his own account. He gladly would have given twice as much to prevent the Director from traveling around Florida to represent St. Francis while wearing that brown reject from a rummage sale. The business manager remembers the Founder's chronic hatlessness fondly, but recently said thoughtfully, "I wonder what he does now that he's a bishop and has to wear a miter?"

Father Bob chuckled the day he overheard a man comment to a drugstore clerk as he paid for his newspaper: "You know, comparatively speaking, those kids at St. Francis are angels." A story on the front page reported that of 105 acts of juvenile delinquency recently recorded in Salina, only one had involved St. Francis youngsters.

That episode happened the Sunday afternoon Father Pete took most of the lads to a horse show. Two boys whose recent behavior had been excellent had asked permission to go to a movie instead; their Dean had felt it safe to tell them to go ahead.

In the middle of the horse show, Father Pete heard his name blared over the loudspeaker. Hurrying to the office, he was given a telephone number to call. He knew it well; it was that of the police department. The desk sergeant supplied the story: officers had found a freshly missing car in an alley behind a drugstore and at the same time surprised the two St. Francis boys trying to force a window of the closed pharmacy. The kids were in jail. Father Pete went to them at once, and was thoroughly grateful that the police wanted only to be rid of them and were happy to let the Homes take them back without charges and without publicity.

The Homes then ran peacefully for another month, when Father Murdoch handed in his resignation. Once again the Director faced the wearisome task of finding a suitable Dean for the Bavaria unit. Temporary deans were enlisted to fill the gap, but the boys, always upset by change, grew increasingly unruly with each shift.

It was discouragingly difficult to locate a man who could operate St. Francis' uniquely open program. He had to be familiar with both group and individual case work and able to build discipline from within rather than by imposing it from without and so treating the boys like inmates of a prison. The new Dean also had to be a man sure of himself and of his faith in order to embody the therapy-in-Christ method of the Homes.

There appeared to be no way to tell in advance whether or not a candidate was suitable; it seemed that only by his fruit could Father Bob know him. One man who applied had excellent references from another institution and a good religious background. The Director liked his kind manner and open compassion for boys in trouble, but the boys in question sized him up even more readily. It took them only one day to discover that their kindly new Dean understood considerably less about running the unit than they did.

Two days after his arrival, two youngsters felt free to go AWOL to another town in Kansas. They telephoned their new Dean to pick them up; he did so immediately, and imposed no penalty whatsoever upon their return. The other boys took the leniency as blanket invitation to wander. The next day four ran away to Oklahoma. The following day, the new Dean resigned; but during his short four-day stay, the structure of discipline in the Bavaria Home had been wrecked. The merry-go-round had started; before it could be stopped, forty boys had taken unauthorized excursions—some of them several times.

Once again Father Bob felt like a passenger in the backseat of a speeding and driverless car. Despite the new clinical setup, the early days seemed to be repeating themselves. During the long hours spent behind the wheel and on foot tracking down runaways, the harassed staff was grateful for one thing: no public offenses had been committed. The Director did not believe the boys intended any harm, although their actions endangered the existence of the Bavaria Home. He explained, "They were just having a good time at the expense of inexperienced leadership. The fault was ours, not theirs."

Things had temporarily calmed down when the news came that Her Imperial Highness Ileana and her two youthful daughters, Magdalena and Elizabeth, planned to visit St. Francis. The boys were enthusiastic at the prospect of receiving royalty who at the same time were girls. There was a rush to get haircuts, and some new boys were disappointed to learn that Father Pete wouldn't give crew cuts or flat tops. "Too many people associate those hair styles with reformatories," he told them. The boys hadn't thought of that. Youngsters like Wally and Richard had new reason to be glad they had had gaudy tattoos removed from their arms and bodies. A few months before, Dr. Chard, a dermatologist, had offered his services free of charge to any of the boys who wished them.

"It hurts to have tattoos removed," the doctor had said, "but those who respect the body as a gift of God should not desecrate it by tattooing." Most of the boys who had cheap or homemade de-signs—and there were many—saw his point and submitted coura-geously to the painful operation.

The youngsters worked hard to clean up the Homes for the royal visit. They spent extra hours decorating the hall for the "Princess" dance they planned. None of the time they spent was wasted, be-

cause the occasion was even more exciting than they had anticipated.

On the day of the Princesses' arrival, the Romanian flag flew by
the side of the Stars and Stripes to welcome the guests to St. Francis Homes. To pick up the visitors at the Kansas City airport, Father Bob took along two of the boys, Jim, a senior, and Ken, only
a junior but an honor member. On the way over in the car, Ken
had asked, "Gee, how do you talk to girls like that, anyway?" "The
same way you talk to any other girls," replied the priest with a
twinkle, and Ken found that he was right. On the way back, he discovered that Elizabeth was quite at home on horseback, so he
promptly dated her to ride all the Home's section line roads with
him.

During their visit, the girls entered joyfully into all the boys'
activities, from ping-pong to chapel, and had to see or hear about
all their hobbies from airplane models to music. "You play a lot
better than I do," said Magdalena to a beaming Pat, after he had
played his piano solo for her.

The girls loved the old colonial house at Ellsworth and considered each meal an adventure—the dining room surging with boys
while each table was served family style by a staff member. They
loved the dogs and the chickens and the horses at Bavaria, too;
and the boys did not find it easy to keep up with their feminine
young guests in any form of athletics. Both girls were not only
expert riders but proficient ping-pong players as well. Many a
young male ego limped away from the table, beaten. Not even the
pool sharks were safe. Princess Ileana, a woman of many talents,
revealed an unsuspected one: she methodically beat the St. Francis
youngsters at billiards and then showed them how it was done—
including a new way to play without using cue sticks.

It would be hard to say whether the boys or the girls had the
better time. "Imperial Highness" would have been their official
title in their homeland of Romania, but they had been raised as
American teen-agers as well as European royalty. All three of the

distinguished visitors joined the boys in their enthusiastic consumption of big, juicy hamburgers with all the onions and catsup the buns would hold.

The girls and their mother had something else in common with the St. Francis lads: the royal family also was on parole, and the boys howled when they heard it. Their offense was not car theft, however. They had fled their communist-held country after the date for permissible entry into the United States had passed. Their visitors' permits had run out, so technically they were in the country on a "good behavior" parole.

Both girls and boys hated to see the four-day visit come to an end. "I just hated to go back to that old jail!" Elizabeth pouted, referring to the well-regarded girls' school she attended.

Father Bob glowed when Princess Ileana said to him as she left, "I've found your boys in many ways better behaved and better mannered than the so-called nice boys I've met." As the visitors were driven away, the world seemed a little less bright to the youngsters, but one ray of sunshine had been left behind. The boy who made up the Princess' bed found her hot water bottle forgotten at its foot! She was a little embarrassed when she discovered in New York City that it was missing. "I needed it not because of any chilliness in the Home," she graciously wrote the Director, "but because of my poor circulation." The boys who won the honor of packaging and mailing the royal hot water bottle felt peculiarly privileged.

"The boys learned as no mere words could teach them," reflected Father Bob, "that in God's Kingdom there is no difference between people. All are his children, regardless of race or rank."

Father Bob always intended to make a real home for his boys; he was determined that it should be neither a reformatory nor a large and impersonal "Children's Home" full of regimented youngsters segregated from the rest of society. His success was apparent when St. Francis' old boys began flocking back, usually unannounced, with such explanations as, "I wanted to come home for Thanksgiving," or "I came to spend my vacation with my family."

Such unheralded returns created problems in an already full house, but somehow a nook or cranny always was available; and old boys were welcomed then as today with the open-armed affection deserved by any member of a close family who has been away and comes home. Every visit is a reunion, with much catching up on family news, inspecting the changes, and meeting new cousins and brothers.

Those who had been at St. Francis in the early days always made a beeline for Father Bob. Seldom did an old boy come within even a semireasonable distance of Salina without looking up his beloved priest. They stopped by to see him, just to see themselves whole in his eyes again. Sometimes they needed help to get a job, or some other favor. They asked and they received, and love was the medium of exchange. His frequent meetings with the "oldsters" compensated the Director a bit for his lack of contact with the boys then living in the Homes.

To be sure, the homecomings were not all happy ones. One Thanksgiving eve, for example, the priest responded to a knock on his door and saw a tall, handsome young man standing there.

Father Bob had to look twice before he recognized one of his first boys, one who had not done well at St. Francis, but the warmth of his welcome was not diminished by his recollection.

"Joe!" he exclaimed. "Is it really *you?* Come in, come in!" With hands outstretched and face alight, he brought the young man in. Only after half an hour of reminiscence did Joe get to the point of his visit.

"Father," he began, "I've been out of work for a long time, but now I've an offer of a job. I can't go looking like this, and I don't have enough money for a meal, much less for a suit. Will you help me?"

The priest jumped to his feet. "Why didn't you say you were hungry sooner? Lets go eat and then we'll see what can be done."

Father Bob watched the young man eat two full meals at a good restaurant nearby, and then the two returned to the Director's house, where the priest handed over what money he could scrape up. He got together all the clothes he could spare and, as usual, some that he couldn't. Having got a handout bigger than any he could have hoped for, Joe disappeared and was heard from no more.

Staff members were angered to hear of such occasions. They begged their Director, for his own and the boys' sake, not to be so easy a mark, and not to let unscrupulous individuals play his emotions like a sure-to-pay slot machine. Father Bob, however, never thought he had been taken advantage of. He did not demand repentance before offering forgiveness, and he did not question the thirst before proffering the cup. One cannot steal what is freely given. The youth who came for five dollars and left with everything the easy mark owned might have despised his benefactor for his weakness, but he also had to see something of the overflowing generosity of divine love.

Father Bob is sentimental, yet he has never been a sentimentalist. He is that most objective of individuals, a practicing Christian. He knew what he was doing and why. He would rather give a beggar a coin than withhold it lest the man be masquerading. Good seed may redeem bad soil: so, with his boys, he was aware of the risk and of the frequency with which he was "taken in." His secret was that it was he who took in the takers-in. The results of his long campaign to overcome evil with good are impressive. For every boy like Joe (and even the Joes are not beyond hope), there was a boy like Bill.

The priest hadn't heard from Bill for nearly a year, when late one night the telephone rang.

CHAPTER 19

"I WAS IN PRISON AND YE CAME UNTO ME." (Matt. 25:36)

"Will you accept a collect call from Bill Jenkins?" queried the operator.

"Of course. Put him on," Father Bob said. Over the wires came a young voice, distraught but tinged with relief.

"Padre, I'm in jail charged with robbery, but I didn't have a thing to do with it. I swear I didn't. Help me, please."

"I'll be there right away."

Bill had been graduated from St. Francis two years before, but he was still one of Father Bob's boys. Within minutes Father Bob was in his car, hurrying to the jail in another state, his mind full of memories of the fifteen-year-old boy he had first known.

Bill was the son of a widowed mother. He came to the Homes after a series of car thefts. The priest vividly recalled the ingratiating youngster with the wide blue eyes. The lad had done well at St. Francis his first year. He had won regional honors in oratory. The priest fondly thought of the bureau Bill had surprised him with, the product of many hours of painstaking labor after school.

"The most beautiful I ever saw," he remembered, and recalled again how the boy had reddened with pleasure when he had told him so.

Bill had returned to his mother the spring after she remarried and seemed to have established a real home. That summer she reported the boy's behavior so encouragingly that the whole St. Francis staff rejoiced. After school started, however, Bill began to spend his after-class hours roaming the streets, until once more he slipped behind the wheel of a stranger's car and was caught by the police. Released on bond, the contrite youngster had come to Father Bob to plead for readmission to the Homes. He recognized his need for someone to protect him from himself.

The court permitted Bill to return, but only under suspended sentence: if he failed to make good at St. Francis, he would serve his term in jail. He made good, however, and when he left the Home, he said tearfully, "Golly, I'll miss it here. Thanks for everything, Padre. I'll never let you or St. Francis down." The Director had believed him, and he reaffirmed his faith in the boy as he drove through the night.

Father Bob listened with interest and sympathy as the disconsolate youth poured out his story in the jail cell.

Bill for some months had held a job in a store in his home town. The shop had been robbed the evening before, and he was accused of the crime when a woman who knew of his former police record had told police that she had seen him run from the scene.

"It wasn't me, Father. Honest!" Then, in a burst of bitterness, "What's the use of trying to be decent, anyway? Jeannie and I were planning to be married next month, but if they send me up now . . ."

Father Bob thought Bill was telling the truth; the problem was to keep him out of jail. He was too old to be readmitted to St. Francis, which in any event was filled to capacity. When it appeared that the youth's innocence could not be clearly established, the priest with great difficulty persuaded the court to release him

217

into his personal custody. With Bill around the house for a while, time seemed to move backward to the days of Eddie, long before the Homes existed.

Soon a suitable job opened up in Salina and Bill applied for it. He came home that night and shouted triumphantly as he opened the front door, "I got it, Padre! I got it!" He did not know that the priest had interceded on his behalf, or that Father Bob had assumed full responsibility to the boy's employer for his integrity.

Bill did well again, as the priest had known he would. He and Jeannie were married, and Kansas now has a respected citizen who, but for a priest's faith, might have been another state's prison statistic.

Leaving St. Francis does not cut off a boy from its interest and help. The Homes help him to find a place in his community by arranging oversight and counseling for the youngster with a home-town social agency. His school, his employer, and his parish priest all are asked to help him over the humps. Although the Homes seek to minimize the risk when a boy leaves St. Francis, he usually returns to the location and memory of his earlier crimes. Thus, as Bill learned, his past is all too likely to rise up and hurt him. In addition, he faces the danger of being caught up in the same old crowd and having to face the same problems at home which had led to trouble in the first place.

A year after leaving St. Francis, Sam sensed that sort of thing happening and wrote the priest a disconsolate letter which ended, "No matter how hard I try, I can't seem to get away from the old gang. Maybe I'd better go away before anything happens." Father Bob understood the boy's discouragement and the battle he was fighting to be himself amid conflicting pressures from family and friends. Sam says Father Bob's answer to his letter set the course of his future.

"We are grateful," the priest wrote, "for all the splendid things you have done for both the Homes and the Church. Because of your years with us, the name of St. Francis ranks higher in the minds of the many who have known you. My advice is to look for work in another town, and I'll help you get a job wherever you say. We count on you to make good in a big way. Love and prayers."

Such genuinely earned praise, the trust expressed in his judgment, and bolstering of his waning self-confidence were precisely what Sam needed. He got a job far from his home town, and began a new life with a renewed sense of purpose. The initiative which led him to enroll in a college extension course five nights a week also enabled him to rise rapidly within his company, and he has become one of St. Francis' proudest success stories.

Some St. Francis oldsters have gone into law, some into the priesthood, some into psychology, and many into business. Several have made military service their career; one has gone to West Point. Not a few of the old boys trace their final rehabilitation to Father Bob's influence upon their lives long after they had left the Homes.

Father Bob often remarked, "It's a great puzzle to know where to concentrate my attention." Somewhere between directing the Homes and personally raising most of their operating funds, he managed to make time to found the National Association of Homes for Boys, to serve as an active member of the Western Conference of Superintendents of State Corrective Schools, and as a member of the National Conference of Superintendents of Training Schools and Reformatories. He attended every such conference held (as does the present Director), yet his first interest was always his own boys, with whom he never lost touch.

Though held aloof from the day-to-day affairs of the new St. Francis lads, the priest continued his therapy-in-Christ method with his old boys through a voluminous correspondence. On their departure from St. Francis, he urged the youngsters to write him frequently, and most did. In return they received a stream of warm, friendly letters from Father Bob, assuring them that they always had someone who loved them and never ceased to be interested in them and their affairs.

To a boy recently out of St. Francis, beginning a new job and scared to death, he wrote, "This note is just to say hello and best wishes for your new job. I'm awfully interested in it, and know you'll do fine. Don't ever hesitate to let me help you any way I can. . . . Lots of love."

To a boy who had distinguished himself in the service: "All of us here—especially me—are busting out at the seams with pride for you."

To a youngster homesick for St. Francis: "Thanks a lot for your letters. Enclosed is your Christmas gift ($1.00) and I only wish it could be more. I miss you a lot. Write soon and often. . . . Love."

To a boy on his twenty-first birthday: "I still think of my kids as in their teens, but you're all getting so all-fired old! I wish that I could express the love and interest my heart holds for all you former St. Francis boys by sending some kind of decent gift on such an important occasion as a twenty-first birthday, but I do want you to know, though, that you are in my heart and prayers."

He also offered good counsel to those he felt needed it, such as the boy who was in the Kansas State Penitentiary. "Your mother telephoned me," he wrote, "to say that you had asked her to get you a job. I feel that was a bad mistake on your part. I've discovered, Vic, that the best thing to do is to just hack away with work by the hour when you first come out of the pen. Then the most recent hour of good workmanship makes a good recommendaion for the next job. In that way, inching along bit by bit, you can build up a reputation anew, instead of looking for recommendations you honestly can't expect at this point."

The important system of follow-up correspondence begun by Father Bob is now in the hands of the deans, who carefully forward letters from the boys he knew to the Bishop of Damaraland. Father Craig is about to reinstitute another of the founder's policies.

Once a year Father Bob sent a questionnaire to the old boys so he could keep abreast of their doings. If any failed to answer he was concerned. Silence usually meant that something was wrong; Lou, for instance, had reason to keep quiet.

Lou had chalked up a poor record during his eighteen months at St. Francis. He had run away several times and was always as near insolence toward the staff as he thought safe, and he repeatedly attempted to make deals with them. He was equally antagonistic and contemptuous toward the other boys.

After he left the Home, Father Bob wrote the youngster a dozen times, to comment on some specific report he'd had from someone else who had run into Lou. There was no answer. The priest sent out two questionnaires: still no answer. Father Bob worried, but at last he had to assume that the lines of communication were closed.

Two years later, an attorney in California wrote that Lou was charged there with armed robbery of a bank. The boy had pleaded guilty on the advice of his attorney, who thought perhaps Father Bob could come to the culprit's aid. The priest, however, knew the boy too well; he is a realist as well as an idealist. "On the basis of Lou's record," he replied, "I could not in good conscience seek a parole for him in Kansas."

Whatever the youth's sins, Father Bob still loved him and again wrote frequently to him. The boy in return seemed anxious to respond; and the priest was happy to note in his letters evidence of a growing interest in religion. The priest was profoundly touched when at Christmastime the federal prisoner enclosed a five-dollar bill in his note: "I'm sorry, Father. You did all you could, but I just couldn't make it. Please take this money and use it for another boy who will not make you ashamed the way I have."

The priest was never ashamed of his boys, only grieved when they failed their attempts to live a responsible life. Somehow he always felt that it was he and not they who had failed.

Some of his most regular correspondents—perhaps because to them his letters meant the most—were his kids who had yet to make good. "I should know by now that neither you nor my

Church would ever forget me," wrote a former boy from a prison in another state after Father Bob had visited him and taken him the sacraments.

"The Church never gives up," Father Bob said again and again. "Secular authorities may call it quits, but the Church, never!" The priest's persistent efforts for Jack Johnson certainly illustrate the point. When the Social Welfare Department had depreciated Jack's chances to succeed at St. Francis, he had refused to give up on the youngster. Neither would Father Bob abandon the boy who called himself "Scarface Johnson," after he had left the Home to live on his own.

The lad had been a full-fledged delinquent at an age when most little boys still believe in Santa Claus, but had improved during his stay at St. Francis. Despite his passionate belief in miracles, no obvious one had taken place in his own life. No optimist would have thought his rehabilitation in any way complete when he left, and a pessimist who observed the boy's behavior over the next few years might have questioned that it had even begun.

When he had been discharged from the Home, Jack still was technically on parole from the State Industrial School; he never quite violated his parole, but he was continually in trouble. He probably would not have remained outside of jail but for the repeated intervention of Father Bob. The priest expressed his unfailing concern to the boy in frequent letters; and he communicated his faith that the boy could and would be reclaimed to everyone who had anything to do with the errant lad. Even though the priest held in mind and prayer the Jack-who-could-be, he never let his love for the Jack-who-was dim his vision. Love is often best shown through firmness—as it was in Father Bob's four-year battle with the boy over his insurance money.

Jack had been awarded seventeen hundred dollars compensation after the automobile accident which had left his face disfigured. As his legal guardian, Father Bob was to hold the money until Jack came of age. The four years after he had left St. Francis, the boy devoted most of his time and energy to trying to wrest his money from the priest: he even attempted to get a court order to obtain it. Father Bob was determined that the money should remain intact, in either his care or that of another state-appointed guardian, until Jack was twenty-one. He might not then be mature enough to spend it wisely, but it was certain that it would be gone in a week if the youngster got his hands on it before that time.

The boy pleaded, cajoled, and threatened. He wanted the money for a thousand reasons on a thousand occasions: to purchase a car, to keep him in cigarettes, to buy clothes. When he asked for it to pay his father's medical expenses, the priest was touched but not blinded, and the county subsequently paid the bill. When the youth said he wanted to give the money to his mother and small sister, the priest acknowledged the nobility of his desire, but discovered that the mother was eligible for state aid, and also he found her a job to supplement her income.

Jack, checked on every move, was bitterly resentful toward Father Bob, and besieged the priest with accusing and vitriolic letters. Still his guardian held firm. He met the threats with dry humor: "I was mighty glad to hear from you, although from the tone of your letter, I wonder if my life is safe. In case it isn't, I enclose a Christmas gift ($2.00) while I'm still here to do it! . . . Lovingly, and with my prayers . . ." Jack was slow to respond to the Gospel in action—hostility met with the other cheek of love— but respond he did, and so demonstrated anew how practical a weapon good is against evil.

On his twenty-first birthday, Jack received his money intact. Whether he or Father Bob was more happy and relieved, it would be difficult to say. A month later, the boy married the girl he had been courting for a year. She had been confirmed in the local parish, and Jack had a steady job as a linotype operator. The hostility, instability, and conflict which had marked his life to that time had become things of the past.

Never had Father Bob been more thankful to God for a reclaimed life than of the night he was able to write: "I can't help expressing my gratification, Jack, that you are now living a respectable and noble life in the eyes of God and man. There is no lad in whom I have had a longer and more sincere interest, even at the critical moments which you and I know better than anyone else! My love to Barbara, and of course to you . . . let me hear from you . . ."

He did. A few months later came a letter from Jack to say that Barbara had died in childbirth. Father Bob wept.

The boy who had seemed destined for tragedy since the age of eight then came home to St. Francis for a brief visit. He talked for long hours with the priest. When he left, he said, "I may not have turned out as good as some of the others in the old St. Francis gang, but a lot of things have come clear at last." He held out both hands to the priest and said, "You don't have to worry about me any more, Padre. I'm all right now for keeps."

Time and time again Father Bob stressed that "there is no permanent healing in therapy unless the boy is incorporated for this life and the life to come into the Mystical Body of Christ, the fellowship of all Christian believers." He was always encouraged, therefore, when a boy's family entered the Church; and many of them did when they began to see the nature of the Church in the changed natures of their sons.

The priest's conviction was that religion is not a department of life, but its focus, and that no program of child training, regardless of its clinical proficiency, can be lastingly effective unless it centers in God. No other part of the boys' development interested him more than their discoveries along the road of faith, which most were traveling for the first time.

Father Bob was delighted one day when fourteen-year-old Chan remarked to him while he was visiting the Ellsworth unit, "You know, Father, it's the funniest thing: a couple of months ago we didn't have chapel services for a few days. First thing we knew, everyone was quarreling and fighting. The very day we started regular services again, everything was O.K."

The same week, the priest told an assembly of boys about a gift presented to the Homes. "What can we ever do to thank our St. Francis friends properly for their generosity?" he asked, more as a rhetorical question than anything else. But a hand shot up and Father Bob, a trifle surprised, nodded to the boy to answer. "We can pray for 'em every day in chapel," said the fifteen-year-old ex-arsonist.

Intercessory prayer is a vital part of the life of every St. Francis boy. They learn its meaning readily because they experience it constantly in action. Hardly a morning arrives that a slip of paper is not found on the altar, deposited there by one of the boys, requesting prayers at the Eucharist or one of the Daily Offices. It may read, "Please pray for my mother—today's her birthday," or "Please pray for my father who drinks too much." Each day intercessions are made for the many needs and petitions which come to the Homes' attention, and the personal prayer requests of many of the donors to St. Francis are offered by the boys and their priests. After a boy leaves the Home, what he has learned of the Faith and of the power of prayer enables him to meet and master the crises of his life with courage, rather than by returning to crime as an easy way out.

Max was a St. Francis graduate who worked his way through college despite discouraging delays caused by the unexpected necessity of having to care for his younger brother. When finally he had earned the master's degree in psychology which would permit him to teach the subject in college, he was a thousand dollars in debt. To save all possible expenses, he built a cottage for his young wife and baby with his own hands. The day before they were to move in, it burned to the ground, uninsured. None of those things daunted him. He had learned at St. Francis to give his problems to God.

Autumn was in the air one September night as Father Bob walked briskly into the Ellsworth Home to attend a meeting called by the most important persons connected with St. Francis. He had been invited by nine boys, all of whom had achieved membership, to "please come over and answer some questions." Wild horses or other engagements could not have kept him from accepting. Still, he entered the meeting room with some trepidation: his services of late had been requested mostly when serious trouble was brewing. He was indeed in for a shock, but not the sort he had anticipated.

Ralph, the president of the group, opened the session with a prayer, and then the questions began. They concerned boys who had boasted of rule-breaking. The nine members present were worried because some of Ellsworth's younger and still supervised boys seemed to have been fascinated and dangerously impressed by the older boys' tales.

"The shock," Father Bob remembers, "was a pleasant one—I had not realized what a high standard of life had been attained by those kids."

Larry (at the Homes because of armed robbery) and Sandy (assault and battery) felt that the boasters were hurting St. Francis and lowering morale among the boys, even though their memberships had been suspended. Larry pointed out that membership was a high honor, hard to attain. "Losing membership here should not be a trivial thing," he said earnestly. "Membership here is *important.*"

When Sandy mentioned that in the last year, one-third of the Ellsworth boys had not received a single demerit, Father Bob's eyes opened wide. "I could hardly believe my ears," he says. "Only the year before, several of the boys with currently spotless records had been on the ropes, almost out for the count."

Fourteen-year-old Ernie commented that people everywhere were so friendly to him that during his last Christmas vacation at La Junta, Colorado, he had asked why. The family he was staying with had replied, "Because you're a St. Francis boy."

"That's the way we want to keep it," he said seriously. "We've got to see that St. Francis keeps its good reputation so people will like us."

An honor member brought the meeting to a close with the cryptic words, "One thing more, guys. *We've* been rough in some ways ourselves—you know what—so let's cut it out."

Father Bob left the meeting still wondering "what," but he didn't really care. As he drove back to Salina he was not content to hum his *Te Deum;* he sang it in full voice!

All the way home he rejoiced, full of new confidence for the future of his boys and that of the Homes. At the curb before his front door, he got out of the car more slowly than usual. He was pondering a sudden idea.

Some months before in Florida, the Archbishop of Cape Town, the Most Rev. Joost de Blank, Primate of the Church in South Africa, had cordially invited him to visit for a few weeks. The idea had seemed impossible at the time, but why couldn't he go now? As the Homes approached their fifteenth anniversary, everything seemed to be in good shape. Father Craig could handle very well anything that might come up. Father Bob hadn't had a vacation in ten years. Wouldn't it be the perfect time to take one?

He thought about it more that night, and became more enthusiastic about the idea. He got out his atlas and studied the maps. His old love of adventure flared into new life. By midnight his mind was made up.

The next morning he stunned the staff in the administrative offices when he strode in, eyes sparkling, and announced his plan. Within two weeks he was off to South Africa, carrying only one smallish suitcase. His little holiday was underway, but not even he knew how far it was to take him.

CHAPTER 20

JUVENILE DELINQUENTS AND CHRIST-CENTERED PSYCHOTHERAPY

"Father Bob certainly must be having a good time," remarked a member of the St. Francis staff as he flipped his desk calendar open to Monday, April 11, 1960. The Director's "few weeks away" had lengthened to nearly six months.

The Homes had run fairly smoothly during his absence, but the entire staff missed him and eagerly anticipated his return to help with plans for the celebration of an important anniversary: St. Francis' doors would have been open on September third exactly fifteen years.

A lot had happened since the desolate poorhouse had been transformed into a refuge for the unforgotten young. Martin was to arrive almost fifteen years to the hour after the first Johnny had trudged up the driveway, but he came to a Home greatly changed from the one Johnny had seen.

The small coupe brought its two passengers into the parking lot of the Ellsworth unit on a warm spring morning. The door opened first on the driver's side, and a county social worker jumped out. Then, very slowly, the door on the other side of the car opened, and hesitatingly Marty stepped out into the bright Kansas sunshine. His gaze took in the staff building, the main house, gracious in design with encircling porches, and the obviously new structure on its right, O'Donnell Hall, the activities building.

His eyes then wandered over the broad campus and beyond. He had not expected to see such green grass, or the cool trees and the rolling hills in the distance. He had come from another state, and had imagined all of Kansas to be flat and barren. At the sight of the nearby baseball field his face brightened for a moment, but then a black cocker spaniel and a coon hound rushed up, leaping and wagging their tails as they barked a noisy welcome. In spite of himself, a half-smile broke across Marty's face as he stooped to pat them, and before he could straighten up he heard someone shout, "Hi!" A boy about his own age was running toward him. "I saw you drive up," he said with a friendly grin. "Welcome to St. Francis!" Just then the commotion brought Father Pete out the door of the staff building. Extending his hand in warm greeting, the big priest proceeded to help the new arrival with his luggage, and led the way to the house. Confused and uncertain, Martin followed. He wished he were a million miles away.

Marty had not deliberately sought the trouble which had landed him at St. Francis. Few of the three per cent of American children who get in trouble with the law do so willfully, at first. Marty's parents had married at eighteen. After Marty was born, his father decided the marriage had been a mistake and deserted his young family. When Marty was fourteen, his mother married a widower with four children. She had failed to discuss her remarriage with her son, and Marty felt left out and abused. He resented his stepfather and his new brothers and sisters, and took refuge from his family in a shell of sullen hostility. He soon became intensely lonely. He wanted to be liked and to belong to someone or something. Like many youngsters in his situation, he found acceptance in a gang. There quickly followed a wild party, a joy ride in a "borrowed" car, a fast police pursuit, a crash, and jail. His priest told the judge about St. Francis, and here he was.

He didn't know all the ins and outs of his admittance, only that he had taken a lot of tests (which included projective tests of personality to determine how deep-seated was his deviation in behavior). There also had been gathered for him a transcript of his three last years at school as well as reports from the court and his parish church. It had all taken several weeks because the evaluation committee, which was headed by the social worker and included the psychologist and Dean of Boys at the unit where Marty would live if accepted, had to receive and study all the material, including a full case history prepared by a professional social worker in the boy's home town. Pending St. Francis' answer, the judge had granted a postponement of trial. Marty didn't care about such details. He had been torn away from the only friends he thought he had and he was bitterly resentful. He would rather have been in jail with the rest of his gang.

The youngster remained impassive when Father Pete took him into the office to tell him what he should know about living at the Home. He didn't trust the priest or like his friendly efforts to make him feel at ease. He had no intention of revealing his feelings by discussing them. He was relieved, however, when Father Pete remarked that only he knew Marty's record, so the youngster could make a completely fresh start at St. Francis.

As soon as the boy unpacked, the priest took him on a tour. He went through the big house where he would live with all the other boys. The eight bedrooms upstairs (two more were in the process of being added on) were nice enough, and the comfortable lounge and TV room were all right, but Marty's eyes widened with pleasure at the sight of the snack bar. Candy bars, Cokes, gum—it was a real store right inside the house. There was a good reason for its being there: psychologists had learned that snacking between meals fulfills a deep emotional need in the troubled adolescent.

When they came to the activities building, Marty forgot to conceal his enthusiasm. It contained a huge and fully equipped gym and a darkroom to develop pictures; there were two craft shops, one for big work (he could hardly wait to get some of the power tools in his hands) and the other for small (a boy was there working on a ship model as they passed by). There was the big recreation hall with a hi-fi, and a small kitchen, Father Pete explained, for the boys and their girl friends to use when they had parties.

At the end of the tour, Marty enjoyed his dinner (except for the turnips, but he learned that every boy had to eat some of everything; when he said he didn't like them, he was given only a tiny portion). He was beginning to think St. Francis might not be so bad as he had anticipated. He was further encouraged to find that St. Francis was no longer a farm, as he had been told.

Most St. Francis boys are, like Martin, from cities, and so the farm emphasis at the Homes gradually had been dropped. The staff came to believe that the therapeutic value of farmwork had been greatly overvalued. Rightly or wrongly, the average city boy looks down on farmwork, and to force him to do "hick" work adds more resentment to a youngster already laden with it.

During his first few weeks, Marty was full of defensive arrogance. His family fostered much of his initial attitude, which had made him unpopular with the boys and rebellious toward the staff. William King, St. Francis' psychologist, explains, "Excessive generosity can be as much of a problem as rejection." His mother and stepfather felt that the boy had got into trouble through their fault, and, perhaps to assuage their guilt, they deluged him with presents and money. The staff frowns on such a practice because it causes the boy to throw his weight around. Each boy at the Homes receives a set allowance which he may supplement only by taking a part-time job when he has earned that privilege. Any extra that he receives from his family may be used to buy necessary clothes, but otherwise must be deposited to his account at St. Francis. Marty's problem thus was doubled: he was resentful because he could not use his parents' gifts, and was increasingly insolent because he knew the money was there.

Money increased the difficulties of Marty's first months in another way. Parents pay what they are able toward their son's maintenance at St. Francis. The sum may range from nothing to, occasionally, several hundred dollars a month. Marty's family paid a hundred and fifty dollars, fifty dollars more than the average.

The staff requests that a family not reveal to the boy what it pays on his behalf, so that each boy may be on an equal footing with the others and expect no special favors. Marty's mother, however, probably to convince her son of the generosity of his stepfather, had disregarded the staff's injunction. As a result, the first time the youngster was disciplined by Father Pete, he stood before the priest, his hands jammed in his pockets in surly defiance, and snarled, "You don't dare do this to me! My family's paying a hundred and fifty bucks a month for me, and I'll do what I please!" Father Pete was some time in convincing him otherwise.

Marty remained at the Home for eighteen months, which under the present clinical setup has proved a satisfactory stay for the average boy. St. Francis boys do not put their gratitude into words any more easily than do other youngsters. The staff is happy if the youngsters go ahead to do well, without looking back with effusive thanks. Director Craig observes, "No one should go into this work thinking he'll be surrounded by grateful kids. He won't. It's not in the nature of children, any of them, to be grateful." Nevertheless, many of the Homes' old boys do think to express their appreciation later, and those reflective letters never fail to warm the hearts of the staff.

"Things have gone well for me since I came home," Marty wrote. "My stepfather and I have developed a good understanding of each other and now I honestly like the guy! Thanks for all your help and patience at St. Francis. The time I spent there sure changed my whole view of life. My main job is pulling up my grades so I can go to college when I graduate."

Although by 1960 the annual cost of caring for forty-six boys had soared to $160,000, the financial supporters of St. Francis were (and still are) much the same as in its early days: private individuals, organizations, and Church groups still contributed approximately eighty per cent, and the remaining twenty per cent came from courts, social agencies, and parents, according to their ability to pay.

The news sheet "Hi-Lites," published twice a year, continues to bring the story of St. Francis' activities and continuing needs before its friends; and at Christmastime a number of American bishops allow the Homes to send an appeal to each address on their diocesan mailing list. Through the prayers and warm interest of people throughout the fifty states, the Homes' requirements somehow manage to be met each year. Recently there has been one slightly helpful change in the financial picture: St. Francis takes an occasional boy from a Federal penal institution (to cross a state line in a stolen car is a Federal offense) and in such a case the Department of Justice pays the full cost. Still and essentially, St. Francis is kept going by the same faith, hope and charity which Father Bob depended upon. However the physical appearance of the Homes may have altered with the passage of time, and the clinical setup, the spirit which pervades them remains unchanged.

Time and again, Father Bob declared to his boys, "The test of a man's character and strength does not lie in what he has done but in what he has overcome." A dedicated staff continues to help its charges "overcome," by a potent combination of psychological therapy and therapy-in-Christ. Each staff member has discovered for himself how valid was Father Bob's conviction that until a boy recognized his complete dependence upon God, his spirit could not be wholly restored.

The Founder at last won his point that a cooperative program of religion, psychology, and social work is necessary for permanent rehabilitation. Over the years, St. Francis' staff has been convinced that a religious Home is much more successful in dealing with juvenile delinquents than a purely secular institution. The rehabilitation rate among St. Francis' boys is better than ninety per cent; in state institutions the average is only twenty to forty per cent.

The present Director of St. Francis is quick to suggest the primary causes of juvenile delinquency among boys: "Lack of adequately expressed love coupled with the lack of an adequate father figure in his home life. That is why it is as beneficial to the boy psychologically as it is formally correct to call the priest who is Dean of his unit 'Father.' That is also why each unit must be kept sufficiently small, so that the boys will feel they have a real home, headed by a father—not by a jailer or even a headmaster."

Father Craig goes on to explain that boys who come to St. Francis seem to have two related things common to their home backgrounds. First, they lack structure in their lives. They are accustomed to drift from one vague activity to another according to the impulse of the moment. At St. Francis, however, they must go to meals (whether or not they do more than taste their food is their business—thus the food itself does not become a symbol of rebellion), and they must go to chapel twice a day (whether or not they participate). Second, they lack a strong and well-integrated family life. It is interesting to note that there is little juvenile delinquency among the Jews and Chinese, whose lives are centered in the family. Poverty of itself plays a minor role in sending children astray; it does so only as it contributes to poor family relationships. There are as many households in which the father is absent, weak, disinterested, or unreasonably harsh among the rich as among the poor.

On the surface, the home environment of Ted Greer, for example, appeared ideal. He was one of three children, all of whom had exceptionally high IQ's. His father was successful in his profession and a prominent layman in his parish church. His mother was a highly intelligent college graduate. They lived in a beautiful home in a fashionable suburb; it did not seem to be an obvious setting for trouble, yet Ted had repeated tangles with the law as he grew older. His problem was not poverty of material things but poverty of affection—and there are many boys like him.

Ted got along well with his mother, but he had a burning dislike for his father. The older man was warm and outgoing with his friends as he went about his many outside activities, but he had little time to give his son. The time he spent with Ted was devoted

234

to berating the boy. Ted was quiet and retiring by nature; his father aggressive and domineering. The man acted as though only one self-evident course were open to him: to force his son to follow in his footsteps and to make the youngster into a carbon copy of himself. The boy's prep school and college were to be the same ones his father had attended, and the child was driven without mercy to excel in the same sports and studies in which his parent had excelled. Ted's interests and abilities lay in different fields, but his father could neither countenance nor understand that fact. He ignored it. He was not harsh physically in disciplining his son, but he did something far worse. He beat the youth psychologically without letup.

The boy's spirit retaliated in the most effective way it knew; it led him to commit a series of delinquent acts. He ran away, he stole a car, he committed a sex offense. He even struck back at his father's religious protestations by robbing the church plates while he served as an acolyte in the same parish where his father was a vestryman.

Upon the recommendation of his priest, Ted was sent to St. Francis and he remained there for almost two years. During that time he was set straight and, more importantly for his future well-being, so was his father. The older man had many conferences with the Homes' psychologist before the boy was returned to him. Ted subsequently went on to a school of his own choice with the full approval of his father, and graduated with top honors. He wrote later to some of his buddies at the Home, "When you look back and think honestly about it, you just want to fall down on your knees and thank the Almighty for the wonderful chance you were given in going to St. Francis in the first place."

All the members of the St. Francis staff are people whose minds and actions are formed on the pattern of their Christian Faith. The business manager is Alfred B. White, who has been with the Homes since 1952 and has done a remarkable job in stabilizing their financial structure. His quiet Christianity in the business office is considered to be as necessary to the work of the Homes as is the more public witness of priest-Director William E. Craig. All the St. Francis staff believe that their religion must be expressed in all their work, and not only in the chapel or in their direct relations with the boys. They recognize the sacraments as their source of grace and see in the Faith the supreme source of moral instruction and spiritual upbuilding.

Psychologist King admits that today's popular ideal of a psychotherapist is one who is accepting and nonjudging; one whose task is only to help the patient uncover the unconscious causes of his behavior, and who assumes that such insight will provide liberation and the ability to alter his behavior. Mr. King, however, disagrees. He states, "That sort of psychotherapy has not been too effective in dealing with undeveloped people with distorted value systems. Delinquent boys need some consistent image of what they should become. They need people who *will* moralize, who *will* pass judgment. In short, they need a moral education at the hands of compassionate people."

The psychologist believes that the dimension added by religion to therapy is to hold lofty goals before the youngsters and to help them avoid the error of regarding all evil merely as illness. Spiritual goals and conviction of personal responsibility are the things which help the boys at St. Francis to change; and, in essence, those are the very things which comprise the Christian precept taught by Father Bob: "See the boy as he is meant to be, not as he is. Let him catch the vision of what he can become through Christ."

Mr. King is acutely aware of the transforming power of love and of the integral part it plays in successful therapy. He observes, "Father Bob always loved *first*, when the boy was most unlovable. That, in my opinion, was the secret of his extraordinary effectiveness in handling juvenile delinquents. When the youngsters realized his love, they became receptive to religion and to other intimate relationships formerly blocked by their suspicious defenses. Their ability to respond to psychotherapy is developed in much the same way."

Jack Horner, the social worker at St. Francis since 1957, adds,

"Much of the therapy-in-Christ method is simply thinking of people as people. It's old-fashioned now to hold parents responsible for all their children's deficiencies. The young offender must accept responsibility for his own behavior as an individual. To live in an environment where he is treated as such a creative person helps him to do so." Father Bob, who had no psychological training and no knowledge of modern clinical techniques, years before had set up just such a basic structure, founded entirely on Christ's teaching.

The staff affirms that the strong St. Francis emphasis on loving one's neighbor and loving God is one of the chief forces in the boys' rehabilitation. "Those who soak up love the most deeply," Mr. Horner observes, "are the most successfully restored."

That Mr. King and Mr. Horner are respectively a Christ-oriented psychologist and a social worker may seem unusual, considering their professions' humanistic reputations, but a great many psychiatrists in Kansas are reputed to be practicing Christians. Mr. Horner says with a smile, "Any psychiatrist who doesn't believe in God should see his analyst!"

Nevertheless, Mr. Horner points out that despite the strong religious convictions of the staff at St. Francis, the religious aspect is the point of lowest pressure of the Homes' entire program. "A boy gets demerits for not keeping his room clean," he comments dryly, "but not for neglecting to worship God. Sure, he gets demerits for not going to chapel, but whether the youngster worships in his heart, none of us can know."

Experience, however, has proved that most of the boys gradually develop the love of God and neighbor, after the stresses and strains of adjusting to their new environment have been worked out. It takes longer for some than others, and some respond more fully than others, but few are the youngsters who pass through St. Francis without responding at all.

Each May, all friends of St. Francis are invited to an open house, held in alternate years at the Bavaria and Ellsworth units. To prepare for the events, the boys scrub and polish the Homes until they gleam, and even the most confirmed city lovers get busy with lawn mower and garden trowel to order the grounds, which are at their loveliest in the spring. The townspeople contribute the results of a mammoth baking spree; and on the big day, picnic tables are set up out of doors to be laden with cakes and cookies and pies which represent the finest achievements of the housewives of western Kansas.

The spring 1960 party, the year of St. Francis' fifteenth birthday, was to be a particularly gala affair: a forerunner, as it were, of the festivities planned for the official anniversary in September. Father Bob was expected home from his African sojourn in plenty of time —he was, in fact, due to return momentarily—and hopes were that Bishop Nichols, then retired, would return to Kansas for the May event as well as for the autumn one. His successor, Bishop Lewis, of course planned to attend. On the last day of April, the Bishop received a bolt out of the blue: an airmail letter bearing a colorful South African stamp.

Bishop Lewis ripped it open and read the single paragraph. He reread it slowly. Then, reaching for the telephone, he called an emergency meeting of the St. Francis Board of Directors.

CHAPTER **21**

THE VISION GOES ON

So URGENT WAS THE SUMMONS that the St. Francis Directors were quickly assembled. Bishop Lewis read them the letter in which Father Bob announced his resignation as Director of the Homes. He offered no explanation. The news was received in stunned silence. There had been no warning of such a move: indeed, the priest's letters had been filled with plans he wanted to put into effect when he returned "in time for the Open House."

For fully five minutes no one said a word. "He must have lost his mind," someone at the far end of the room said at last.

"He can't mean it," said another.

"We all know how impulsive he is. He probably already regrets having mailed the letter."

"I can't believe he really has any intention of resigning."

The members of the board talked on, but the general feelings of all had been expressed in the first reactions. Father Bob had often acted impulsively in the past and then changed his mind. They could not imagine that the letter before them was final. For that reason they decided not to seek a new Director from the outside. One commented, "It would be pretty embarrassing to bring in a new Director and have Father Bob show up the next week."

Still, there was the resignation before them, and something had to be done. After much discussion, the board moved to accept it, effective January 1, 1961, with "deep regret," and appointed a committee to confer privately with Father Craig. He was as shocked as they had been, and as unable to picture St. Francis without its founder. Hoping that Father Bob would reconsider, he agreed to assume what he expected to be a very short-lived directorship.

Not until three months later was the mystery of Father Bob's sudden resignation resolved. The Homes received a telegram which announced that he had been chosen Bishop of Damaraland, in South-West Africa. He had known that he was to be elected when he submitted his resignation, but could not reveal the news until the Archbishop of Cape Town, the Most Reverend Joost de Blank, had made the official announcement.

Father Bob had kept the secret well. Not even his sister had known, although she had been warned that something was about to happen by a note from Africa which asked her to plan to be in Cape Town on November twenty-eighth.

"I knew something pretty important was in the wind," she said, "or Bob would never have asked me to spend my money on that long trip."

The thought had flashed across her mind that perhaps he had been tapped for the episcopate, but she did not seriously consider the possibility. Less than a handful of American priests has been chosen to be bishops in other provinces of the worldwide Anglican Communion. She did not know what it was all about until the day a wire came to her house addressed to Father Bob. She opened it, saw it was from her daughter in Boston, and read the message: "Congratulations, Uncle Bob, on your election to be Bishop of Damaraland." Marge was still baffled; she didn't even know where Damaraland was. She immediately telephoned her daughter, who had read the announcement in *The New York Times*. Marge then cabled her brother in Africa, and learned that with his usual absentmindedness, he had just forgotten to let his family know. His reply contained the welcome news that he would be on his way home within two weeks, and would be at St. Francis for its fifteenth anniversary as he had promised. He would then return to Africa to be consecrated on November twenty-eighth. Thus, in the sixteenth year of St. Francis' existence, the founder would enter the third stage of his ministry—once again in response to a plea for help.

The decision had not been easy for Father Bob to make. For years the Homes had been his life; the boys, his family; their welfare, his ministry. Yet gradually and gently he had been disengaged from their affairs until he was only the head fund raiser and administrator of the Homes. No longer was he "Father Bob" to the lost and lonely. His only family relationship recently had been with his staff. Most importantly, he no longer felt that he was doing the work of a priest.

"I have never lost my hunger to guide souls," he said during his visit home. "As a swivel-chair official, I was deprived of the pastoral relationship I wanted and had been accustomed to in my earlier ministry.

"The truth is," he said after a moment's thought, "I was never able to adjust myself, as the director of a growing institution should, to the clinical program. It seemed that it continually threatened to take the therapy of the Homes out of the Church. The ever-increasing budget was another matter. I frankly was tired of the never-ending ecclesiastical begging."

Father Bob did not mention the most obvious reason to let St. Francis go: the challenge had been met and conquered, and he thrived on attempting the impossible. The Homes were well established and functioning evenly under a competent and devoted staff led by Father Craig. God's will in their particular area seemed to have been fulfilled.

Father Bob longed for new fields, new souls to win for Christ, to build something again from nothing. In one of the last uncivilized areas in Africa, he saw a new opportunity to advance the Kingdom.

Today his life has come full circle, for his ministry as a bishop of the Church is very similar to the poverty and sacrifice of his early days as the only priest in one corner of Kansas. He is today a Father-in-God indeed, bringing the Church to spiritually thirsty parishioners in a wide and impoverished land. Eighty per cent of his people live in Ovamboland on the northern border of South-West Africa. Distances, finances, and problems are impossible; Father Bob is happy.

The founder has no qualms about his Homes; he is confident that they are in good hands. He knows Father Craig will see that the therapy-in-Christ program is carried on without compromise. The present director is no less aware than was his great predecessor that a clinical program, however excellent, cannot adequately answer the needs of young people whose chief problem is ignorance of both human and divine love. Unfortunately, there seems to be no certain way to ensure that the religious emphasis at St. Francis will continue unbroken. The Articles of Incorporation state that the Bishop of Western Kansas shall be ex-officio a member and Chairman of the Board of Directors and President of the Corporation, but Faith is held by individuals, and it cannot be written into the bylaws.

Father Craig hopes to insure the continuity of St. Francis' program by selecting an assistant director who, when the time comes, will step into his shoes and maintain the Homes' traditions. He believes that such personal selection of successors is the only way that the present program of the Homes may be strengthened and protected. Even a legal requirement that all directors be priests of the Church does not provide an ironclad guarantee of continued Christian emphasis. Father Craig remembers too well the deacon and his wife who instituted a program which was almost entirely clinical and the devastating result. More reversions occurred than ever before in the history of St. Francis, and that under the leadership of an apparently well-qualified man in Holy Orders. At the time, only Father Bob's stubborn determination and Bishop Nichols' active support brought the situation back to the original vision. The Homes' most reliable safeguards would seem to be continuity of persons, a sort of Franciscan Succession, rather than unenforceable regulations.

William Ellwood Craig, Ph.D., came to the Homes in 1956 to be assistant director in charge of promotion, after fifteen years' varied experience as a parish priest and diocesan officer. He says with a laugh, "I'm certainly glad I didn't read that survey report first, or I'd never have come! I still remember the day—I'd been at St. Francis about a week—that Father Bob handed me the report to read. He spoke of its contents in horror!"

Father Craig is a decisive and energetic man who has much of the founder's enthusiasm. He is an able executive as well as dedicated priest; he knows how to delegate responsibility, and to his staff he is more a colleague than a "director."

"After all," he comments, "the staff members are all professionals. They know their jobs and don't need to be 'directed.' Emergencies frequently arise that I must call them about; and that, in my opinion, keeps us sufficiently in touch." To help his staff members stay abreast of thinking in their fields, Father Craig makes certain that each one attends a professional conference every year; he himself takes in three.

Father Craig and the St. Francis board push ahead the development of the Homes as rapidly as finances will permit. On May 6, 1962, the Bavaria unit's new activities building was dedicated by Bishop Lewis. It is named Mize Hall after Father Bob and is located at the end of the campus, where its sturdy red brick walls, punctuated by vertical bands of glass and Madonna-blue enameled panels, finally close in the quadrangle as if to announce that one St. Francis Boys' Home, at least, is complete.

A number of small additions are being planned, but the major project currently underway is the building of the new St. Nicholas Chapel at Ellsworth. Soon the Bishop of Western Kansas will be able to pronounce the stirring words, "Now set your heart and your soul to seek the Lord your God; arise therefore and build ye the Sanctuary of the Lord God . . ." as the chapel site is blessed and ground broken.

A third Home is being planned and the search is now in progress for a site suitable both in location and price. Even a third unit, however urgently required, will not meet the demand, for St. Francis can now accept only one boy from every ten who apply for admission. To ease the situation a little, St. Francis has begun to place some of its boys in carefully selected foster homes. "In that way," Father Craig explains, "we can get boys out of St. Francis more quickly and make room for boys whose need is present and serious. Some of our boys are ready to leave, but cannot be released because they have no place to go. Their own homes are broken, overcrowded, or otherwise undesirable. A good foster home to see them through high school seems to us a happy solution."

St. Francis has obtained its license from the state to place in private homes those youngsters who no longer need institutional care. The sort of private homes to which the boys are sent is very different from the typical state-licensed foster home.

Before licensing such a home, the state does all it can to investigate so that the children placed there may be protected, but such investigation necessarily is rather superficial. The true flavor of the family's home life and the real motivation (often purely financial) of husband and wife for taking in children can be and frequently is concealed. St. Francis, however, is in a favorable position to seek out well-adjusted, loving families through local parish priests.

Neither is the pairing of youngster and family made on a haphazard basis as often it must be when only the state is involved. The St. Francis social worker visits the home recommended by the local priest, explains the needs of one particular boy, and so tries to tailor the boy to the family. Money cannot be a consideration; it is never mentioned until the family has expressed its willingness and demonstrated its ability to care for the boy offered them. The Homes pay no less than $100 a month for the support of a youngster, however, and are prepared to pay more if necessary.

(The State of Kansas pays $90 and most others from which boys come pay less.)

The boy who goes to a foster home is carefully chosen by the staff. He must be out of the habit of lying and stealing, and must be a good and regular scholar; St. Francis cannot cope from a distance with school problems. So far, only three such foster homes have been developed. They are widely separated, but all are in Kansas. They are continuously supervised by the social workers who knew the boys at the mother Homes. Foster home placement promises to be an excellent solution for the introverted boy who is willing to extend his personality, and who needs the ego-support of a normal family environment.

Recently St. Francis has moved to improve its help and expression of concern to the boy who has left the Homes to go on to a technical training school or college. Such youngsters now remain under the supervision of the Homes, and psychologist King visits them at regular intervals for as long as seems necessary. The arrangement has worked well, for as Mr. King comments, "It obviates the risk of a boy's being thrown completely on his own immediately after finishing high school."

The present Director is no more content than was Father Bob to let St. Francis rest on its laurels. "Save a boy and make a man" is the Homes' motto, but the staff has a private objective: to serve more boys better.

The influence of the founding priest is not confined to continuance of his objectives for St. Francis. His teaching and example have touched the inner lives of the staff as unmistakably as they have his boys'. "His is the sort of goodness," remarks Chief Social Work Director Jack Horner, "which rubs off on everyone. The lives Father Bob has been a part of can never be quite the same again."

As one speaks with one after another of the staff members about Father Bob, one may be perplexed by the paradox of each opening statement.

"He's a saint," was the unanimous opinion which always was

245

followed by the equally unanimous conclusion, "but he certainly was hard to work for!" It is not difficult to understand what they meant.

Father Bob was never a contented administrator—he was visionary and a true Franciscan. Because he enjoyed a Spartan existence and took no pleasure in physical comforts, he neither recognized nor comprehended the wider needs of his employees. He required little sleep, had no family responsibilities and no regular habits; and he expected his co-workers to put in the same exertion and endless hours of work he exacted of himself. His demands on his extraordinarily dedicated group of men and his inability to delegate authority to people who were, after all, experts in their own field were difficult for them to accept with good grace. So far he fell below true sainthood, which is, in the words of the Prayer Book, "always mindful of the needs of others." Yet they all stayed on. Why?

"Over and above his often unreasonable requirements," says Mr. Horner, "there was the irresistible appeal of his personality: his warmth, his shining love of people, and the realization that everything he did and said was for only one reason: to help boys in need."

Father Bob, then, was so intent on serving his children that he considered his co-workers mostly as extensions of himself and thus was indisputably a hard taskmaster. Nevertheless, as Christians, his staff saw in him the power of God working through man. They remembered the words of Christ ". . . if therefore thine eye be single, thy whole body shall be full of light." However little Father Bob took thought for his or their health and private life, they recognized in him a man with a single eye, fulfilling the function God had intended for him. In his drive to do one thing perfectly, to love his boys and make them whole, they saw the fire and inspiration of the Holy Spirit.

William King tells how Father Bob influenced his life; the psychologist is himself a Roman Catholic but has brought up his four children in the Episcopal Church. "The first time they went to the Episcopal church school," he recalls, "Father Bob stopped by the house early and took them himself so that my daughters would feel at home."

Mr. King once was cynical about the Church's over-regard for respectability and disillusioned by the worldly clergymen he had known, but he found in Father Bob a man who actually lived by the precepts of Jesus Christ and who was ready to give up his life for his convictions. The priest, to be sure, was a mixed package, like all humans: thoughtless but sensitive, hard-driving but sympathetic, autocratic but humble. Above all else, however, he was truly a priest, with Christ standing in the center of his life. Faith was the central fact of his existence.

"The love of Christ seems to radiate from him," says Mr. King, "and I doubt that anyone who comes within his orbit can fail to be touched by it."

The Homes' psychologist and their social worker often speak of the hours in which they and Father Bob discussed together how the different viewpoints of psychology and religion might be reconciled. "It was in these talks," they say, "that we learned through a man of dazzling vision what therapy-in-Christ means, how it works, and what is its inestimable value in the treatment of delinquency."

All of his colleagues agree that Father Bob frequently saved the day with a flash of humor when he was dealing with an overtired and often overwrought staff, even though his quick temper as often threatened to lose it.

One says, "No matter what the occasion of his outburst, none of us really held it against him. He always apologized immediately, and we knew how hard he had to struggle against his own impatience." The speaker also muses, "Sometimes we almost wished to be one of the boys—he almost never lost his temper with them. His patience there was absolutely remarkable."

The staff further appreciated his loyalty. He was quick to praise their work; and if he was as quick to criticize, he felt that to be his own prerogative and would permit it to be usurped by no one else.

When someone outside the Homes once had disparaged a staff action, Father Bob indignantly retorted, "All those men are consecrated persons, and I don't mean consecrated boobs, as I've been called. They're all brilliant men and know their jobs."

Another member of the staff adds, "Perhaps none of us have caught in its entirety the vision Father Bob had, but we do our best." They do indeed carry on the Christianity-in-action which Father Bob taught and which is the foundation of the Homes. They express the love of God through men, and the boys respond to them as other boys did to the founder.

CHAPTER 22

THE LOST SHALL BE FOUND

LONG BEFORE DAYLIGHT on a cold winter morning, the eighteen notes of the Angelus shiver on the frosty air, and lights appear one by one in the windows of St. Francis. Boys dart like shadows from their rooms and scurry to the chapel to offer worship to God.

The priest who is the Home's Dean of Boys enters the sanctuary to celebrate the Eucharist. As he places the chalice on the altar, he notes a slip of paper lying on the holy table. He reads, "Please pray for Mom this morning," and places it with the other intercessions for the day.

He steps back to the foot of the altar to prepare himself for the Holy Sacrifice, and is conscious of the sound of scuffling. The corners of his lips turn up—Jimmy's cocker spaniel has followed him into chapel again and is being evicted! Soon the only sounds are breathing and restless knees: the day is about to begin as does every day at St. Francis, at the altar of God.

The boys in the chapel entered the Homes typed by society and themselves as hostile, resentful, destructive young hoodlums. Nearly all will leave with a new picture of themselves as well-integrated young citizens and members of a Christian family in which they enjoy a new and intimate relationship with Christ.

The practicality of men of great vision is seldom visible to the eyes of the world. Bishop Nichols has remarked, "Had Bob been 'practical,' there never would have been a St. Francis."

If Father Bob did not conform to the earthly ideal of a good businessman, he was very close to the heavenly idea of one. As our Lord told St. Paul, "My grace is sufficient for thee: for my strength is made perfect in weakness." The founder of St. Francis was considered by everyone, including himself, to be a poor administrator, but at last he assembled the thoroughly competent staff which carries on the Homes today in his absence. Someone said that he had one foot in heaven and the other off the ground. However, St. Francis is a convincing witness—spiritually, physically, and sociologically—that the Christian Faith is both practical and powerful when it simply is lived and not diluted with other standards.

The original single brick house in each unit is now encircled by supplementary buildings, thirteen in all. Some fourteen hundred boys from every state in the Union, of most colors and beliefs, have gone through the Homes to date, and most have left to lead successful and constructive lives. The Homes' high rate of rehabilitation suggests no lack of realism in Father Bob's therapy-in-Christ method, which is now supplemented by other techniques, but which remains the essential approach to the salvation of wasted lives.

The priest has not had to retract the claim on which he founded St. Francis, that the historic Church is a wise old mother, with nineteen hundred years of experience in effective techniques and disciplines of rehabilitation. His work has shown that where the Church is alive in Christ, God's grace makes miracles to be everyday occurrences. The first miracle-minded Jack, his disorderly past long behind him, recently remarked, "It was a real miracle when He led Father Bob to establish the Homes."

The most remarkable element at St. Francis is its therapy-in-Christ, the therapy which begins the moment the boy enters the Home and continues long after he has left, the therapy which never gives up on a boy, however uneconomical or hopeless the effort my seem.

A youngster does not walk through the doors of St. Francis as an inmate, or a case or a patient, but only as a child of God, the beloved son of an all-loving Father. He is taught who he is, what Body he is a member of, how he may discharge his responsibilities, and how, through sacrament, prayer, and service to others, he may approach and know God. He is taught the reality of sin and salvation, and to beware of sentimentality and superstition. He is taught the reality of the Church as the Mystical Body of Christ, that it is not a proud club of self-sufficient people, but a company of weak sinners, very like himself, made strong and sure by God. He is taught the love of God, which offers him responsible, non-sentimental forgiveness when he is most unworthy and which love is never withheld or forgiveness refused, whatever the transgression.

The idea that forgiveness of itself was a dynamic instrument of rehabilitation in the beginning caused much skepticism among the townspeople and the welfare agencies. Father Bob's philosophy that forgiveness should be offered immediately, before the culprit exhibited the least contrition, caused much disapproval. "That priest sure puts the cart before the horse," was the general sentiment.

As usual, the priest turned to scripture. "Mary Magdalene wasn't brought to our Lord by her contrition," he pointed out again and again. "It was His forgiveness which made her penitent." Father Bob perceived that the Magdalene was not an isolated example but the illustration of the first law of love. So with his boys: through his forgiveness, they first understood that repentance is necessary and began to experience it, where before they had merely been sorry that they got caught and landed in jail.

Like St. Francis of Assisi for whom the Homes are named and who began his work in an empty Church, Father Bob started in an abandoned poorhouse. Both were willing to be thought fools for Christ's sake. Both had to save their work from followers who considered themselves more practical than the founders. The first little poor man of God became one of the most renowned of the saints. The second is on his way to becoming a legend in only his fifty-seventh year of life and labor.

Father Bob has always been a man of many contradictions, but perhaps the greatest paradox is that the man who is a simple Franciscan at heart now finds himself a prelate of the Church. The constancy of his faith underlies the confusion of qualities in his personality. That he is a bishop has not changed him; indeed he began his bishopric in typical Father Bob fashion.

Near the end of the reception following his consecration, he heard a voice say, "My Lord." For a second he didn't realize that the formal title was addressed to him; he still is not accustomed to it. Then he turned at a gentle tap on his shoulder, and saw that one of the guests wished to say good-bye. It was a Zulu chief flanked by three bodyguards. Sister Marge, who was present, re-members that he was "a most charming man in every respect. He spoke with the most beautiful English accent, and obviously was highly cultured."

The new Bishop held out his hand for a cordial handshake, but the chief dropped to his knees to kiss the bishop's ring. Father Bob looked down at his hand and realized that he had failed to put his ring on. "Oh, I forgot my ring!" he exclaimed, and rushed up-stairs to get it. Fortunately it was in plain sight on his bureau and, hastily slipping it on his finger, he ran downstairs; but he was too late. The chief had departed with greater dignity than had the bishop.

Bishop Mize honors his office and delights in the beauty and the pomp of the traditional ceremonial which his people want and need, but his private life of sacrifice remains unchanged. He embraces personal poverty no less ardently than he did thirty years ago. Following in the footsteps of his patron saint, "Lady Poverty" is his lifelong love. His family still does not quite approve. Marge says, "As a bishop he should have nice things in his house, but the last I heard he still didn't have any proper living room furniture. He's the same old Bob—won't accept a cent for anything he considers 'personal.'"

He still is always in a hurry. In the winter of 1963, he nearly lost his life because of his impatience. Steady rains had broken the territory's drought, and normally dry ravines near the see city of Windhoek were filled with the water. The Bishop had an important meeting scheduled in a distant native residential section. Disregarding the flood danger, he jumped into his new Land Rover and took off. He thought that cars turning back from a flooded ravine had crossed it safely, so he drove on. His car was swept downstream by the swirling current until it finally was jammed against the concrete support of a small footbridge. As the Bishop tried to crawl out of his car, it tipped over, and he was trapped beneath the door for ten minutes before the car finally shifted sufficiently to allow several Africans at the scene to pull him out.

Bishop and successor to the Apostles he may be, but to those who know him best, he will always be "Father Bob"—the same whether he wears an unpressed, secondhand suit or a richly ornamented cope and miter. Only the thinning hair and the ring tell whether it is the African or the Kansan plain as the Mizes' second son drives an old car at breakneck speed down a dirt road while he reads his Prayer Book; whether it is Bishop Mize or Father Bob who runs down the station platform to catch a train at the last minute without the price of a cup of coffee in his pocket, his coat out at the elbows, and holes in his shoes; whether it is the priest or the prelate who puts his arm around the shoulder of a child in trouble.

The Bishop left a large part of his heart and life at St. Francis when he went to Africa: the Homes were the only real home he had ever had. "The boys there are still my boys, every one of 'em, and they always will be," he declares. He does not exaggerate; he is thousands of miles away, but his philosophy and his influence pervade St. Francis. Each boy there is touched by his spirit. They continue to be the beneficiaries of a therapy which is more than a successful technique to its administrators: it is a way of life.

In an age when secularism is exalted and humanism glorified, and an era when Christianity is often so watered down with both that it is blamed for their failures, the St. Francis Boys' Homes still witness to the power of the Faith and its Author, and the cry of a boy in the night, "Help me, Father!" has been answered over and over again by the divine gift of joy and peace.

St. Francis Homes are a monument to the vision and the faith of a priest affectionately known as Father Bob, and the transformed lives of once-lost boys are his legacy. Still, perhaps his early request that he be left out of the story's telling was more practical than it seemed. The achievement which reflects such honor on him points even more clearly to the God whose power, purpose, and love upholds, directs, and sustains all His servants who will take Him at His Word.